STERLING
Test Prep

ATI TEAS
Science Questions

Practice Questions
with Detailed Explanations

2nd edition

2   1

ISBN-13: 978-1-9547251-4-0

Sterling Test Prep products are available at quantity discounts.

Contact info@sterling–prep.com

Sterling Test Prep
6 Liberty Square #11
Boston, MA 02109

Published by Sterling Test Prep

 Printed in the U.S.A.

Congratulations on joining thousands of students using our study aids to achieve high TEAS scores!

Scoring well on TEAS VI is essential for admission to a competitive nursing program to pursue a fulfilling career in health care. This book helps you develop the knowledge to quickly answer questions tested on the science section. Understanding key concepts, extracting and analyzing information from questions, and distinguishing between similar choices are more effective than merely memorizing terms.

This book provides high-yield practice questions with detailed explanations that cover all science topics tested on TEAS VI. Science instructors with years of teaching experience prepared these questions by analyzing the test content and developing material that builds your knowledge and skills crucial for a high score. Our editors reviewed and systematized the content to ensure adherence to the current test requirements. These experts prepare students for standardized tests and have coached thousands of students on test preparation and successful admission strategies.

The detailed explanations contain the science material necessary for targeted TEAS VI preparation. By reading these explanations thoroughly, you will learn the important foundations and essential details. This prepares you for the test and will significantly improve your TEAS VI score.

We look forward to being an essential part of your exam preparation and wish you great success in nursing program admissions!

STERLING
Test Prep

211001cfr

For best results, use ATI TEAS Science Review

A thorough review of science topics tested on TEAS VI. Learn the important foundations and essential details for targeted test preparation to *increase your score.*

Visit our Amazon store

HESI A2 prep books

- Biology, Anatomy & Physiology Review
- Biology, Anatomy & Physiology Practice Questions
- Chemistry and Physics Review
- Chemistry and Physics Practice Questions

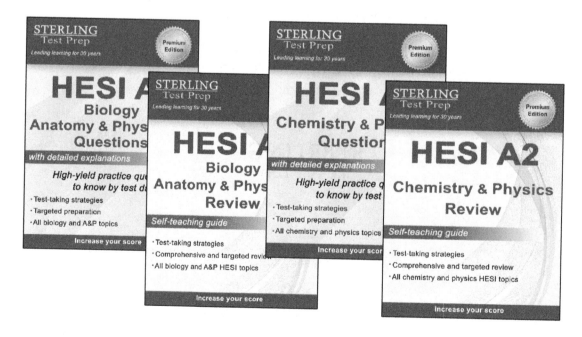

Table of Contents

Table of Contents (*continued*)

Part II: Answer Keys and Detailed Explanations (*continued*)

Section I: Human Anatomy and Physiology (*continued*)

Section II: Life and Physical Sciences 261

Section III: Scientific Reasoning 357

ATI TEAS Preparation and Test-Taking Strategies

Test preparation strategies

The best way to do well on the science section of TEAS is to be good familiar with the material in this book. There is no way around this, so proper preparation is the key to success. Prepare for the test to answer with confidence as many questions as possible.

Study in advance. Plan to devote 3 to 6 months studying for ATI TEAS VI. The information is manageable by studying at regular intervals during the weeks before the test. Cramming is not a successful tactic. However, do not study too far in advance. Studying more than six months ahead is not advised and may result in fatigue and poor knowledge retention.

Develop a realistic study and practice schedule. Cramming eight hours a day is unfeasible and leads to burnout, which is detrimental to performance. Commit to a realistic study and practice schedule.

Remove distractions. During this preparation period, temporarily eliminate distractions. However, it is crucial not to neglect physical well-being, as well as social or family life. Balance is key. Prepare with full intensity but do not jeopardize your health or emotional well-being.

Develop an understanding over memorization. When studying, devote time to each topic. After a study session, write a short outline of the concepts. The act of writing clarifies relationships and increases knowledge retention.

Make flashcards. Consider using self-made flashcards to develop knowledge retention and to quiz what you know. Avoid commercial flashcards because making cards helps build and retain knowledge.

Find a study partner. Occasionally studying with a friend who is preparing for the test can motivate and provide accountability. Explaining concepts to another improves and fine-tunes your understanding, integrates knowledge, bolsters competence, and identifies deficiencies in comprehension.

Take practice tests. Do not take practice tests too early. First, develop a broad and detailed understanding of concepts. In the last weeks, use practice tests to fine-tune your final preparation. If you are not scoring well on practice tests, you want time to improve without undue stress.

Alternate the days for studying and practicing. This steadily increases knowledge retention and identifies areas that require further study. Also, it accustoms you to the challenges of test-taking.

Test day strategies

Be well-rested. Get a full night's sleep before the test for proper mental and physical capacity. If you are up late the night before (i.e., you are not well prepared), you will not feel fresh and alert and will have difficulty concentrating and focusing on the test.

Eat the right foods. Avoid foods and drinks that lead to drowsiness (carbohydrates and protein) or drinks high in sugar, causing the glucose spike and crash.

Pack in advance. Check what you are allowed to bring to the test. Pay attention to the required check-in items (e.g., printed confirmation, identification). Pack the day before, so you are not frantically looking for things on test day. Prepare your clothes to avoid the stress of looking for matching socks.

Arrive at the testing center early. Allow time to check-in and remain calm before the test begins. Starting off the right way is an advantage. Map and test your route to the center in advance and determine parking locations, if applicable. If you are not familiar with the test location, visit before the test day to practice and avoid travel errors. Plan your route correctly to arrive at the center without delays or encountering additional challenges and unnecessary stress.

Maintain a positive attitude. Avoid falling into a mental spiral of negative emotions. Too much worry leads to underperformance. If you become anxious, chances are higher for lower performance in preparation and during the test. To do well on the test requires logical, systematic, and analytical thinking, so relax and remain calm. This inner peace helps during preparation and the high-stakes test.

Focus on your progress. Do not be concerned with other test-takers. If someone appears to be proceeding rapidly through the test, it does not matter; they may be rushing or guessing on questions.

Take breaks. Do not skip the available timed breaks. Your mind and body will appreciate them. If time allows, eat a light snack to replenish your energy. These refreshing breaks help you finish strong.

Pause to breathe deeply. The best approach to any test is *not* to keep your head down the whole session. While there is no time to waste, take a few seconds between questions to breathe deeply and momentarily clear your thoughts to relax your mind and muscles.

Time management strategies

Besides good preparation, time management is the critical strategy to know for the exam.

Average time per question. In advance, determine the average time allotted for each question. Use two different approaches depending on which phase of preparation you are working on.

During the first phase of preparation, acquire, fortify, and refine your knowledge. Timed practice is not the objective at this stage. While practicing, note how many questions you would have completed in the allotted time. During this regimented practice, use the time needed to develop your analytical and thought processes related to specific questions. Work systematically and note your comprehension compared to the correct answers to learn the material and identify conceptual weaknesses. Do not overlook the value of explanations to questions; these can be a great source of content, analysis, and interdependent relationships.

During the second phase of preparation, when taking practice tests, do not spend more than the average allotted time on each question. Pacing your response time helps develop a consistent pace, so you complete the test within the allotted time. If you are time-constrained during the final practice phase, you need to work more efficiently, or your score will suffer.

Focus on the easy questions and skip the unfamiliar. You get the same points for answering easy or difficult questions. This means more points for three quickly answered questions than for one hard-earned victory. Everyone has their strengths and weaknesses. For an unfamiliar question on the exam, skip it on the first round because these challenging questions require more than the average allotted time. Use your time first to answer all familiar (i.e., easy), so if time runs out, you maximized points.

On the second review, questions that you cannot approach systematically or lack fundamental knowledge will likely not be answered through analysis. Use the strategy of elimination and educated guessing to select an answer and move on to another question.

Do not overinvest in any question. You may encounter questions that consume more time than the average and make you think that you will get it right by investing more time. Stop thinking that way. Do not get entangled with questions while losing track of time. The test is timed, so you cannot spend too much time on any question.

Look at every question on the exam. It would be unfortunate not to earn points for a question you could have quickly answered because you did not see it. If you are still in the first half of the test and are spending more than the required average on a question, select the best option, note the question number, and move on. You do not want to rush through the remaining questions, causing you to miss more answers. If time allows, return to marked questions and take a fresh look. However, unless you have a reason to change the original answer, do not change it. University studies show that students who hastily change answers often replace the correct answer with an incorrect answer.

Multiple-choice questions strategies

For multiple-choice questions, what matters is how many questions were answered correctly, not how much work went into selecting the answers. An educated guess earns the same points as an answer known with confidence.

On the test, you need to think and analyze information quickly. This skill cannot be gained from a college course, review prep course, or textbook. Working efficiently and effectively is a skill developed through focused effort and applied practice.

There are strategies, approaches, and perspectives to apply when answering multiple-choice questions on the science section of TEAS VI. These strategies help maximize points. Many strategies are known by you and seem like common sense. However, under the pressure of a timed test, these helpful approaches might be overlooked. While no strategy replaces the importance of comprehensive preparation, applying them increases the probability of successful guessing on unfamiliar questions.

Understand the question. Know what the question is asking before selecting an answer. This seems obvious, but it is surprising how many students do not read (and reread) a question carefully and rush to select the wrong answer. The test-makers anticipate these hasty mistakes, and many enticing answers are included among the specious choices.

A successful student reads the question and understands it precisely before looking at the answers. Separate the vital information from distracters and understand the design and thrust of the question. Answer the question posed and not merely pick a factually accurate statement or answer a misconstrued question.

Rephrasing the question helps articulate what precisely the correct response requires. When rephrasing, do not change the meaning of the question; assume it is direct and to the point as written. After selecting the answer, review the question and verify that the choice selected answers the question.

Answer the question before looking at choices. This valuable strategy is applicable if the question asks for generalized factual details. Answer the question by forming a thought response first, then look for the choice that matches your preordained answer. Select the predetermined statement as it is likely correct.

Factually correct, but wrong. Questions often have incorrect choices that are factually correct but do not answer the question. Therefore, with applied thought, predetermine the answer and not select a choice merely because it is a factually correct statement. Verify that the choice answers the question.

Do not fall for the familiar. When in doubt, it is comforting to choose what is familiar. If you recognize a term or concept, you may be tempted to pick that choice impetuously. However, do not go with familiar answers merely because they are familiar. Think through the answer and how it relates to the question before selecting it.

Know the equations. Since many exam questions require scientific equations, memorize the needed ones and understand when to use each. As you work with this book, learn to apply formulas and equations and use them in many questions.

Manipulate the formulas. Know how to rearrange the formulas. Many questions require manipulating equations to calculate the correct answer. Familiarity includes manipulating the terms, understanding relationships, and isolating variables.

Estimating. For quantitative questions, estimating helps choose the correct answer quickly if you have a sense of the order of magnitude. This is especially applicable to questions where the answer choices have different orders of magnitude; save time by estimating instead of computing. In most instances, estimation enables the correct answer to be identified quickly compared to the time needed for calculations.

Evaluate the units. For quantitative problems, analyze the units in the answers to build relationships between the question and the correct answer. Understand what value is sought and eliminate wrong choices with improper units.

Make visual notes. Write, draw, or graph to dissect the question. This helps determine what information is provided, the question's objective, and the concept tested by the question. Even if a question does not require a graphic answer, a graph, chart, or table often allows a solution to become apparent.

Experiments questions. Determine the purpose, methods, variables, and controls of the experiment. Understanding the presented information helps answer the question. With multiple experiments, understand variations of the same experiment by focusing on the differences. For example, focus on the changes between the first and second experiments, second and third, and first and third. This helps organize the information and apply it to the answer.

Words of caution. The words *"all," "none,"* and *"except"* require attention. Be alert with questions containing these words as they require an answer that may not be apparent on the first read of the question.

Process of elimination. If the correct answer is not immediately apparent, use the process of elimination. Use the strategy of educated guessing by eliminating one or two answers. Usually, at least one answer choice is easily identified as wrong. Eliminating even one choice increases the odds of selecting the correct one. Eliminate as many choices as possible.

- Use proportional estimations for quantitative questions, eliminate the choices unreasonably high or low.

- Eliminate answers that are "almost right" or "half right." Consider "half right" as "wrong" since these distractor choices are purposely included.

- If two answers are direct opposites, the correct answer is likely one of them. Therefore, you can typically eliminate the other choices and narrow the search for the correct one. However, note if they are direct opposites too, or there is another reason to consider them correct.

- With factual questions where answers are numbers, eliminate the smallest and largest numbers (unless you have a reason to choose it as correct).

- *Roman numeral questions.* These questions present several statements and ask which is/are correct. These questions are tricky for most test-takers because they present more than one potentially correct statement, often included in combinations with more than one answer. Eliminating a wrong Roman numeral statement eliminates all choices that include it.

Correct ways to guess. Do not assume you must get every question right; this will add unnecessary stress during the exam. You will (most likely) need to guess some questions. Answer as many questions correctly as possible without wasting time that should be used to maximize your score.

For challenging questions, random guessing does not help. Use educated guessing after eliminating one or two choices. Guessing is a form of "partial credit" because while you might not be sure of the correct answer, you have the relevant knowledge to identify some wrong choices.

For example, if you randomly entered responses for the first 20 questions, there is a 25% chance of correctly guessing since questions have four choices. Therefore, the odds are guessing 5 questions correctly and 15 incorrectly.

After eliminating one answer as wrong, you have a 33% chance of being right. Therefore, your odds move to 6-7 questions right and 13-14 questions wrong. While this may not seem like a dramatic increase, it can make an appreciable difference in your score. If you confidently eliminate two wrong choices, you increase the chances of guessing the correct answer to 50%!

- Do not rely on gut feelings alone to quickly answer questions. Understand and recognize the difference between *knowing* and a *gut feeling* about the answer. Gut feelings should sparingly be used after the process of elimination.

- Do not fall for answers that sound "clever," and do not choose "bizarre" answers. Choose them only if you have a reason to believe they may be correct.

- *Roman numeral questions.* A workable strategy for Roman numeral questions is to guess the wrong statement. For example:

    A. I only

    B. III only

    C. I and II only

    D. I and III only

Notice that statement II does not have an answer dedicated to it. This indicates that statement II is likely wrong and eliminates choice C, narrowing your search to three choices. However, if you are confident that statement II is the answer, do not apply this strategy.

Double-check the question. After selecting an answer, return to the question to ensure the selected choice answers the question as asked and not as misconstrued for convenience.

Fill the answers carefully. This is simple but crucial. Many mistakes happen when filling in answers. Be attentive to the question number and enter the answer accordingly. If you skip a question, skip it on the answer sheet.

ATI TEAS
Science Questions

Part I

Practice Questions

Section I

Human Anatomy and Physiology

Anatomy & Physiology; Basic Biology

Respiratory System

Cardiovascular and Hematological Systems

Immune System

Digestive System

Nervous System

Skeletal System

Muscular System

Reproductive System

Integumentary System

Endocrine System

Genitourinary System

Anatomy & Physiology; Basic Biology

1. The abdomen is […] to the head; the chin is […] to the navel.

   A. superior; inferior
   B. inferior; superior
   C. lateral; medial
   D. distal; proximal

2. The heart is […] to the arm; arms are […] to the chest.

   A. medial; lateral
   B. proximal; distal
   C. lateral; medial
   D. superior; inferior

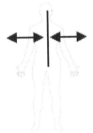

3. The wrist is […] to the elbow; the knee is […] to the ankle.

   A. superior; inferior
   B. proximal; distal
   C. anterior; posterior
   D. distal; proximal

4. The breastbone is […] to the spine; the heart is […] to the breastbone.

   A. medial; lateral
   B. posterior; anterior
   C. anterior; posterior
   D. proximal; distal

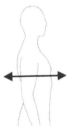

5. The two basic types of cells are:

   A. plant and animal
   B. bacterial and animal
   C. nervous and muscle
   D. prokaryotic and eukaryotic

6. Type of cell junction that connects a cell to a basement membrane:

   A. tight junction
   B. adherence junction
   C. gap junction
   D. hemidesmosome

7. Plant cells, unlike animal cells, are characterized by the presence of:

    A. cell wall

    B. plasma membrane

    C. nuclear envelope

    D. ribosomes

8. The endosymbiotic theory involves:

    A. larger cell engulfing virus

    B. larger cell engulfing smaller cell

    C. fertilization of large cell by smaller cell

    D. larger cell parasitizing on smaller cell

9. Krebs cycle occurs in the:

    A. mitochondria

    B. Golgi apparatus

    C. nucleus

    D. cytoplasm

10. Making mRNA from DNA "blueprint" is known as:

    A. translation

    B. processing

    C. transcription

    D. replication

11. All cells of the human body have a nucleus except:

    A. stem cell

    B. ovum

    C. sperm

    D. red blood cell

12. Organelle that synthesizes protein from mRNA is:

    A. mitochondria

    B. ribosome

    C. peroxisome

    D. nucleolus

13. Which of the following is/are NOT able to readily diffuse through the plasma membrane of a cell without the aid of a transport protein?

    I. water

    II. small hydrophobic molecules

    III. small ions

    IV. neutral gas molecules

    A. I only

    B. I and II only

    C. I and III only

    D. III and IV only

14. If a membrane-bound vesicle that contains hydrolytic enzymes is isolated, most likely it is a:

    A. vacuole

    B. lysosome

    C. chloroplast

    D. phagosome

15. Which cellular substituent is produced within the nucleus?

A. Golgi apparatus

B. lysosome

C. ribosome

D. rough endoplasmic reticulum

16. Both prokaryotes and eukaryotes contain:

    I. a plasma membrane

    II. ribosomes

    III. peroxisomes

A. I only

B. II only

C. I and II only

D. I, II and III

17. All of the following statements are true about cytoskeleton, EXCEPT that it:

A. is not required for mitosis

B. maintains the cell's shape

C. gives the cell mechanical support

D. is composed of microtubules and microfilaments

18. Which of the following involves the post-translational modification of proteins?

A. peroxisomes

B. smooth ER

C. Golgi complex

D. lysosomes

19. The width of a typical animal cell is closest to:

A. 1 millimeter

B. 20 micrometers

C. 1 micrometer

D. 10 nanometers

20. Which organelle is identified by the sedimentation coefficient S (Svedberg) units?

A. peroxisome

B. ribosome

C. mitochondrion

D. nucleus

21. The best definition of active transport is the movement of:

A. solutes across a semipermeable membrane down an electrochemical gradient

B. solutes across a semipermeable membrane up a concentration gradient

C. substances across a membrane following the Donnan equilibrium

D. solutes via osmosis across a semipermeable membrane from high to low concentration

22. All of the following processes take place in the mitochondrion, EXCEPT:

A. oxidation of pyruvate

B. Krebs cycle

C. electron transport chain

D. glycolysis

23. Which eukaryotic organelle is NOT membrane-bound?

    A. nucleus

    B. plastid

    C. centriole

    D. chloroplast

24. During which phase of mitotic division do spindle fibers split the centromere and separate the sister chromatids?

    A. anaphase

    B. telophase

    C. prophase

    D. metaphase

25. A cell division where each of the two daughter cells receives a chromosome complement identical to that of a parent is:

    A. mitosis

    B. crossing-over

    C. meiosis

    D. replication

26. Which of the following processes is NOT an example of apoptosis?

    A. Reabsorption of a tadpole's tail during metamorphosis into a frog

    B. Formation of the endometrial lining of the uterus during the menstrual cycle

    C. Formation of the synaptic cleft by triggering cell death in brain neuronal cells

    D. Formation of fingers in the fetus by the removal of tissue between the digits

27. Which of the following tissues is/are an example(s) of connective tissue?

    I. bone

    II. cartilage

    III. nervous

    A. II only

    B. I and II only

    C. II and III only

    D. I, II and III

28. Which of these organelles undergoes self-replication?

    A. nucleus

    B. mitochondria

    C. nucleolus

    D. ribosomes

29. Tissues are composed of cells, and a group of tissues functioning together makes up:

    A. organs

    B. membranes

    C. organ systems

    D. organelles

30. An organ is defined as a structure that has a recognizable shape, has specific functions, and is composed of two or more different types of:

    A. tissues

    B. cells

    C. germ layers

    D. mesoderm

31. Which of the following is NOT classified as one of the four primary (basic) types of tissue?

    A. connective

    B. blood

    C. muscle

    D. nervous

32. Which connective tissue stores triglycerides and provides cushioning and support for organs?

    A. endothelial

    B. muscle

    C. connective

    D. adipose

Notes for active learning

Respiratory System

1. Which of the following is NOT a function of the respiratory system?

    A. Helping to expel abdominal contents during defecation and childbirth

    B. Helping to transport gases to tissues

    C. Allowing the exchange of O_2 between blood and air

    D. Contributing to the maintenance of the pH balance

2. The loudness of a person's voice depends on:

    A. force with which air rushes across the vocal folds

    B. strength of the intrinsic laryngeal muscles

    C. length of the vocal folds

    D. thickness of vestibular folds

3. Air moves out of the lungs when the pressure inside the lungs is:

    I. higher than the intra-alveolar pressure

    II. higher than the pressure of the atmosphere

    III. less than the pressure in the atmosphere

    A. I only

    B. II only

    C. III only

    D. I and II only

4. During breathing, inhalation results from:

    A. forcing air from the throat down into the lungs

    B. contracting the diaphragm

    C. relaxing the muscles of the rib cage

    D. muscles of the lungs expanding the alveoli

5. What maintains the openness (i.e., patency) of the trachea?

    A. relaxation of smooth muscle

    B. C-shaped cartilage rings

    C. surfactant production

    D. surface tension of water

6. Intrapulmonary pressure is:

   A. negative pressure in the intrapleural space

   B. the difference between atmospheric pressure and respiratory pressure

   C. pressure within the pleural cavity

   D. pressure within the alveoli of the lungs

7. The gas exchange between the blood and tissues takes place in:

   A. arteries, arterioles, and capillaries

   B. the entire systemic circulation

   C. capillaries only

   D. pulmonary veins only

8.. In a healthy person, the most potent respiratory stimulus for breathing is:

   A. acidosis

   B. alkalosis

   C. a decrease of oxygen in tissues

   D. an increase of carbon dioxide in the blood

9. After inhalation, the lungs pull away from the thorax wall during elastic recoil due to:

   A. natural tendency for the lungs to recoil and transpulmonary pressure

   B. compliance and the surface tension of the alveolar fluid

   C. elastic fibers of the connective tissue and the surface tension of the alveolar fluid

   D. compliance and transpulmonary pressure

10. Which of the following would cause an increased breathing rate?

   A. Low partial pressure of CO_2 in blood

   B. High partial pressure of CO_2 in blood

   C. High partial pressure of O_2 in blood

   D. High pH of the blood

11. Lung compliance is determined by:

   A. alveolar surface tension

   B. muscles of inspiration

   C. flexibility of the thoracic cage

   D. airway opening

12. Tidal volume is the amount of air:

   A. forcibly inhaled after regular inspiration

   B. forcibly expelled after normal expiration

   C. remaining in the lungs after forced expiration

   D. exchanged during normal breathing

13. Which is a possible cause of hypoxia?

   A. taking several rapid, deep breaths

   B. very cold climate

   C. low atmospheric oxygen levels

   D. obstruction of the esophagus

14. Where does the lower respiratory tract begin?

   A. bronchioles

   B. primary bronchi

   C. choanae

   D. trachea

15. All of the following are stimuli for breathing, EXCEPT:

   I. decrease in plasma pH

   III. elevated blood pressure

   II. decreased O_2 levels

   IV. elevated CO_2 levels

   A. I only

   B. II only

   C. III only

   D. I and IV only

16. Which of these structures would NOT be affected by a respiratory tract infection?

   A. alveoli

   B. bronchi

   C. esophagus

   D. trachea

17. Respiratory control centers are located in the:

   A. pons and midbrain

   B. upper spinal cord and medulla

   C. midbrain and medulla

   D. medulla and pons

18. Which of the following sequences is correct for air movement during exhalation?

   A. alveoli → trachea → bronchi → bronchioles → larynx → pharynx

   B. alveoli → bronchi → bronchioles → trachea → pharynx

   C. alveoli → bronchioles → bronchi → trachea → larynx → pharynx

   D. alveoli → bronchi → trachea → bronchioles → pharynx → larynx

19. The projection from the inside of the nose into the breathing passage is called:

    A. meatus

    B. conchae

    C. vibrissae

    D. naris

20. In the lungs and through cell membranes, oxygen and carbon dioxide are exchanged through the process of:

    A. active transport

    B. filtration

    C. diffusion

    D. osmosis

21. Which physiological process is generally passive?

    I. gas exchange   II. inhalation   III. exhalation

    A. I only

    B. I and II only

    C. I and III only

    D. I, II and III

22. The point of division of the trachea into the right and left primary bronchi is the:

    A. trachea

    B. esophagus

    C. carina

    D. glottis

23. All of these statements regarding the respiratory system are true, EXCEPT:

    A. when the pulmonary pressure is less than atmospheric pressure, air flows out of the lungs

    B. thoracic cavity enlargement causes the pressure of air within the lungs to decrease

    C. contraction of the diaphragm enlarges the thoracic cavity

    D. ciliated nasal membranes warm, moisten and filter inspired air

24. Most inhaled particles (e.g., dust) do not reach the lungs because of the:

    A. action of the epiglottis

    B. porous structure of turbinate bones

    C. abundant blood supply to the nasal mucosa

    D. ciliated mucous lining in the nose

25. Which is NOT a part of the pharynx?

    A. laryngopharynx

    B. oropharynx

    C. nasopharynx

    D. larynx

26. Why is the air that enters the lungs of a patient who has a tube inserted directly into the trachea colder and dryer than usual and often causes lung crusting and infection?

    A. Because the larynx does not adequately humidify it

    B. Because it is not filtered as it enters the respiratory system

    C. Because it does not flow past the mouth and tongue

    D. Because it does not flow through the nasal passageways

27. The airway from the nose to the larynx is the:

    A. lower respiratory tract

    B. posterior lung system

    C. respiratory division

    D. upper respiratory tract

28. The smallest passageways in the lungs to have ciliated epithelia are:

    A. tertiary bronchi

    B. alveolar ducts

    C. terminal bronchioles

    D. respiratory bronchioles

29. Which of the following factors influences the rate and depth of breathing?

    A. stretch receptors in the alveoli

    B. temperature of alveolar air

    C. thalamic control

    D. voluntary cortical control

30. Which structure is most important in keeping food out of the trachea?

    A. vocal folds

    B. soft palate

    C. epiglottis

    D. glottis

31. Why are there rings of hyaline cartilage in the trachea?

    A. To prevent choking

    B. To keep the passageway open for the continuous flow of air

    C. To provide support for the mucociliary escalator

    D. To provide support for the passage of food through the esophagus

32. All of the following statements about CO_2 are correct, EXCEPT:

    A. more is carried by erythrocytes than is dissolved in blood plasma as bicarbonate

    B. its concentration is higher in venous blood than in arterial blood

    C. its concentration in the blood decreases by hyperventilation

    D. it stimulates breathing

Notes for active learning

Cardiovascular and Hematological Systems

1. In a healthy individual, the highest blood pressure would most likely be in the:

   A. superior vena cava

   B. aorta

   C. pulmonary capillaries

   D. systemic capillaries

2. Oxygenated blood is pumped by:

   A. left ventricle and left atrium

   B. left ventricle and right atrium

   C. left and right atria

   D. left and right ventricles

3. The osmotic pressure at the arterial end of a capillary bed:

   I. results in a net outflow of fluid

   II. is less than the hydrostatic pressure

   III. is greater than the hydrostatic pressure

   A. I only   **C.** I and II only

   B. II only   **D.** I and III only

4. All of these statements about the circulatory system are true, EXCEPT:

   A. veins have a strong pulse

   B. oxygenated blood is typically transported in arteries

   C. mammals have a four-chambered heart

   D. the thoracic duct returns lymphatic fluid to the circulatory system

5. Which of the following is the *correct* path of blood flow through the heart?

   A. Superior/inferior vena cava → left atrium → left ventricle → pulmonary artery → lungs → pulmonary vein → right atrium → right ventricle → aorta

   B. Superior/inferior vena cava → right atrium → left ventricle → pulmonary artery → lungs → pulmonary vein → left atrium → right ventricle → aorta

   C. Superior/inferior vena cava → right atrium → right ventricle → pulmonary vein → lungs → pulmonary artery → left atrium → left ventricle → aorta

   D. Superior/inferior vena cava → right atrium → right ventricle → pulmonary artery → lungs → pulmonary vein → left atrium → left ventricle → aorta

6. Which of the following is a protective role of blood?

   A. maintenance of pH in body tissue

   B. maintenance of body temperature

   C. prevention of blood loss

   D. maintenance of adequate fluid volume

7. Which blood component is involved in clot formation?

   A. erythrocytes   **C.** platelets

   B. macrophages   **D.** T cells

8. Which of the following is characteristic of a capillary?

      I. hydrostatic pressure is higher at the arteriole end than at the venule end

      II. osmotic pressure is higher in the blood plasma than in the interstitial fluid

      III. hydrostatic pressure results from heart contractions

   A. I only   **C.** II and III only

   B. I and II only   **D.** I, II and III

9. All of the below statements about blood are correct, EXCEPT:

   A. mature erythrocytes lack a nucleus

   B. blood platelets are involved in the clotting process

   C. erythrocytes develop in the adult spleen

   D. leukocytes undergo phagocytosis of foreign matter

10. Which of the following is a normal blood flow pathway?

   A. inferior vena cava to the left atrium

   B. right ventricle to the aorta

   C. pulmonary veins to the left ventricle

   D. pulmonary veins to the left atrium

11. In an infant born with a congenital heart defect, which of the following most likely results from blood mixing between the right and left ventricles?

   A. recurrent fever

   B. hemoglobin deficiency

   C. poor oxygenation of the tissues

   D. low blood pressure

12. Which statement is accurate regarding blood plasma?

  A. It is over 90% water

  B. It contains about 20 dissolved components

  C. It is the same as the serum but without the clotting proteins

  D. The main protein component is hemoglobin

13. Which of these vessels has the highest partial pressure of oxygen in a healthy person?

  A. aorta

  B. coronary veins

  C. superior vena cava

  D. pulmonary arteries

14. Which of these structures would be reached LAST by a tracer substance injected into the superior vena cava?

  A. tricuspid valve

  B. pulmonary veins

  C. left ventricle

  D. right ventricle

15. In the mammalian heart, semi-lunar valves are found:

  A. where the blood goes from the atria to ventricles

  B. on the right side of the heart, only

  C. where the pulmonary veins attach to the heart

  D. where blood leaves via the aorta and pulmonary arteries

16. Which statement is correct about the atrioventricular (AV) node?

  A. It regulates the contraction rhythm of cardiac cells

  B. It delays the contraction of the heart ventricles

  C. It is the parasympathetic ganglion located in the left atrium of the heart

  D. It conducts action potentials from the vagus nerve to the heart

17. Stenosis is a condition whereby the valve's opening is narrowed and results in decreased blood flow through the valve. If diagnosed with stenosis of the mitral valve, where would a patient experience the highest blood pressure increase?

  A. right atrium

  B. aorta

  C. left ventricle

  D. left atrium

18. Which of the following would result from a significant loss of blood due to a hemorrhage?

  A. No change in blood pressure but a slower heart rate

  B. No change in blood pressure but a change in respiration

  C. Lowering of blood pressure due to change in cardiac output

  D. Rise in blood pressure due to change in cardiac output

19. What is the correct order for the cardiac conduction pathway?

    A. Purkinje fibers → SA node→ AV node → bundle of His

    B. SA node → bundle of His → Purkinje fibers → AV node

    C. SA node → AV node → bundle of His → Purkinje fibers

    D. AV node → SA node → bundle of His → Purkinje fibers

20. Which of these heart structures has blood with the highest O_2 content?

    A. right atrium

    B. left ventricle

    C. pulmonary artery

    D. thoracic duct

21. Which of these heart structures has blood with the lowest O_2 content?

    A. thoracic duct

    B. left ventricle

    C. pulmonary artery

    D. inferior vena cava

22. In which of the following vessels has the highest protein concentration?

    A. proximal tubule   **C.** afferent arteriole

    B. renal artery   **D.** vasa recta

23. Which blood cell is responsible for coagulation?

    A. leukocyte   **C.** lymphocyte

    B. erythrocyte   **D.** platelet

24. Which of the following is NOT correct about the hepatic portal system?

    A. It branches from the inferior vena cava

    B. It consists of a vein connecting two capillary beds

    C. Its major vessels are the superior mesenteric, inferior mesenteric, and splenic veins

    D. It carries nutrients to the liver for processing

25. Which of the following is valid according to Starling's capillary physiology hypothesis?

    A. Filtration occurs where the hydrostatic pressure is less than the osmotic pressure

    B. Ultrafiltrate is returned to the bloodstream by the lymphatic system

    C. Hydrostatic pressure is lower at the arteriolar end

    D. Osmotic pressure drives fluid out of the capillary

26. Which of the following is correct about the hemoglobin molecule of the red blood cell?

    A. It does not bind CO_2

    B. It has a higher O_2 affinity in adults compared with fetal hemoglobin

    C. It does not bind CO

    D. It exhibits positive cooperative binding for O_2

27. All of the following are functions of blood, EXCEPT:

    A. transport of salts to maintain blood volume

    B. transport of hormones to their target organs

    C. transport of metabolic wastes from cells

    D. delivery of O_2 to body cells

28. All of the following statements are true regarding blood, EXCEPT:

    A. It carries body cells to injured areas for repair

    B. Its pH usually is between 7.34 and 7.45

    C. It contains albumins to regulate osmolarity

    D. It is denser and more viscous than water

29. When inhaled, carbon monoxide (CO) can be lethal because it:

    A. irritates the pleura

    B. blocks electron transport within the cytochrome system

    C. binds with a strong affinity to hemoglobin

    D. is insoluble in the bloodstream

30. The site of O_2 absorption in the capillaries of the lungs is:

    A. alveoli   **C.** bronchi

    B. pleura   **D.** bronchioles

31. Which of the following statements is valid for cardiac muscle?

    A. It is multi-nucleated

    B. It is not striated

    C. It is under involuntary control

    D. It is innervated by the somatic motor nervous system

Notes for active learning

With each topic, reinforce learning by reading review chapters in your *ATI TEAS Science Review* book.

Visit our Amazon store

Immune System

1. A person lacking gamma globulins would have:

A. diabetes

B. hemophilia

C. severe allergies

D. low resistance to infection

2. Humoral immunity depends on the function of:

A. erythrocytes

B. cytotoxic T cells

C. immunoglobulins

D. albumin

3. Which cell type produces antibodies?

A. neurons

B. T cells

C. B cells

D. macrophages

4. Inflammatory responses may include which of the following?

A. clotting proteins migrating away from the site of infection

B. increased activity of phagocytes in an inflamed area

C. reduced permeability of blood vessels to conserve plasma

D. release of substances that decrease the blood supply to an inflamed area

5. Which innate immune response is exhibited by a patient initially exposed to a pathogen?

A. T killer cells

B. neutrophils

C. T helper cells

D. B lymphocytes

6. Which of the following would be impaired due to HIV infecting and killing helper CD4$^+$ T lymphocytes?

    I. humoral immunity

    II. cell-mediated immunity

    III. non-specific immunity

A. I only

B. I and II only

C. I and III only

D. II and III only

7. What are antigens?

A. proteins in the blood that cause foreign blood cells to clump

B. proteins embedded in B cell membranes

C. proteins that consist of two light and two heavy polypeptide chains

D. foreign molecules that trigger the production of antibodies

8. Which cells are responsible for secreting virus-neutralizing antibodies?

A. T cells

B. plasma cells

C. macrophages

D. thymus cells

9. All of the following is a T cell type, EXCEPT:

A. memory

B. regulatory

C. cytotoxic

D. antigenic

10. B lymphocytes develop immunocompetence in:

A. lymph nodes

B. bone marrow

C. the spleen

D. the thymus

11. The inflammatory response is involved in all of the following processes, EXCEPT:

A. disposing of cellular debris and pathogens

B. setting the stage for repair processes

C. preventing the spread of the injurious agent to nearby tissue

D. replacing injured tissues with connective tissue

12. B cells are dormant in lymph nodes and other lymphoid tissues until activated by specific lymphocyte antigens. When activated, B cells produce:

A. cytotoxic T cells

B. lymphokines

C. antibodies

D. macrophages

13. All of the following are examples of innate immunity, EXCEPT:

A. phagocytotic cells

B. digestive enzymes and stomach acid

C. memory B cells

D. skin as a physical barrier to antigens

14. Which statement is true regarding interferons?

A. Interferon produced against one virus would not protect cells against another virus

B. They act by increasing the rate of cell division

C. They interfere with viral replication within cells

D. They are used in nasal sprays for the common cold

15. White blood cells at the scene of a wound:

A. produce the blood clot

B. secrete scar tissue fibers

C. stimulate the epidermal cells to divide

D. engulf microbes and cell debris

16. A patient with AB blood type is the *universal recipient* because this patient's blood:

    A. contains neither antibody

    B. contains both antibodies

    C. is the most common blood type

    D. is the least common blood type

17. A patient with O type blood is the *universal donor* because this patient's blood:

    A. contains neither antigen

    B. contains both antigens

    C. is the least common

    D. is the most common

18. Antibodies that function against a particular foreign substance are released by:

    A. lymph nodes

    B. natural killer cells

    C. T lymphocytes

    D. plasma cells

19. Which statement about lymphocytes is correct?

    A. T cells are the precursors of B cells

    B. T cells are the only form of lymphocytes in lymphoid tissue

    C. The two main types are T cells and macrophages

    D. B cells differentiate into plasma cells that secrete antibodies into the blood

20. What is the function of lymph nodes?

    A. breaking down hemoglobin

    B. filtering of lymph

    C. facilitating the absorption of amino acids

    D. increasing glucose concentrations in blood

21. All of the following are functions of the lymphatic system, EXCEPT:

    A. regulation of erythropoiesis

    B. destruction and removal of foreign particles

    C. removal of proteins from interstitial spaces

    D. absorption of lipids from the small intestine

22. Antibodies act by:

    A. aiding in phagocytosis of antigens

    B. binding to antigens via the variable portion

    C. inhibiting stem cell production in the bone marrow

    D. binding to plasma cells and marking them for destruction via phagocytosis

23. The correct sequence of events in phagocytosis is:

    A. ingestion → adherence → chemotaxis → digestion → killing

    B. chemotaxis → adherence → ingestion → digestion → killing

    C. chemotaxis → ingestion → digestion → adherence → killing

    D. adherence → digestion → killing → ingestion → chemotaxis

24. The reason for *swollen glands* in the neck of a patient with a cold is that:

    A. blood pools in the neck to keep it warm

    B. lymph nodes swell during infection as white blood cells proliferate within them

    C. inflammation is initiated by the infection that causes fluid to be drained from the area

    D. fever initiates a general expansion of the tissues of the head and neck

Digestive System

1. All of the following processes take place in the liver, EXCEPT:

   A. glycogen storage

   B. detoxification of poisons

   C. synthesis of adult erythrocytes

   D. conversion of amino acids to urea

2. What cartilaginous structure prevents food from going down the trachea?

   A. tongue

   B. larynx

   C. glottis

   D. epiglottis

3. The chemical and mechanical receptors that control digestion are located in the:

   A. pons and medulla

   B. oral cavity

   C. glandular tissue that lines the organ lumen

   D. walls of the tract organs

4. Which system is involved in distributing the absorbed lipids to the peripheral tissue?

   A. digestive

   B. integumentary

   C. lymphatic

   D. nervous

5. Which organ is the primary site of fatty acid synthesis?

   A. smooth muscle

   B. spleen

   C. kidney

   D. liver

6. Which organ is the site of bile production?

   A. large intestine

   B. small intestine

   C. liver

   D. gallbladder

7. Which of the following is the correct order (from the lumen) of the four underlying layers making up walls of every organ in the alimentary canal?

   A. mucosa → submucosa → muscularis externa → serosa

   B. submucosa → serosa → muscularis externa → mucosa

   C. serosa → mucosa → submucosa → muscularis externa

   D. muscularis externa → serosa → mucosa → submucosa

8. The primary site of water absorption is the:

   A. duodenum

   B. large intestine

   C. jejunum

   D. ileum

9. Which of these processes does NOT occur in the mouth?

A. moistening of food

B. mechanical digestion

C. bolus formation

D. chemical digestion of proteins

10. All of the following statements about bile are correct, EXCEPT that:

A. it functions to carry bilirubin formed from the breakdown of worn-out RBCs

B. it contains enzymes for digestion

C. it is an excretory product and a digestive secretion

D. it functions to emulsify fats

11. Structures found at the esophagus-stomach, stomach-duodenum, and ileum-colon junction sites are:

A. sphincters

B. regions of dense villi

C. Peyer's patches

D. sites for peristalsis

12. Which of these statements is NOT accurate about the digestive system?

A. Peristalsis is a wave of smooth muscle contractions that proceeds along the digestive tract

B. Digestive enzymes from the pancreas are released via a duct into the duodenum

C. Low pH of the stomach is essential for the functioning of carbohydrate digestive enzymes

D. Villi in the small intestine absorb nutrients into the lymphatic and circulatory systems

13. In addition to mechanical breakdown and storage of food, the stomach:

A. initiates protein digestion and denatures proteins

B. is the first site where absorption takes place

C. is the site of lipid digestion

D. is the site of carbohydrate and lipid digestion

14. All of the following match nutrients to the specific digestive enzymes correctly, EXCEPT:

A. proteins – ptyalin (salivary amylase)

B. proteins – chymotrypsin

C. proteins – carboxypeptidase

D. carbohydrates _– pancreatic amylase

15. The acid secretions in the stomach are stimulated by the presence of:

A. lipids and fatty acids

B. simple carbohydrates and alcohols

C. protein and peptide fragments

D. starches and complex carbohydrates

16. The gastrointestinal tract is made up of three layers: mucosa, submucosa, and muscularis mucosae. The latter is composed of which type of muscle?

A. voluntary skeletal

B. voluntary smooth

C. involuntary smooth

D. involuntary skeletal

17. All of the following are functions of hepatocytes, EXCEPT:

A. producing digestive enzymes

B. processing nutrients

C. storing fat-soluble vitamins

D. detoxifying chemicals

18. Which is an example of an enzyme that is secreted as an inactive precursor and is converted into its active form in the lumen of the small intestine?

A. protease

B. salivary amylase

C. trypsinogen

D. bicarbonate

19. What is the site of amino acid absorption?

A. stomach

B. gallbladder

C. large intestine

D. small intestine

20. What is the function of bicarbonate within the mucus secreted into the gastrointestinal tract by the epithelium?

    I. Digestion of proteins

    II. Functioning as a buffer for the contents within the gastrointestinal tract

    III. Preventing the gastrointestinal tract from becoming acidic

A. I only

B. I and II only

C. II and III only

D. I, II and III

21. Which of the following is a function of goblet cells?

A. Protection against disease-causing organisms, such as bacteria, entering the digestive tract in food

B. Secretion of buffers to keep the pH of the digestive tract close to neutral

C. Producing mucus protecting digestive organs from protease enzymes needed for food digestion

D. Absorption of nutrients from digested food

22. Which of the following is NOT an end product of digestion?

A. amino acids

B. lactose

C. fructose

D. fatty acids

23. Bacteria of the large intestine play an essential role in:

A. synthesizing vitamin K and some B vitamins

B. synthesizing vitamin C

C. producing gas

D. absorption of bilirubin

24. Which of these controls the flow of material from the esophagus into the stomach?

    A. gallbladder

    B. pyloric sphincter

    C. epiglottis

    D. cardiac sphincter

25. Which organ secretes intrinsic factors and absorbs caffeine?

    A. liver

    B. pancreas

    C. duodenum

    D. stomach

26. Which statement is true for bile?

    A. It is an emulsifying agent

    B. It is a protein

    C. It is an enzyme

    D. It is a hormone

27. Most digestion of food in humans takes place in the:

    A. liver

    B. small intestine

    C. mouth

    D. stomach

28. Which organ detoxifies the body like peroxisomes detoxify the cell?

    A. spleen

    B. liver

    C. kidneys

    D. stomach

29. Which nutrients yield 4 calories per gram?

    A. glucose and proteins

    B. fats and glucose

    C. proteins and lipids

    D. glucose, proteins and fats

Nervous System

1. Which of these effects would result from the stimulation of the parasympathetic nervous system?

   A. Relaxation of the bronchi

   B. Dilation of the pupils

   C. Increased gut motility

   D. Increased heart rate

2. The autonomic nervous system is comprised of:

   A. sensory neurons that supply the digestive tract

   B. sensory neurons that convey information from somatic receptors for special senses of vision, hearing, taste, and smell

   C. CNS motor fibers that conduct nerve impulses from the CNS to skeletal muscles

   D. motor fibers that conduct nerve impulses from the CNS to smooth muscle, cardiac muscle, and glands

3. The central nervous system determines the strength of a stimulus by the:

   A. amplitude of action potentials

   B. frequency of action potentials

   C. type of stimulus receptor

   D. origin of the stimulus

4. All of the following is correct about neurons, EXCEPT that they:

   A. are mitotic

   B. have high metabolic rates

   C. conduct impulses

   D. have extreme longevity

5. The autonomic nervous system's motor pathway contains:

   A. three neurons

   B. many neurons

   C. a single long neuron

   D. two neurons

6. Which of the following is most characteristic of an accident victim who sustained isolated damage to the cerebellum?

   A. loss of muscular coordination

   B. loss of speech

   C. loss of voluntary muscle contraction

   D. loss of sensation in the extremities

7. The somatic nervous system:

   A. innervates the skeletal muscles

   B. innervates the glands

   C. innervates the cardiac muscle

   D. innervates smooth muscle of the digestive tract

8. Which of the following is NOT a location where the white matter would be found?

    A. pyramidal tracts

    B. outer portion of the spinal cord

    C. corpus callosum

    D. cerebral cortex

9. Which function would be significantly impaired by destroying the cerebellum?

    A. thermoregulation

    B. coordinated movement

    C. sense of smell

    D. urine formation

10. Which of these systems, when stimulated, results in increased heart rate, blood pressure, and blood glucose levels?

    A. central nervous system

    B. somatic nervous system

    C. sympathetic nervous system

    D. parasympathetic nervous system

11. The brain stem consists of:

    A. midbrain

    B. pons, medulla, midbrain and cerebellum

    C. pons, medulla and midbrain

    D. cerebrum, pons, and medulla

12. All of the following are in normal cerebrospinal fluid, EXCEPT:

    A. potassium

    B. protein

    C. glucose

    D. red blood cells

13. Cell bodies of the sensory neurons of the spinal nerves are in the:

    A. sympathetic ganglia

    B. thalamus

    C. ventral root ganglia of the spinal cord

    D. dorsal root ganglia of the spinal cord

14. The part of the cerebral cortex involved in cognition, personality, intellect, and recall is:

    A. the limbic association area

    B. combined primary somatosensory cortex and somatosensory association

    C. the prefrontal cortex

    D. the cortex posterior association area

15. Which of these processes is controlled by the sympathetic nervous system?

    A. increased gastric secretions

    B. increased respiration

    C. constriction of pupils

    D. decreased heart rate

16. The region on neurons that brings the graded potential to the neuronal cell body is:

A. axon

B. dendrite

C. T-tubule

D. node of Ranvier

17. Which statement correctly describes the role of the myelin sheath in action potential transmission?

A. Saltatory conduction dissipates current through specialized leakage channels

B. Oligodendrocytes cover the nodes of Ranvier to prevent backflow of current

C. Protein fibers cover the axon and prevent leakage of current across the membrane

D. Lipids insulate the axons, while membrane depolarization occurs within the nodes

18. Which structure in humans is analogous to an electrical device that allows current to flow only in one direction?

A. dendrite

B. axon process

C. myelin sheath

D. synaptic cleft

19. The myelin sheath around the axons of the peripheral nervous system is produced by:

A. axon hillock

B. nerve cell body

C. nodes of Ranvier

D. Schwann cell

20. The specific region of the neuron that connects to the axon and sums the graded inputs before the propagation of the all or none depolarization is:

A. axon hillock

B. nerve cell body

C. node of Ranvier

D. axon terminus

21. Myelin covers axons and is responsible for:

A. initiating the action potential

B. allowing pumping of Na^+ out of the cell

C. maintaining the resting potential

D. allowing faster conduction of impulses

22. What is the function of the nodes of Ranvier within the neuron?

A. To provide a binding site for acetylcholine

B. To provide a space for Schwann cells to deposit myelin

C. To regenerate the anterograde conduction of the action potential

D. To permit the axon hillock to generate a stronger action potential

23. In a myopic eye, the inverted image formed by the lens falls:

A. on the optic nerve

B. in front of the retina

C. behind the retina

D. on the retina

24. The fovea has a high concentration of:

    A. cones

    B. axons leaving the retina for the optic nerve

    C. rods

    D. blood vessels

25. The phenomenon of being able to distinguish objects 5-10 min after bright lights are turned off is due to:

    A. sudden bleaching of cones

    B. sudden bleaching of rods

    C. sudden bleaching of rhodopsin

    D. slow unbleaching of rods

26. Which of the following results from parasympathetic stimulation?

    A. Piloerection of the hair of the skin

    B. Contraction of the abdominal muscles during exercise

    C. Production of saliva

    D. Increased heart rate

27. Most refraction (bending of light in the eye) is accomplished by:

    A. the pupil

    B. photoreceptors

    C. the vitreous humor

    D. the cornea

28. When light strikes the eye, photoreceptors:

    A. depolarize

    B. enter refractory

    C. hyperpolarize

    D. release neurotransmitter

29. Which condition is NOT an eye disorder?

    A. glaucoma

    B. otitis

    C. myopia

    D. hyperopia

30. Which of the following structures contain(s) hair cells that detect motion?

    I. the skin

    II. the organ of Corti

    III. the semicircular canals

    A. I only

    B. III only

    C. II and III only

    D. I, II and III

Skeletal System

1. The vertebral curves function to:

   A. improve the cervical center of gravity
   B. accommodate the weight of the pelvic girdle
   C. provide resilience and flexibility
   D. accommodate muscle attachment

2. The purpose of synovial fluid in a synovial joint is to:

   A. hydrate osteocyte cells
   B. create a rigid connection between opposing flat bones
   C. reduce friction between the ends of opposing bones
   D. create the structure for the necessary morphology of joints and bones

3. Which region of the human vertebral column bears most of the weight of the body and receives the most stress?

   A. thoracic region
   B. lumbar region
   C. cervical region
   D. sacral region

4. During bone maturation, osteoblasts are trapped in their matrix and then turn into which cells as they stop producing more matrix?

   A. matrixocytes
   B. trabeculocytes
   C. osteoclasts
   D. osteocytes

5. Which of the following is characteristic of short bones?

   A. Consist mainly of hyaline cartilage
   B. Consist mostly of dense bone
   C. Consist of both spongy and dense bone
   D. Consist mostly of spongy bone

6. The primary function of the axial skeleton is to:

   A. provide central support for the body and protect internal organs
   B. provide a space for the significant digestive organs
   C. provide a conduit for the peripheral nerves
   D. provide an attachment point for muscles to allow movement

7. The skeletal system performs all of the following functions, EXCEPT:

   A. production of Vitamin C
   B. storage and release of minerals
   C. protection of the viscera
   D. production of the blood

8. Which bone tissue is most adapted to support weight and withstand tension stress?

A. compact bone

B. trabecular bone

C. spongy bone

D. irregular bone

9. During bone formation, a deficiency of growth hormone can cause:

A. decreased proliferation of the epiphyseal plate cartilage

B. increased osteoclast activity

C. inadequate calcification of bone

D. decreased osteoclast activity

10. Connective tissue holding the bones together in a synovial joint is:

A. osteocyte

B. ligament

C. cartilage

D. periosteum

11. The typical histological makeup of bone is concentric lamellae called:

A. periosteum

B. endosteum

C. osteon

D. trabeculae

12. Which of these is NOT in compact bone?

A. yellow marrow

B. canaliculi

C. Haversian canals

D. Volkmann's canals

13. The process when bone develops from hyaline cartilage is:

A. periosteal ossification

B. intramembranous ossification

C. intermembranous ossification

D. endochondral ossification

14. The connective tissue that connects bones is:

A. synovium

B. osteoprogenitor cells

C. ligaments

D. sockets

15. The process of bones increasing in width is:

A. concentric growth

B. appositional growth

D. closing of the epiphyseal plate

C. epiphyseal plate opening

16. Which type of tissue is bone classified as?

    A. epithelial

    B. connective

    C. muscle

    D. skeletal

17. The shaft of long bones is:

    A. cortex

    B. medulla

    C. epiphysis

    D. diaphysis

18. Which of these is the critical function of the spongy bone of the hips?

    A. storage of fats

    B. synthesis of lymph fluid

    C. synthesis of erythrocytes

    D. storage of erythrocytes

19. The structural unit of spongy bone is:

    A. trabeculae

    B. osseous lamellae

    C. osteons

    D. Haversian canals

20. The narrow space of hyaline cartilage that is the site of long bone growth until the end of puberty is:

    A. chondrocyte line

    B. epiphyseal plate

    C. medullary cavity

    D. mineralization

21. What is the structure on the ends of bones that looks bluish-white and reduces friction:

    A. hyaline cartilage

    B. elastic cartilage

    C. areolar connective tissue

    D. fibrocartilage

22. Which type of bone cell produces the matrix of the bone?

    A. osteoclasts

    B. osteocytes

    C. osteoblasts

    D. endothelial

23. Synovial fluid within joint cavities of freely movable joints contains:

    A. hydrochloric acid

    B. hyaluronic acid

    C. lactic acid

    D. pyruvic acid

24. Which connective tissue is used for the attachment of muscle to bone?

    A. origin

    B. ligament

    C. aponeurosis

    D. tendon

25. Which of these is NOT the function of bone?

A. storage of lipids

B. regulation of blood temperature

C. structural support

D. storage of minerals

26. Tendon sheaths:

A. are extensions of periosteum

B. help anchor the tendon to the muscle

C. act to reduce friction

D. are lined with dense irregular connective tissue

27. The inorganic matter in the matrix of osseous tissue is primarily:

A. calcium carbonate

B. glycosaminoglycans

C. collagen

D. hydroxyapatite

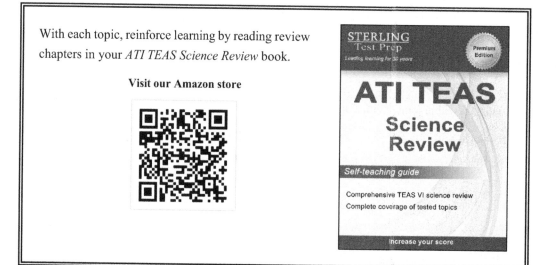

Muscular System

1. How are cardiac muscle cells different from smooth and skeletal muscle cells?

   A. It is often branched
   B. It has T tubules

   C. It is under involuntary control
   D. It has a striated appearance

2. Which of the following takes place during muscular contraction?

   A. Neither the thin nor the thick filament contracts
   B. The thin and thick filaments contract
   C. The thin filament contracts, while the thick filament remains constant
   D. The thin filament remains constant, while the thick filament contracts

3. Most skeletal muscles consist of:

   A. predominantly slow oxidative fibers
   B. predominantly fast oxidative fibers

   C. muscle fibers of the same type
   D. a mixture of fiber types

4. Which of the following does NOT happen during muscle contraction?

   A. H band shortens or disappears
   B. I band shortens or disappears

   C. A band shortens or disappears
   D. sarcomere shortens

5. Shivering functions to increase core body temperature because it:

   A. increases the contractile activity of skeletal muscles
   B. signals the hypothalamus that body temperature is higher than the actual
   C. causes bones to rub together to generate heat
   D. signals the body that the core temperature is low and encourages behavioral modification

6. Which is NOT a property of muscle tissue?

   A. extensibility
   B. contractility

   C. communication
   D. excitability

7. Which of the following muscle types are involuntary muscles?

   I. cardiac
   II. smooth
   III. skeletal

   A. I only
   B. II only

   C. I and II only
   D. II and III only

8. Myoglobin:

A. phosphorylates ADP directly

B. stores oxygen in muscle cells

C. produces the endplate potential

D. breaks down glycogen

9. During an action potential, a cardiac muscle cell remains depolarized much longer than a neuron to:

A. prevent a neuron from depolarizing twice in rapid succession

B. permit adjacent cardiac muscle cells to contract at different times

C. prevent the initiation of another action potential during contraction of the heart

D. ensures that Na^+ voltage-gated channels remain open, so Na^+ exits the cell

10. A characteristic of cardiac muscle that can be observed with the light microscope is:

A. somatic motor neurons

B. no nuclei

C. intercalated discs

D. single cells

11. Muscles undergo movement at joints by:

A. decreasing in length and moving the origin and insertion of the muscle closer

B. filling with blood and increasing the distance between the ends of a muscle

C. increasing in length and pushing the origin and insertion of the muscle apart

D. depolarizing neurons which initiate electrical twitches at the tendons

12. Wavelike contraction produced by the smooth muscle is:

A. peristalsis

B. myeloblastosis

C. vasodilation

D. circulitus

13. The striations of a skeletal muscle cell are due to:

A. T tubules

B. sarcoplasmic reticulum

C. arrangement of myofilaments

D. thickness of the sarcolemma

14. For the movement of a pair of antagonistic muscles, one of the muscles:

A. contracts in an isometric action

B. acts synergistically by contracting to stabilize the moving bone

C. contracts in an isotonic action

D. relaxes

15. What structure connects the biceps muscle to the radius bone?

A. biceps cartilage

B. biceps ligament

C. biceps tendon

D. annular ligament of the radius

16. The enteric nervous system controls which action of the muscle?

    A. Contraction of the diaphragm

    B. Peristalsis of the gastrointestinal tract

    C. Conduction of cardiac muscle action potentials

    D. The reflex arc of the knee jerk response when the patella is struck

17. Which of the following is NOT present in a skeletal muscle?

    A. sarcoplasmic reticulum

    B. multinucleated cells

    C. individual innervations of each muscle fiber

    D. intercellular conductivity of action potentials

18. All of the following statements are true for smooth muscle, EXCEPT:

    A. Its contractions are involuntary

    B. It does not require calcium for contraction

    C. Its contractions produce a chemical change near the smooth muscle

    D. Its contractions are longer than the contractions in skeletal muscle

19. Which of the following muscles is under voluntary control?

    A. smooth muscle in the gastrointestinal tract

    B. iris of the eye

    C. diaphragm

    D. cardiac tissue

20. Which of the following statements describes the structure of smooth muscle?

    A. Multicellular units of muscle tissue are under voluntary control

    B. Peristalsis results from single-unit muscle cells within the gastrointestinal tract

    C. Ca^{2+} distribution occurs via an extensive network of T-tubules

    D. Ca^{2+} binds to troponin and changes the conformation of the tropomyosin

21. Which of the following is a true statement about muscle?

    A. Striated muscle cells are long and cylindrical with many nuclei

    B. Cardiac muscle cells are in the heart, and large blood vessels

    C. Cardiac muscle cells have many nuclei

    D. Smooth muscle cells have T tubules

22. A typical skeletal muscle:

    A. is innervated by the somatic nervous system

    B. is innervated only by the autonomic nervous system

    C. is innervated only by the parasympathetic and sympathetic nervous system

    D. has myosin and actin that lack a striated appearance

23. A protein in muscle cells that binds oxygen is:

    A. tropomyosin   **C.** myoglobin

    B. glycogen   **D.** myosin

24. This muscle type is always characterized by multinucleated cells.

      I. skeletal muscle

      II. smooth muscle

      III. cardiac muscle

    A. I only   **C.** I and III only

    B. III only   **D.** II and III only

25. Which of the following statements is/are correct about cardiac muscle?

      I. It acts as a functional syncytium

      II. It is under the control of the autonomic nervous system

      III. It is striated due to the arrangement of actin and myosin filaments

    A. I only   **C.** II and III only

    B. III only   **D.** I, I and III

26. The point of attachment of a nerve to muscle fiber is the:

    A. contraction point   **C.** relaxation point

    B. synapse   **D.** neuromuscular junction

27. All of these statements are true for muscles, EXCEPT:

    A. Resting muscle is completely relaxed

    B. Tonus is the state of partial contraction which occurs in a resting muscle

    C. Isometric contraction means that the length of the muscle is constant

    D. Isotonic contraction means that the length of the muscle shortens

Reproductive System

1. Which of the following events is/are essential for the menstrual cycle?

      I.   adrenal medulla releases norepinephrine

      II. FSH stimulates ovarian follicle development

      III. progesterone stimulates the formation of the endometrial lining

A. II only

B. III only

C. I and II only

D. II and III only

2. All of the following about human gamete production is true, EXCEPT:

A. meiosis in females produces four egg cells

B. sperm develop in the seminiferous tubules within the testes

C. eggs develop in the ovarian follicles within the ovaries

D. FSH stimulates gamete production in males and females

3. All of these statements regarding the menstrual cycle are true, EXCEPT:

A. Graafian follicle, under the influence of LH, undergoes ovulation

B. follicle secretes estrogen as it develops

C. corpus luteum develops from the remains of the post-ovulatory Graafian follicle

D. The posterior pituitary secretes FSH and LH

4. Which of the following is the initial site of spermatogenesis?

A. seminiferous tubules

B. seminal vesicles

C. vas deferens

D. epididymis

5. Which statement correctly describes the role of LH in the menstrual cycle?

A. stimulates the ovary to increase LH secretions

B. inhibits secretions of GnRH

C. stimulates the development of the endometrium for implantation of the zygote

D. induces the corpus luteum to secrete estrogen and progesterone

6. What is the most likely cause of a condition in which the testes do not fully descend into the scrotum due to abnormal testicular development?

A. cortisol deficiency

B. testosterone deficiency

C. excess LH

D. excess estrogen

7. Testosterone is synthesized primarily by:

   A. sperm cells

   B. hypothalamus

   C. Leydig cells

   D. anterior pituitary gland

8. Which of these conditions is the LEAST likely cause of male infertility?

   A. acrosomal enzymes denaturation

   B. immotility of cilia

   C. abnormal mitochondria

   D. testosterone deficiency

9. Which of the following can result from scars formed in the reproductive system of women with a high risk of infections (e.g., chlamydia)?

   A. elevated levels of estrogen

   B. decreased ovulation

   C. infertility

   D. decreased levels of estrogen

10. The primary difference between estrous and menstrual cycles is that:

   A. in the estrous cycle, the endometrium is shed and reabsorbed by the uterus, while in the menstrual cycle, the shed endometrium is excreted from the body

   B. behavioral changes during estrous cycles are much less apparent than those of menstrual cycles

   C. season and climate have less pronounced effects on the estrous cycle than they do on menstrual cycles

   D. copulation commonly occurs across the estrous cycle, whereas in menstrual cycles, copulation only occurs during the period surrounding ovulation

11. Progesterone is primarily secreted by the:

   A. primary oocyte

   B. hypothalamus

   C. corpus luteum

   D. anterior pituitary gland

12. One of the functions of estrogen is to:

   A. induce the ruptured follicle to develop into the corpus luteum

   B. stimulate testosterone synthesis in males

   C. maintain female secondary sex characteristics

   D. promote the development and release of the follicle

13. The epididymis functions to:

   A. synthesize and release testosterone

   B. store sperm until they are released during ejaculation

   C. initiate the menstrual cycle by secreting FSH and LH

   D. provide a conduit for the ovum as it moves from the ovary into the uterus

14. What is the purpose of the cilia that cover the inner linings of the Fallopian tubes?

   A. Preventing polyspermy by immobilizing additional incoming sperm after fusion

   B. Facilitating the movement of the ovum towards the uterus

   C. Removing particulate matter that becomes trapped in the mucus layer

   D. Protecting the ovum from pH fluctuations

15. Decreasing progesterone during the luteal phase of the menstrual cycle results in:

   A. increased secretion of estrogen in the follicle followed by the menstruation phase

   B. degeneration of the corpus luteum in the ovary

   C. increased secretion of LH, which produces the luteal surge and onset of ovulation

   D. thickening of the endometrial lining in preparation for implantation of the zygote

16. Which of the following sequences correctly represents the pathway of anatomical structures passed by a probe inserted into the urethra of a male patient?

   A. urethra → vas deferens → prostate → ejaculatory duct → seminiferous tubules →_epididymis

   B. urethra → prostate → vas deferens → ejaculatory duct → seminiferous tubules →_epididymis

   C. urethra → ejaculatory duct → prostate → vas deferens → epididymis → seminiferous tubules

   D. urethra → prostate → ejaculatory duct → vas deferens → epididymis → seminiferous tubules

Notes for active learning

Integumentary System

1. The primary role of melanin in the skin is to:

   A. provide a waterproof layer for the skin

   B. shield the nucleus from damage by UV radiation

   C. be an integral component of collagen fibers

   D. keep the body cool via evaporation

2. Which layer is NOT part of the skin?

   A. hypodermis

   B. papillary

   C. dermis

   D. epidermis

3. Which of the following are the sites where the apocrine glands are found?

   A. Palms of the hands and soles of the feet

   B. Under the arms and in the external genitalia areas

   C. Beneath the flexure lines in the body

   D. All body regions, buried deep in the dermis

4. Which layer of the skin is composed of dense, irregular connective tissue?

   A. reticular layer of the dermis

   B. hypodermis

   C. epidermis

   D. papillary layer of the dermis

5. An essential function of the eccrine sweat gland is:

   A. body temperature regulation

   B. earwax production

   C. milk production

   D. stress-induced sweating

6. What causes "goosebumps" (the hair standing on end)?

   A. contraction of the epidermal papillae

   B. contraction of the epidermal ridges

   C. contraction of the arrector pili

   D. contraction of the dermal papillae

7. In addition to waterproofing and lubricating the skin, a vital function of sebum is protecting against:

   A. abrasions or cuts to the skin

   B. harmful bacteria

   C. overheating

   D. overexposure to UV light

8. Which glands are numerous throughout most of the body and produce a watery sweat that cools the body?

   A. merocrine (eccrine) glands
   B. apocrine glands
   C. ceruminous glands
   D. sebaceous glands

9. Which layer of the skin has no blood vessels?

   A. papillary
   B. hypodermis
   C. epidermis
   D. dermis

10. Which of the following is NOT associated with the dermis?

    A. elastin
    B. keratin
    C. blood vessels
    D. collagen

11. The outside layer of the skin is the:

    A. epidermis
    B. dermis
    C. apocrine layer
    D. lamellar layer

12. The inside layer of the two main layers of the skin is the:

    A. epidermis
    B. dermis
    C. lamellar layer
    D. apocrine layer

13. Which kind of cells comprises up to 30 or more layers of stratum corneum?

    A. keratinized
    B. tactile Merkel
    C. non-keratinized
    D. stem

14. Which skin gland is a holocrine gland?

    A. sebaceous
    B. sudoriferous
    C. endocrine
    D. ceruminous

15. The factor in the hue of the skin is the amount of:

    A. oxygen in the blood
    B. blood vessels
    C. keratin
    D. melanin

16. What layer of the integumentary system contains adipose tissue?

    A. dermis
    B. subcutaneous layer
    C. epidermis
    D. muscular layer

17. In which order would a needle pierce the epidermal layers of the skin?

    A. corneum → lucidum → granulosum → spinosum → basale

    B. granulosum → basale → spinosum → corneum → lucidum

    C. basale → spinosum → lucidum → granulosum → corneum

    D. basale → spinosum → granulosum → lucidum → corneum

18. Which layer of the skin is responsible for fingerprints?

    A. hypodermis

    B. papillary dermis

    C. reticular dermis

    D. epidermis

19. The hypodermis acts as a shock absorber because:

    A. cells that make up the hypodermis secrete a protective mucus

    B. major part of its makeup is adipose tissue

    C. the basement membrane can absorb shock

    D. it is located just below the epidermis and protects the dermis from shock

20. Keratinocytes protect the skin from UV damage by:

    A. maintaining the appropriate pH for the melanocyte to synthesize melanin granules

    B. maintaining the appropriate temperature so melanocyte proteins are not denatured

    C. providing the melanocyte with nutrients necessary for melanin synthesis

    D. accumulating melanin granules on their superficial portion

21. Which of the following layers is responsible for cell division and replacement?

    A. stratum basale

    B. stratum spinosum

    C. stratum granulosum

    D. stratum corneum

22. Which of these thermoregulation mechanisms is NOT involved in heat conservation?

    A. blood vessel constriction

    B. shivering

    C. perspiration

    D. piloerection

23. The touch sensors of the epidermis are:

    A. nociceptors

    B. dendritic cells

    C. tactile cells

    D. keratinocytes

24. Which degree of burn destroys the epidermis and dermis and frequently requires a skin graft?

    A. first-degree burn

    B. second-degree burn

    C. third-degree burn

    D. fourth-degree burn

25. Which of the following is NOT a function of the integument?

    A. thermoregulation   **C.** barrier to UV energy

    B. vitamin E synthesis   **D.** infection resistance

26. Which cutaneous receptor is utilized for the reception of touch or light pressure?

    A. Ruffinian endings   **C.** Meissner's corpuscles

    B. end-bulbs of Krause   **D.** Pacinian corpuscles

Endocrine System

1. Molecular signals that travel to distant cells are known as:

A. paracrine signals

B. parasitic signals

C. autocrine signals

D. hormones

2. The class of hormones affecting cellular targets by starting or ending transcription is:

A. steroids

B. eicosanoids

C. peptides

D. amino acids

3. Which of the following is TRUE about hormones?

A. They regulate cellular functions and are generally controlled via negative feedback

B. The circulating level is held constant through a series of positive feedback loops

C. Lipid-soluble and water-soluble hormones bind to intracellular protein receptors

D. The ducts of endocrine organs release their contents into the bloodstream

4. Given that parathyroid hormone plays a vital role in the control of blood Ca^{2+} ion levels, it is an essential hormone for:

    I.   bone density

    II. renal calcium reabsorption

    III. blood calcium concentration

A. I only

B. I and II only

C. I and III only

D. I, II and III

5. All of the following statements are characteristic of peptide hormone activity, EXCEPT:

A. hormone is transmitted via blood circulation

B. the target organ is at a distant site from the release of the hormone

C. cellular effects within cells often require the activity of a protein kinase

D. hormones pass into the target cell's membrane and enter the nucleus

6. A hormone released by the posterior pituitary is:

A. TSH

B. prolactin

C. oxytocin

D. progesterone

7. Deficiency of which hormone causes female infertility due to the ovulation of immature ova?

    A. oxytocin
    B. estrogen

    C. FSH
    D. LH

8. Which endocrine gland synthesizes ACTH?

    A. hypothalamus
    B. thalamus

    C. anterior pituitary
    D. medulla

9. The thyroid secretes all of the following, EXCEPT:

    A. triiodothyronine
    B. TSH

    C. thyroxine
    D. all of the above

10. A gland that produces exocrine and endocrine secretions is:

    A. adrenal
    B. pancreas

    C. parathyroid
    D. pituitary

11. During stress, the adrenal cortex responds by secreting the following hormone:

    A. adrenaline
    B. norepinephrine

    C. ACTH
    D. cortisol

12. The hypothalamus controls the anterior pituitary through:

    A. cytokines
    B. second messengers

    C. releasing hormones
    D. antibodies

13. The concentration of blood Ca^{2+} is raised by:

    A. calcitonin
    B. parathyroid hormone

    C. aldosterone
    D. glucagon

14. Which of the following is an example of antagonistic endocrine relationships that maintain homeostasis?

    A. ACTH — TSH
    B. oxytocin — prolactin

    C. vitamin D — parathyroid hormone
    D. insulin — glucagon

15. What is the classification of a feedback system where a response enhances the original stimulus?

    A. enhancing
    B. responsive

    C. negative
    D. positive

16. Which of these hormones directly affects blood sugar?

    A. calcitonin

    B. estrogen

    C. glucagon

    D. oxytocin

17. Which endocrine gland synthesizes melatonin?

    A. pineal

    B. hypothalamus

    C. anterior pituitary

    D. posterior pituitary

18. Which hormone, secreted by the delta cells of the GI tract, inhibits the release of insulin and glucagon?

    A. cortisol

    B. trypsin

    C. somatostatin

    D. pepsin

19. Which statement is true for epinephrine?

    A. It is released by the adrenal medulla

    B. It is released during parasympathetic stimulation

    C. It is a steroid hormone

    D. It is synthesized by the adrenal cortex

20. Which gland produces growth-hormone-releasing hormone (GHRH) that stimulates the transcription of the growth hormone gene?

    A. parathyroid

    B. anterior pituitary

    C. hypothalamus

    D. liver

21. Which of the following basic categories is the correct chemical classification for hormones?

    A. female and male hormones

    B. peptides and steroids

    C. carbohydrates, proteins and steroids

    D. steroid, peptide, and amines

22. Insulin and aldosterone are secreted by these endocrine organs, respectively:

    A. pancreas and adrenal cortex

    B. spleen and red bone marrow

    C. liver and pancreas

    D. adrenal gland and kidney

23. The ability of a tissue or organ to respond to the presence of a hormone depends on:

    A. nothing; hormones stimulate cells because they are powerful and nonspecific

    B. the location of the tissue or organ to the circulatory path

    C. the membrane potential of the cells of the target organ

    D. the presence of the appropriate receptors on/in the target tissue or the organ cell

24. The parathyroid gland is one of two glands controlling blood calcium levels and is anatomically located:

A. superior to the kidney

B. connected to the hypothalamus

C. posterior in the neck, near the larynx

D. within the duodenum of the small intestine

25. Which endocrine gland releases vasopressin, a hormone involved in water balance?

A. posterior pituitary

B. hypothalamus

C. thyroid

D. adrenal cortex

26. Which of these regulates temperature?

A. cerebrum

B. hypothalamus

C. medulla oblongata

D. pons

27. A patient who has gained 35 lbs in the past 3 months visits her physician and complains of fatigue. She is diagnosed with a goiter and decreased metabolic rate. Based on this, which hormone is most likely to be deficient in this patient?

A. estrogen

B. cortisol

C. thyroxine

D. aldosterone

28. During periods of dehydration, the main activating factor of aldosterone secretion is:

A. ACTH

B. renin

C. sympathetic nervous system

D. spontaneous adrenal release

Genitourinary System

1. A structure originating from the renal pelvis and extending to the urinary bladder is:

   A. urethra

   B. major calyx

   C. ureter

   D. vas deferens

2. Which of the choices below is NOT a function of the urinary system?

   A. Eliminates solid undigested wastes and salts and excretes CO_2 and H_2O

   B. Maintains blood osmolarity

   C. Regulates blood glucose levels and produces hormones

   D. Helps maintain homeostasis by controlling blood volume

3. Which of the following statements about ureters is correct?

   A. Ureters are innervated by only parasympathetic nerves

   B. Ureters are capable of peristalsis

   C. The epithelium is stratified squamous like the skin, which allows distensibility

   D. Ureters contain sphincters at the entrance to the bladder to prevent the backflow of urine

4. Gout is manifested by decreased excretion of uric acid. Which organ is mainly responsible for the elimination of uric acid?

   A. spleen

   B. large intestine

   C. kidney

   D. liver

5. Which area of the kidney is the site of passive diffusion of Na^+?

   A. thick segment of ascending limb

   B. distal convoluted tubule

   C. loop of Henle

   D. proximal convoluted tubule

6. Hydrolysis of which of the following produces nitrogenous waste as urea, uric acid, or ammonia?

   A. vitamins

   B. fats

   C. sugars

   D. proteins

7. Which of the following is part of the excretory and reproductive systems of male mammals?

   A. urethra

   B. ureter

   C. prostate

   D. vas deferens

8. Which of the following nephron structures is/are the site(s) of removing H_2O to concentrate the urine?

      I.   ascending loop of Henle
      II. descending loop of Henle
      III. proximal convoluted tubule

A. II only

B. III only

C. II and III only

D. I, II and III

9. Which of the following sequences correctly represents the pathway of anatomical structures passed by a probe inserted into the urethra of a female patient?

A. urethra → bladder → opening to the ureter → ureter → prostate → renal pelvis

B. ureter → opening to the ureter → prostate → vas deferens → epididymis

C. urethra → bladder → opening to the ureter → ureter → renal pelvis

D. kidney → ureter → opening to the bladder → bladder → urethra

10. Angiotensin II functions to:

A. decrease water absorption

B. decrease arterial blood pressure

C. decrease aldosterone production

D. constrict arterioles and increase blood pressure

11. Renin is a polypeptide hormone that:

A. is produced in response to increased blood volume

B. is produced in response to decreased blood pressure

C. acts on the pituitary gland

D. is produced in response to concentrated urine

12. If a concentrated NaCl solution is infused directly into the renal tubules of a healthy person, what is the most likely effect?

A. Urine volume decreases because of decreased filtrate osmolarity

B. Urine volume increases because of decreased filtrate osmolarity

C. Urine volume increases because of increased filtrate volume

D. Urine volume decreases because of increased filtrate osmolarity

13. Which of the following is NOT typically contained in the blood after it has been filtered through the glomerulus in the kidney?

A. sodium ions

B. blood cells

C. amino acids

D. glucose

14. Which statement most accurately describes the expected levels of aldosterone and vasopressin in the blood of a dehydrated patient compared to a healthy individual?

    A. Aldosterone levels are higher, and vasopressin levels are lower

    B. Aldosterone levels are lower, and vasopressin levels are higher

    C. Aldosterone and vasopressin levels are higher

    D. Aldosterone and vasopressin levels are lower

15. Which of the following is a function of the loop of Henle?

    A. Absorption of water into the filtrate

    B. Absorption of electrolytes by active transport and water by osmosis in the same segments

    C. Forming a small volume of concentrated urine

    D. Forming a large volume of concentrated urine

16. If the renal clearance value of substance X is zero, it means that:

    A. usually, all substance X is reabsorbed

    B. the value is relatively high in a healthy adult

    C. the substance X molecule is too large to be filtered via the kidneys

    D. most of substance X is filtered via the kidneys and is not reabsorbed in the convoluted tubules

17. All of these statements about aldosterone are correct, EXCEPT that it:

    A. stimulates the secretion of Na^+

    B. stimulates the secretion of K^+

    C. results in the production of concentrated urine

    D. is produced by the adrenal cortex

18. Which of the following is NOT reabsorbed by secondary active transport in the proximal convoluted tubule?

    A. phosphate   **C.** glucose

    B. urea   **D.** amino acids

19. Most electrolyte reabsorption by the renal tubules is:

    A. in the proximal convoluted tubule

    B. in the descending loop of Henle

    C. not limited by a transport maximum

    D. in the distal convoluted tubule

Notes for active learning

Section II

Life and Physical Sciences

Basic Macromolecules in a Biological System

Chromosomes, Genes, and DNA

Mendel's Laws of Heredity

Basic Atomic Structure

Characteristic Properties of Substances

Changing States of Matter

Chemical Reactions

Basic Macromolecules in a Biological System

1. What is the correct sequence of energy sources used by the body?

    A. fats → glucose → other carbohydrates → proteins

    B. glucose → other carbohydrates → fats → proteins

    C. glucose → other carbohydrates → proteins → fats

    D. glucose → fats → proteins → other carbohydrates

2. Hemoglobin is an example of a protein that:

    A. is initially inactive in the cell

    B. has a quaternary structure

    C. carries out a catalytic reaction

    D. has only tertiary structure

3. All proteins:

    A. are post-translationally modified

    B. have a primary structure

    C. have catalytic activity

    D. contain prosthetic groups

4. Glycogen is:

    A. degraded by glycogenesis

    B. synthesized by glycogenolysis

    C. the storage polymer of glucose

    D. found in both plants and animals

5. All of these statements apply to proteins, EXCEPT:

    A. they regulate cell membrane trafficking

    B. they catalyze chemical reactions

    C. they can be hormones

    D. they undergo self-replication

6. In general, phospholipids contain:

    A. a glycerol molecule

    B. saturated fatty acids

    C. unsaturated fatty acids

    D. a cholesterol molecule

7. Which of the following is NOT involved in osmosis?

    A. H_2O spontaneously moves from a hypertonic to a hypotonic environment

    B. H_2O spontaneously moves from an area of high solvent to low solvent concentration

    C. H_2O spontaneously moves from a hypotonic to a hypertonic environment

    D. Transport of H_2O

8. The presence of which element differentiates a protein from a carbohydrate molecule?

A. carbon

B. hydrogen

C. nitrogen

D. oxygen

9. Which of these choices is the correct statement about lipids?

A. They are composed of elements C, O, N & H

B. Their secondary structure is composed of α helices and β pleated sheets

C. They are molecules used for long term energy storage in animals

D. Elements of C:H:O are in the ratio of 1:2:1

10. Which element is NOT found within nucleic acids?

A. nitrogen

B. oxygen

C. phosphorus

D. sulfur

11. In general, phospholipids contain:

A. a glycerol molecule

B. saturated fatty acids

C. unsaturated fatty acids

D. a cholesterol molecule

12. All of the following are lipid derivatives, EXCEPT:

A. carotenoids

B. albumins

C. waxes

D. steroids

13. The linear sequence of amino acids along a peptide chain determines its:

A. primary structure

B. secondary structure

C. tertiary structure

D. quaternary structure

14. There are [   ] different types of major biomolecules used by humans.

A. a few dozen

B. four

C. several thousand

D. several million

15. Insulin is an example of a(n):

A. hormone

B. storage protein

C. structural protein

D. enzyme

16. What type of protein structure corresponds to a spiral alpha-helix of amino acids?

    A. primary

    B. secondary

    C. tertiary

    D. quaternary

17. Proteins are characterized by the fact that they:

    A. always have quaternary structures

    B. retain their conformation above 35-40 °C

    C. have a primary structure formed by covalent linkages

    D. are composed of a single peptide chain

18. Members of which class of biomolecules is the building block of proteins?

    A. fatty acids

    B. amino acids

    C. glycerols

    D. monosaccharides

19. Proteins are polymers. They consist of monomer units which are:

    A. keto acids

    B. amide

    C. amino acids

    D. ketones

20. Collagen is an example of a (an):

    A. storage protein

    B. transport protein

    C. enzyme

    D. structural protein

21. The coiling of a chain of amino acids describes a protein's:

    A. primary structure

    B. secondary structure

    C. tertiary structure

    D. quaternary structure

22. Which of the following is an essential amino acid in the human diet?

    A. aniline

    B. valine

    C. glycine

    D. serine

23. Which of the following macromolecules are composed of polypeptides?

    A. amino acids

    B. proteins

    C. carbohydrates

    D. fats

24. The function of cholesterol in a cell membrane is to:

    A. act as a precursor to steroid hormones

    B. take part in the reactions that produce bile acids

    C. maintain structure due to its flat rigid characteristics

    D. attract hydrophobic molecules to form solid deposits

25. The biochemical roles of lipids are:

    A. short-term energy storage, transport of molecules, and structural support

    B. storage of excess energy, component of cell membranes, and chemical messengers

    C. catalysis, protection against outside invaders, motion

    D. component of cell membranes, catalysis, and structural support

26. Which of the following is a lipid?

    A. lactose   **C.** nicotine

    B. aniline   **D.** estradiol

27. Which statement regarding fatty acids is NOT correct? Fatty acids:

    A. are always liquids   **C.** are usually unbranched chains

    B. are long-chain carboxylic acids   **D.** usually have an even number of carbon atoms

28. Triacylglycerols are compounds that contain combined:

    A. cholesterol and other steroids   **C.** fatty acids and glycerol

    B. fatty acids and phospholipids   **D.** fatty acids and choline

29. When dietary triglycerides are hydrolyzed, the products are:

    A. glycerol and fatty acids   **C.** amino acids

    B. carbohydrates   **D.** alcohols and lipids

30. How many fatty acids are in a phospholipid molecule?

    A. 0   **C.** 2

    B. 1   **D.** 3

31. Which of the following is NOT a function of lipids within the body?

    A. cushioning to prevent injury   **C.** energy reserve

    B. insulation   **D.** precursor for glucose catabolism

32. Which of the following molecules is a disaccharide?

A. lactose

B. cellulose

C. amylose

D. glucose

33. What is the major biological function of the glycogen biomolecule?

A. It is used to synthesize disaccharides

B. It is the building block of proteins

C. It stores glucose in animal cells

D. It is a storage form of sucrose

34. A carbohydrate can be defined as a molecule:

A. composed of carbon atoms bonded to water molecules

B. composed of amine groups and carboxylic acid groups bonded to a carbon skeleton

C. composed mostly of hydrocarbons and soluble in nonpolar solvents

D. that is an aldehyde or ketone and has more than one hydroxyl group

35. Disaccharides are best characterized as:

A. two monosaccharides linked by a nitrogen bond

B. two peptides linked by a hydrogen bond

C. two monosaccharides linked by an oxygen bond

D. two amino acids linked by a peptide bond

36. Which of these choices is the correct statement about lipids?

A. They are composed of elements C, O, N & H

B. Their secondary structure is composed of α helices and β pleated sheets

C. They are molecules used for long-term energy storage in animals

D. Elements of C:H:O are in the ratio of 1:2:1

37. Which nutrients yield four calories per gram?

A. glucose and proteins

B. fats and glucose

C. proteins and lipids

D. lipids and sugars

38. Which of the following is NOT an end product of digestion?

A. amino acids

B. lactose

C. fructose

D. fatty acids

39. Consider the following types of compounds:

       I. amino acid

      II. nitrogen-containing base

      III. phosphate group

      IV. five-carbon sugar

From which of the above compounds are the monomers (i.e., nucleotides) of nucleic acids formed?

A. I only

B. I and II only

C. II and IV only

D. II, III and IV only

40. The nucleotide sequence, T–A–G, stands for

A. threonine-alanine-glutamine

B. thymine-adenine-guanine

C. tyrosine-asparagine-glutamic acid

D. thymine-adenine-glutamine

Chromosomes, Genes, DNA

1. DNA and RNA differ because:

    A. only DNA contains phosphodiester bonds

    B. only RNA contains pyrimidines

    C. DNA is in the nucleus, and RNA is in the cytosol

    D. RNA is associated with ribosomes, and DNA is associated with histones

2. Tumor-suppressor genes normally control:

    A. cell differentiation

    B. necrosis

    C. cell proliferation or activation of apoptosis

    D. sister chromatid separation

3. In the genetic code, deciphered by Nobel laureate Marshall W. Nirenberg, each amino acid is coded for by three nucleotides (codons). How many possible codons exist in nature encoding 20 amino acids in polypeptides?

    A. 4

    B. 20

    C. 27

    D. 64

4. Which of the following statements does NOT apply to protein synthesis?

    A. The process does not require energy

    B. rRNA is required for proper binding of the mRNA message

    C. tRNA molecules shuttle amino acids that are assembled into the polypeptide

    D. The mRNA is synthesized from 5' → 3'

5. Which stage of cell division is the stage when chromosomes replicate?

    A. prophase

    B. interphase

    C. anaphase

    D. metaphase

6. Which of these statements is NOT correct about DNA replication?

    A. DNA polymerase synthesizes and proofreads the DNA

    B. RNA primers are necessary for the hybridization of the polymerase

    C. Ligase relaxes positive supercoils that accumulate as the replication fork opens

    D. DNA polymerase adds Okazaki fragments in a 5' → 3' direction

7. If a particular RNA sequence has a cytosine content of 25%, what is its adenine content?

    A. 50%

    B. cannot be determined

    C. 12.5%

    D. 25%

8. Which of the following statements is TRUE for the base composition of DNA?

   A. In double-stranded DNA, the number of G bases equals the number of T bases

   B. In double-stranded DNA, the number of A bases equals the number of T bases

   C. In double-stranded DNA, the number of C bases equals the number of T bases

   D. In every single strand, the number of A bases equals the number T bases

9. Which of the following is NOT a part of post-translational modification of protein?

   A. addition of a 3' poly-A tail

   B. phosphorylation

   C. methylation

   D. glycosylation

10. Which of the following is an exception to the principle of the *central dogma* of molecular biology?

    A. yeast

    B. retroviruses

    C. bread mold

    D. skin cells

11. Chromosome regions with few functional genes are:

    A. heterochromatin

    B. mid-repetitive sequences

    C. euchromatin

    D. chromatids

12. If a drug inhibits ribosomal RNA synthesis, which of these eukaryotic organelles would be most affected by this drug?

    A. Golgi apparatus

    B. lysosome

    C. mitochondria

    D. nucleolus

13. Which of these macromolecules would be repaired rather than degraded?

    A. triglyceride

    B. polynucleotide

    C. polypeptide

    D. polysaccharide

14. Which of the following is the correct sequence occurring during polypeptide synthesis?

    A. DNA generates tRNA → tRNA anticodon binds to the mRNA codon in the cytoplasm → tRNA is carried by mRNA to the ribosomes, causing amino acids to join in a specific order

    B. DNA generates mRNA → mRNA moves to the ribosome → tRNA anticodon binds to the mRNA codon, causing amino acids to join in their appropriate order

    C. Specific RNA codons cause amino acids to line up in a specific order → tRNA anticodon attaches to mRNA codon → rRNA codon causes the protein to cleave into specific amino acids

    D. DNA regenerates mRNA in the nucleus → mRNA moves to the cytoplasm and attaches to the tRNA anticodon → operon regulates the sequence of amino acids in the appropriate order

15. After the new DNA strands are synthesized, which enzyme is needed to complete the process of DNA replication?

A. ligase

B. primase

C. helicase

D. reverse transcriptase

16. What is the number of double-stranded DNA molecules in a single mouse chromosome immediately after the gametes are formed?

A. 0

B. 1

C. 2

D. 4

17. What distinguishes meiosis from mitosis?

I. Genetic recombination

II. Failure to synthesize DNA between successive cell divisions

III. Separation of homologous chromosomes into distinct cells

A. I only

B. II only

C. I and III only

D. II and III only

18. SRY gene encoding for the testis-determining factor is the master sex-determining gene that resides on:

A. pseudoautosomal region of the Y chromosome

B. short arm of the Y chromosome, but not in the pseudoautosomal region

C. X chromosome

D. pseudoautosomal region of the X chromosome

19. The number of chromosomes contained in a human primary spermatocyte is:

A. 23

B. 46

C. 92

D. 184

20. 47, XXY is a condition known as:

A. Turner syndrome

B. double Y syndrome

C. trisomy X syndrome

D. Klinefelter syndrome

21. Translation, transcription, and replication take place in which phase of the cell cycle:

A. G1

B. G2

C. metaphase

D. S

22. Which type of inheritance has the pattern where an affected male has all affected daughters but no affected sons?

A. X-linked recessive

B. Y-linked

C. X-linked dominant

D. Autosomal recessive

23. Which cell division process results in four genetically different daughter cells that contain one haploid set of chromosomes?

A. interphase

B. meiosis

C. cell division

D. mitosis

24. Which of the following is a type of genetic mutation?

I. insertion
II. frameshift
III. nonsense
IV. missense

A. I and II only

B. I, II and III only

C. II and IV only

D. I, II, III and IV

25. A DNA damage checkpoint arrests cells in:

A. M/G2 transition

B. S/G1 transition

C. G1/S transition

D. anaphase

26. If a segment of a double-stranded DNA has a low ratio of guanine-cytosine (G-C) pairs relative to adenine-thymine (A-T) pairs, it is reasonable to assume that this nucleotide segment:

A. requires less energy to separate the two DNA strands than a comparable segment with a high C-G ratio

B. requires more energy to separate the two DNA strands than a comparable segment with a high C-G ratio

C. contains more cytosine than guanine

D. contains more adenine than thymine

27. A failure in which stage of spermatogenesis produces nondisjunction resulting in a male having an XXY karyotype?

A. prophase I

B. metaphase

C. anaphase I

D. telophase

28. Which of the following stages is when human cells with a single unreplicated copy of the genome are formed?

    A. mitosis

    B. meiosis II

    C. meiosis I

    D. interphase

29. In transcription:

    A. the mRNA contains the genetic information from DNA

    B. uracil pairs with thymine

    C. a double helix containing one parent strand and one daughter strand is produced

    D. the mRNA produced is identical to the parent DNA

30. The two new DNA molecules formed in replication:

    A. contain one parent and one daughter strand

    B. both contain only the parent DNA strands

    C. both contain only two new daughter DNA strands

    D. are complementary to the original DNA

31. The main role of DNA is to provide instructions on how to build:

    I. lipids

    II. carbohydrates

    III. proteins

    A. I only

    B. II only

    C. III only

    D. I and II only

32. Nucleic acids are polymers of [   ] monomers.

    A. monosaccharide

    B. fatty acid

    C. DNA

    D. nucleotide

33. During DNA transcription, a guanine base on the template strand codes for which base on the growing RNA strand?

    A. guanine

    B. thymine

    C. adenine

    D. cytosine

34. What intermolecular force connects strands of DNA in the double helix?

    A. hydrogen bonds

    B. ionic bonds

    C. amide bonds

    D. ester bonds

35. What is the term for the process of a DNA molecule synthesizing an identical molecule of DNA?

A. transcription

B. translation

C. duplication

D. replication

36. Translation is the process whereby:

A. protein is synthesized from DNA

B. protein is synthesized from mRNA

C. DNA is synthesized from DNA

D. DNA is synthesized from mRNA

37. Which of the following is the correct listing of DNA's constituents in the order of increasing size?

A. Nucleotide, codon, gene, nucleic acid

B. Nucleic acid, nucleotide, codon, gene

C. Nucleotide, codon, nucleic acid, gene

D. Gene, nucleic acid, nucleotide, codon

38. What is the process in which the DNA double helix unfolds, and each strand serves as a template for the synthesis of a new strand?

A. translation

B. replication

C. transcription

D. complementation

39. Which of the following illustrates the direction of flow for protein synthesis?

A. RNA → protein → DNA

B. DNA → protein → RNA

C. RNA → DNA → protein

D. DNA → RNA → protein

40. The three-base sequence in mRNA specifying the amino acid is called:

A. rRNA

B. an anticodon

C. a codon

D. tRNA

41. DNA is a(n):

A. peptide

B. protein

C. nucleic acid

D. enzyme

Mendel's Laws of Heredity

1. Which of the following stages is when human cells with a single unreplicated copy of the genome are formed?

A. mitosis

B. meiosis II

C. meiosis I

D. interphase

2. During which phase of mitotic division do spindle fibers split the centromere and separate the sister chromatids?

A. anaphase

B. telophase

C. prophase

D. metaphase

3. In mice, short hair is dominant over long hair. What can be concluded if a short-haired individual is crossed with a long-haired individual and both long and short-haired offspring?

A. Short-haired individual is homozygous

B. Short-haired individual is heterozygous

C. Long-haired individual is homozygous

D. Long-haired individual is heterozygous

4. Several eye colors are characteristic of *Drosophila melanogaster*. Red eyes are dominant over sepia or white eyes. What percent of offspring of a sepia-eyed fly will have sepia-eyes if that fly mated with a red-eyed fly that was a cross of red-eyed and sepia-eyed parents?

A. 0%

B. 25%

C. 50%

D. 75%

5. All of the following are necessary conditions for the Hardy-Weinberg equilibrium, EXCEPT:

A. forward mutation rate equals backward mutation rate

B. random emigration and immigration

C. large gene pool

D. random mating

6. Mendel's crossing of spherical-seeded pea plants with wrinkled-seeded pea plants resulted in progeny that all had spherical seeds. This indicates that the wrinkled-seed trait is:

A. codominant

B. dominant

C. recessive

D. penetrance

7. The result of mitosis is the production of:

A. two (1N) cells identical to the parent cell

B. two (2N) cells identical to the parent cell

C. four (1N) cells identical to the parent cell

D. four (2N) cells identical to the parent cell

8. The degree of genetic linkage is often measured by the:

A. frequency of nonsense mutations

B. histone distribution

C. frequency of missense mutations

D. probability of crossing over

9. If two species with the AaBbCc genotype reproduce, what is the probability that their progeny have the AABBCC genotype?

A. 1/2

B. 1/4

C. 1/16

D. 1/64

10. What is the pattern of inheritance for a rare recessive allele?

A. Every affected person has an affected parent

B. Unaffected parents can produce children who are affected

C. Unaffected mothers have affected sons and daughters who are carriers

D. Every affected person produces an affected offspring

11. If tall height and brown eye color are dominant, what is the probability for a heterozygous tall, heterozygous brown-eyed mother and a homozygous tall, homozygous blue-eyed father to have a tall child with blue eyes? Note: the genes for eye color and height are unlinked.

A. 3/4

B. 1/8

C. 1/4

D. 1/2

12. Recombination frequencies:

A. arise from completely random genetic exchanges

B. are the same for *cis* and *trans* heterozygotes

C. decrease with distance

D. are the same for all genes

13. How many different gametes can be produced from the genotype *AaBbCc*, assuming independent assortment?

A. 4

B. 6

C. 8

D. 16

14. What is the pattern of inheritance for a rare dominant allele?

   A. Every affected person has an affected parent

   B. Unaffected parents can produce children who are affected

   C. Unaffected mothers have affected sons and daughters who are carriers

   D. Every affected person produces an affected offspring

15. People that are homozygous for a recessive autosomal mutation accumulate harmful amounts of lipids. Jane and her parents are not afflicted. However, Jane's sister accumulates lipids. What is the probability that Jane is heterozygous for the mutation?

   A. 1/4

   B. 1/3

   C. 2/3

   D. 1/2

16. What is the risk of having a child affected by a disease with autosomal dominant inheritance if the mother and father have one mutant gene for that disease?

   A. 0%

   B. 25%

   C. 50%

   D. 75%

17. Which of these statements is/are valid for an autosomal dominant inheritance?

   I. A single allele of the mutant gene is needed to exhibit the phenotype

   II. transmission to the son by the father is not observed

   III. autosomal dominant traits do not skip generations

   A. II only

   B. I, II and III

   C. I only

   D. I and III only

18. All of these cell types contain the diploid (2N) number of chromosomes EXCEPT:

   A. primary oocyte

   B. spermatogonium

   C. spermatid

   D. zygote

19. The probability that all children in a four-children family will be males is:

   A. 1/2

   B. 1/4

   C. 1/8

   D. 1/16

20. Common red-green color blindness is an X-linked trait. When a woman whose father is color blind has a son with a non-afflicted man, what is the probability that their son will be color blind?

   A. 0

   B. 1/4

   C. 1/2

   D. 3/4

21. Since the gene responsible for color blindness is on the X chromosome, what is the chance that a son of a color-blind man and a woman-carrier will be color-blind?

A. 75%

B. 100%

C. 25%

D. 50%

22. A recessive allele may appear in a phenotype due to:

A. gain-of-function mutation

B. acquired dominance

C. senescence

D. the loss of heterozygosity

23. Mendel concluded that each pea has two units for each characteristic, and each gamete contains one unit. Mendel's "unit" for traits is now referred to as:

A. gene

B. genome

C. codon

D. DNA

24. Which cross must produce all green, smooth peas if green (G) is dominant over yellow (g) and smooth (S) is dominant over wrinkled (s)?

A. GgSs × GGSS

B. GgSS × ggSS

C. Ggss × GGSs

D. GgSs × GgSs

25. What is the probability that a cross between a true-breeding pea plant with a dominant trait and a true-breeding pea plant with a recessive trait will result in all F_1 progeny having the dominant trait?

A. 50%

B. 25%

C. 0%

D. 100%

Basic Atomic Structure

1. Based on experimental evidence, Dalton postulated that:

    A. atoms of different elements have the same mass
    B. not all atoms of a given element are identical
    C. atoms can be created and destroyed in chemical reactions
    D. each element consists of indivisible minute particles called atoms

2. When an atom is most stable, how many electrons does it contain in its valence shell?

    A. 4   C. 8
    B. 6   D. 10

3. According to John Dalton, atoms of an element:

    A. are divisible   C. are identical
    B. have the same shape   D. have different masses

4. What is the term for the number that characterizes an element and indicates the number of protons in the nucleus of the atom?

    A. Mass number   C. Atomic mass
    B. Atomic number   D. Neutron number

5. The number of neutrons in an atom is equal to:

    A. the mass number   C. mass number minus the atomic number
    B. the atomic number   D. atomic number minus the mass number

6. The term nucleon refers to:

    A. the nucleus of a specific isotope
    B. both protons and neutrons
    C. positrons that are emitted from an atom that undergoes nuclear decay
    D. electrons that are emitted from a nucleus in a nuclear reaction

7. How many neutrons are in a Beryllium atom with an atomic number of 4 and an atomic mass of 9?

    A. 4   C. 9
    B. 5   D. 13

8. What is the term for the chemical formula of a compound that expresses the actual number of atoms of each element in a molecule?

    A. molecular formula

    B. empirical formula

    C. elemental formula

    D. atomic formula

9. Elements have the same number of:

    A. electrons

    B. neutrons

    C. protons and neutrons

    D. protons

10. Almost all of the mass of an atom exists in its:

    A. electrons

    B. nucleus

    C. outermost energy level

    D. first energy level

11. Element X has an atomic number of 7 and an atomic mass of 13. Neutral element X has:

    A. 6 neutrons

    B. 6 electrons

    C. 6 protons

    D. 13 electrons

12. An atom with an electrical charge is referred to as a(n):

    A. element

    B. ion

    C. compound

    D. isotope

13. Isotopes have the same number of:

    A. neutrons, but a different number of electrons

    B. protons, but a different number of neutrons

    C. protons, but a different number of electrons

    D. neutrons and electrons

14. What must be the same if two atoms represent the same element?

    A. number of neutrons

    B. atomic mass

    C. number of electron shells

    D. atomic number

15. Isotopes of an element possess the same:

    A. number of electrons, atomic number, and mass, but have nothing else in common

    B. atomic number and mass, but have nothing else in common

    C. chemical properties and mass, but have nothing else in common

    D. number of electrons, atomic number, and chemical properties

16. Which characteristics describe a neutron's mass, charge, and location, respectively?

    A. Approximate mass 1 amu; charge 0; inside the nucleus

    B. Approximate mass 5×10^{-4} amu; charge 0; inside the nucleus

    C. Approximate mass 1 amu; charge +1; inside the nucleus

    D. Approximate mass 1 amu; charge –1; inside the nucleus

17. The three isotopes of hydrogen have different numbers of:

    A. neutrons   **C.** protons

    B. electrons   **D.** charges

18. Atoms of an element have the same:

    A. atomic number and chemical properties, but not necessarily the same mass

    B. chemical properties and mass, but lack other similarities

    C. number of electrons, the atomic number, and mass but lack other similarities

    D. mass and chemical properties, but lack other similarities

19. Which of the following is an ion?

    A. A molecule such as galactose

    B. An atom that has an electrical charge

    C. A substance formed by the combination of two elements

    D. Another term for an atom

20. Which statement about a neutron is FALSE?

    A. It is a nucleon

    B. It is often associated with protons

    C. It has a charge equivalent but opposite to an electron

    D. It is much more massive than an electron

21. An atom containing 29 protons, 29 electrons, and 34 neutrons has a mass number of:

    A. 5   **C.** 34

    B. 29   **D.** 63

22. Two different isotopes of a neutral element as isolated atoms must have the same number of:

    I. protons   II. neutrons   III. electrons

    A. I only   **C.** I and III only

    B. II only   **D.** I, II and III

23. Which of the following statements best describes the role of neutrons in the nucleus?

  A. The neutrons stabilize the nucleus by attracting protons
  B. The neutrons stabilize the nucleus by balancing charge
  C. The neutrons stabilize the nucleus by attracting other nucleons
  D. The neutrons stabilize the nucleus by repelling other nucleons

24. The atomic number of an atom identifies the number of:

  A. excited states   **C.** neutrons
  B. electron orbits   **D.** protons

25. What is the name for the sum of the number of protons and neutrons in the nucleus of an atom?

  A. Atomic weight   **C.** Mass number
  B. Atomic number   **D.** Atomic mass

26. Isotopes are atoms of an element with similar chemical properties but with different:

  A. numbers of electrons   **C.** numbers of protons
  B. atomic numbers   **D.** masses

27. Periods on the periodic table represent elements:

  A. in the same group   **C.** known as isotopes
  B. with consecutive atomic numbers **D.** with similar chemical properties

28. What is the number of known nonmetals relative to the number of metals?

  A. About two times greater   **C.** About five times less
  B. About fifty percent   **D.** About twenty-five percent greater

29. The attraction of the nucleus on the outermost electron in an atom tends to:

  A. decrease from right to left and bottom to top on the periodic table
  B. decrease from left to right and bottom to top on the periodic table
  C. decrease from left to right and top to bottom of the periodic table
  D. decrease from right to left and top to bottom on the periodic table

30. Which of the following elements is a nonmetal?

  A. Sodium   **C.** Aluminum
  B. Chlorine   **D.** Magnesium

31. What is the name for elements in the same column of the periodic table with similar chemical properties?

A. congeners

B. stereoisomers

C. diastereomers

D. epimers

32. An atom that contains 47 protons, 47 electrons, and 60 neutrons is an isotope of:

A. Nd

B. Bh

C. Ag

D. Al

33. Rank the elements below in order of decreasing atomic radius.

A. Al > P > Cl > Na > Mg

B. Cl > Al > P > Na > Mg

C. Mg > Na > P > Al > Cl

D. Na > Mg > Al > P > Cl

34. Which element has the lowest electronegativity?

A. Mg

B. Al

C. Cl

D. Br

35. Which of the following elements is NOT correctly classified?

A. Mo – transition element

B. Sr – alkaline earth metal

C. Po – halogen

D. Ar – noble gas

36. Which element listed below has the greatest electronegativity?

A. I

B. Fr

C. H

D. F

37. ^{65}Cu and ^{65}Zn have the same:

A. mass number

B. number of neutrons

C. number of ions

D. number of electrons

38. Which of the following elements is in Period 5 and Group IIIA on the periodic table?

A. In

B. As

C. Tl

D. Y

39. What happens to the properties of elements across a period of the periodic table?

      I. Elements become more metallic because of the increase in atomic number

      II. The properties of the elements change gradually across a period

      III. Elements become larger because of the addition of more protons

  A. I only

  B. II only

  C. III only

  D. I and II only

40. Which characteristic is NOT a property of the transition elements?

  A. Colored ions in solution

  B. Form complex ions

  C. Multiple oxidation states

  D. Nonmetallic in character

41. Elements with atomic numbers of 84 and higher are radioactive because:

  A. strong attractions between their nucleons make them unstable

  B. their atomic numbers are larger than their mass numbers

  C. strong repulsions between their electrons make them unstable

  D. strong repulsions between their protons make their nuclei unstable

Characteristic Properties of Substances

1. Referring to the periodic table, which of the following is NOT a solid metal under normal conditions?

A. Ce

B. Os

C. Ba

D. Hg

2. Metalloids:

      I. have some metallic and some nonmetallic properties

      II. may have low electrical conductivities

      III. contain elements in group IIIB

A. I and III only

B. II only

C. II and III only

D. I and II only

3. Which element would most likely be a metal with a low melting point?

A. K

B. B

C. N

D. C

4. Refer to the periodic table and predict which of the following is a solid nonmetal under normal conditions.

A. Cl

B. F

C. Se

D. As

5. Which choice below represents an element?

A. glucose

B. sodium chloride

C. methanol

D. hydrogen

6. Which of the following represent(s) a compound rather than an element?

      I. O_3 II. CCl_4 III. S_8

A. I and III only

B. II only

C. I and II only

D. III only

7. Which of the following statements best describes an element?

A. has consistent physical properties

B. consists of more than one type of atom

C. consists of one type of atom

D. material that is pure

8. What is the name for the attraction between water molecules?

A. adhesion

B. polarity

C. cohesion

D. van der Waals

9. Why does H_2O have a relatively high boiling point compared to H_2S?

A. Hydrogen bonding

B. Van der Waals forces

C. H_2O molecules pack more closely than H_2S

D. Covalent bonds are stronger in H_2O

10. Which of the following demonstrate colligative properties?

    I. Freezing point   II. Boiling point   III. Vapor pressure

A. I only

B. II only

C. III only

D. I, II and III

11. Which of the following is characteristic of gases?

    I. Formation of homogeneous mixtures, regardless of the nature of non-reacting gas components

    II. Relatively long distances between molecules

    III. High compressibility

    IV. No attractive forces between gas molecules

A. I and II only

B. II and III only

C. II, III, and IV only

D. I, II, III, and IV

12. Which of the following statements best describes a solid?

A. Indefinite shape, but definite volume

B. Definite shape, but indefinite volume

C. Definite shape and volume

D. Indefinite shape and volume

13. Identify the decreasing ordering of attractions among particles in the three states of matter.

A. gas > liquid > solid

B. gas > solid > liquid

C. solid > liquid > gas

D. liquid > solid > gas

14. A nonvolatile liquid would have:

A. a highly explosive propensity

B. strong attractive forces between molecules

C. weak attractive forces between molecules

D. a high vapor pressure at room temperature

15. Matter is nearly incompressible in which of these states?

    I. solid   II. liquid   III. gas

A. I only

B. II only

C. I and II only

D. I, II, and III

16. The boiling point of a liquid is the temperature:

A. where sublimation occurs

B. where the vapor pressure of the liquid is less than the atmospheric pressure over the liquid

C. equal to or greater than 100 °C

D. where the vapor pressure of the liquid equals the atmospheric pressure over the liquid

17. Why does a beaker of water begin to boil at 22 °C when placed in a closed chamber, and a vacuum pump is used to evacuate the air from the chamber?

A. The vapor pressure decreases

B. Air is released from the water

C. The atmospheric pressure decreases

D. The vapor pressure increases

18. Which of the following describes a substance in the liquid physical state?

    I. It has a variable shape

    II. It compresses negligibly

    III. It has a fixed volume

A. I only

B. II only

C. I and III only

D. I, II and III

19. Which characteristics best describe a liquid?

A. Volume and shape of the container; no intermolecular attractions

B. Definite volume; the shape of the container; no intermolecular attractions

C. Definite shape and volume; strong intermolecular attractions

D. Definite volume; the shape of the container; moderate intermolecular attractions

20. Which of the following statements best describes a gas?

A. Definite shape, but indefinite volume

B. Indefinite shape, but definite volume

C. Indefinite shape and volume

D. Definite shape and volume

21. What happens to the kinetic energy of a gas molecule when the gas is heated?

A. Depends on the gas

B. Kinetic energy increases

C. Kinetic energy decreases

D. Kinetic energy remains constant

22. The following statements concerning temperature change as a substance is heated are correct, EXCEPT:

   A. As a liquid is heated, its temperature rises until its boiling point is reached

   B. When liquid changes to a gaseous state, temperature gradually increases until all the liquid is changed

   C. As a solid is heated, its temperature rises until its melting point is reached

   D. During the time for a solid to melt to a liquid, the temperature remains constant

23. Which of the following explains why bubbles form on the inside of a pot of water when the pot of water is heated?

   A. As temperature increases, the vapor pressure increases

   B. As temperature increases, the atmospheric pressure decreases

   C. As temperature increases, the solubility of air decreases

   D. As temperature increases, the kinetic energy decreases

24. What is the term that refers to liquids that do not dissolve in one another and separate into two layers?

   A. Soluble   **C.** Insoluble

   B. Miscible   **D.** Immiscible

25. Of the following, which can serve as the solute in a solution?

      I. solid   II. liquid   III. gas

   A. I only   **C.** I and II only

   B. II only   **D.** I, II, and III

26. Which of the following can function as the solvent in a solution?

      I. solid   II. liquid   III. gas

   A. I only

   B. II only   **C.** I and II only   **D.** I, II and III

27. Which of the following properties is NOT characteristic of an acid?

   A. It is neutralized by a base   **C.** It produces H^+ in water

   B. It has a slippery feel   **D.** It tastes sour

28. Which of the following is a general property of an acidic solution?

   A. Turns litmus paper blue   **C.** Tastes bitter

   B. Feels slippery   **D.** None of the above

29. What is the term given for the mass percent of each element in a compound?

A. mass composition

B. percent composition

C. compound composition

D. elemental composition

30. Which property primarily determines the effect of temperature on the solubility of gas molecules?

A. Ionic strength of the gas

B. Molecular weight of the gas

C. Polarity of the gas

D. Kinetic energy of the gas

31. Which of the following statements is/are true?

      I. A gaseous solution consists of a gaseous solute and a gaseous solvent

      II. A solid solution consists of a solid solute and a solid solvent

      III. A liquid solution results from a gaseous solute and a liquid solvent

A. I only

B. II only

C. I and II only

D. I, II and III

32. Which statement is true regarding gases when compared to liquids?

A. Gases have lower compressibility and higher density

B. Gases have lower compressibility and lower density

C. Gases have higher compressibility and lower density

D. Gases have higher compressibility and higher density

33. Why does water boil at a lower temperature when at high altitudes?

A. Vapor pressure of water is increased at high altitudes

B. Ambient room temperature is higher than at low altitudes

C. Atmospheric pressure is lower at low altitudes

D. Atmospheric pressure is lower at high altitudes

34. Which of the following is/are a characteristic of metals?

      I. conduction of heat   II. high density   III. malleable

A. I only

B. II only

C. I and II only

D. I, II, and III

35. Metals are good heat conductors and electrical conductors because of the:

A. relatively high densities of metals

B. high elasticity of metals

C. ductility of metals

D. looseness of outer electrons in metal atoms

36. Which of the following is/are a general characteristic of a nonmetal?

        I. low density   II. heat conduction   III. brittle

    A. I only   **C.** III only

    B. II only   **D.** I and III only

37. The reason a water solution of sucrose (i.e., table sugar) does not conduct electricity is because sucrose is a:

    A. semiconductor   **C.** strong electrolyte

    B. non-electrolyte   **D.** weak electrolyte

38. An object is sinking in a fluid. What is the weight of the fluid displaced by the sinking object when the object is completely submerged?

    A. Dependent on the viscosity of the liquid   **C.** Greater than the weight of the object

    B. Equal to the weight of the object   **D.** Less than the weight of the object

39. When soup gets cold, it often tastes greasy because oil spreads out on the surface of the soup instead of staying in small globules. This is explained in terms of the:

    A. increase in the surface tension of water with decreasing temperature

    B. Archimedes' principle

    C. decrease in the surface tension of water with decreasing temperature

    D. Joule-Thomson effect

40. Density is:

    A. inversely proportional to both the mass and volume

    B. proportional to mass and inversely proportional to the volume

    C. inversely proportional to the mass and proportional to the volume

    D. proportional to both the mass and volume

41. Ice has a lower density than water because ice:

    A. molecules vibrate at lower rates than water molecules

    B. is denser and therefore sinks when in liquid water

    C. is made of open-structured, hexagonal crystals

    D. molecules are more compact in the solid state

42. The moderate temperatures of islands throughout the world have much to do with water's:

    A. high evaporation rate   **C.** vast supply of thermal energy

    B. high specific heat capacity   **D.** poor conductivity

43. In liquid water of a given temperature, the water molecules are moving randomly at different speeds. Electrostatic forces of cohesion tend to hold them. Occasionally one molecule gains enough energy through multiple collisions to pull away and escape from the liquid. Which of the following is an illustration of this phenomenon?

    A. When a large steel suspension bridge is built, gaps are left between the girders

    B. When a body gets too warm, it produces sweat to cool itself down

    C. Increasing the atmospheric pressure over a liquid causes the boiling temperature to decrease

    D. If snow begins to fall when Mary is skiing, she feels colder than before it started to snow

44. The process whereby heat flows through molecular collisions is known as:

    A. radiation   **C.** conduction

    B. inversion   **D.** convection

45. The process in which heat flows by the mass movement of molecules from one place to another is:

      I. conduction   II. convection   III. radiation

    A. I only   **C.** III only

    B. II only   **D.** I and II only

46. The process whereby heat flows in the absence of any medium is known as:

    A. radiation   **C.** conduction

    B. inversion   **D.** convection

47. Which method of heat flow requires the movement of energy through solid matter to a new location?

      I. Conduction   II. Convection   III. Radiation

    A. I only   **C.** III only

    B. II only   **D.** I and II only

48. On a cold day, a piece of steel feels much colder to the touch than a piece of plastic. This is due to the difference in which one of the following physical properties of these materials?

    A. Mass   **C.** Density

    B. Thermal conductivity   **D.** Specific heat

49. By what primary heat transfer mechanism does one end of an iron bar become hot when the other end is placed in a flame?

    A. Convection   **C.** Conduction

    B. Diffusion   **D.** Radiation

50. Warm air rises because it tends to move to regions of less:

      I. density   II. pressure   III. friction

    A. I only   **C.** II and III only

    B. II only   **D.** I and II only

51. Energy transfer by convection is primarily restricted to:

      I. liquids   II. gases   III. solids

    A. I only   **C.** II and III only

    B. II only   **D.** I and II only

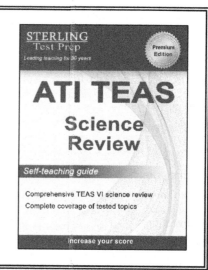

Changing States of Matter

1. What is the term for a change of state from a liquid to a gas?

   A. vaporization

   B. melting

   C. deposition

   D. condensing

2. Which is a true statement about H_2O as it begins to freeze?

   A. Hydrogen bonds break

   B. Number of hydrogen bonds decreases

   C. Number of hydrogen bonds increases

   D. Molecules move closer together

3. Under what conditions are graphite converted to diamond?

   A. low temperature, high pressure

   B. high temperature, low pressure

   C. high temperature, high pressure

   D. low temperature, low pressure

4. If the pressure and temperature of a gas are halved, the volume is:

   A. halved

   B. the same

   C. doubled

   D. quadrupled

5. Which transformation describes sublimation?

   A. solid → liquid

   B. solid → gas

   C. liquid → solid

   D. liquid → gas

6. An ideal gas differs from a real gas because the molecules of an ideal gas have:

   A. no attraction to each other

   B. no kinetic energy

   C. molecular weight equal to zero

   D. appreciable volumes

7. Which of the following is a true statement regarding evaporation?

   A. Increasing the surface area of the liquid decreases the rate of evaporation

   B. The temperature of the liquid changes during evaporation

   C. Decreasing the surface area of the liquid increases the rate of evaporation

   D. Molecules with greater kinetic energy escape from the liquid

8. According to the kinetic theory of gases, which of the following is the average kinetic energy of the gas particles directly proportional to?

   A. temperature

   B. molar mass

   C. volume

   D. pressure

9. According to the kinetic theory, what happens to the kinetic energy of gaseous molecules when the temperature of a gas decreases?

    A. Increase as does velocity

    B. Decreases as does velocity

    C. Increases and velocity decreases

    D. Decreases and velocity increases

10. What is the term for a direct change of state from a solid to a gas?

    A. sublimation

    B. vaporization

    C. condensation

    D. deposition

11. For a fixed quantity of gas, gas laws describe the relationships between pressure and which two variables?

    A. chemical identity; mass

    B. volume; chemical identity

    C. temperature; volume

    D. temperature; size

12. Which of the following increases the pressure of a gas?

    I. Decreasing the volume

    II. Increasing the number of molecules

    III. Increasing temperature

    A. I only

    B. I and II only

    C. II and III only

    D. I, II, and III

13. Which of the following is NOT an endothermic process?

    A. Condensation of water vapor

    B. Boiling liquid

    C. Water evaporating

    D. Ice melting

14. Which of the following quantities is needed to calculate the amount of heat energy released as water turns to ice at 0 °C?

    A. Heat of condensation for water and the mass

    B. Heat of vaporization for water and the mass

    C. Heat of fusion for water and the mass

    D. Heat of solidification for water and the mass

15. In which of the following pairs of physical changes are both processes exothermic?

    A. Melting and condensation

    B. Freezing and condensation

    C. Sublimation and evaporation

    D. Freezing and sublimation

16. Which of the following has the same numerical magnitude?

   A. Heats of sublimation and deposition

   B. Heats of solidification and condensation

   C. Heats of fusion and deposition

   D. Heats of sublimation and condensation

17. Which transformation describes evaporation?

   A. solid $\rightarrow$ liquid

   B. solid $\rightarrow$ gas

   C. liquid $\rightarrow$ solid

   D. liquid $\rightarrow$ gas

18. As the strength of the attractive intermolecular force increases, [ ] decreases.

   A. melting point

   B. vapor pressure of a liquid

   C. density

   D. normal boiling temperature

19. Which of the following terms does NOT involve the solid state?

   A. solidification

   B. sublimation

   C. evaporation

   D. melting

20. Which is an assumption of the kinetic molecular theory of gases?

   A. Nonelastic collisions

   B. Constant interaction of molecules

   C. Elastic collisions

   D. Gas particles occupy space

21. Boiling occurs when the:

   A. internal pressure of a liquid is less than the sum of external pressures

   B. vapor pressure of a liquid is greater than the external pressure

   C. internal pressure of a liquid is greater than the atmospheric pressure

   D. internal pressure of a liquid is greater than the external pressure

22. The reason why ice floats in a glass of water is that, when frozen, H_2O is less dense due to:

   A. strengthening of cohesive forces

   B. high specific heat

   C. increased number of hydrogen bonds

   D. weakening of cohesive forces

23. At constant pressure, what effect does decreasing the temperature of a liquid by 20 °C have on the magnitude of its vapor pressure?

   A. Inversely proportional

   B. Decrease

   C. Increase

   D. No effect

24. What is the relationship between temperature and volume of a fixed amount of gas at constant pressure?

A. Equal

B. Indirectly proportional

C. Directly proportional

D. Decreased by a factor of 2

25. Which of the following is true of an ideal gas, according to the kinetic theory?

A. All molecular collisions have the same energy

B. All molecules have the same kinetic energy

C. All molecules do not have the same velocity

D. All molecules have the same individual temperature

26. If a researcher is working with a sample of neon at 278 K, what phase change is observed when the pressure is reduced from 60 atm to 38 atm?

A. liquid → solid

B. solid → liquid

C. solid → gas

D. liquid → gas

27. Phase changes occur as the temperature of the matter:

I. decreases   II. increases   III. remains the same

A. I only

B. II only

C. III only

D. I and II only

28. The heat required to change a substance from the solid to the liquid state is the heat of:

A. condensation

B. freezing

C. fusion

D. vaporization

29. What is the term for a change of state from a gas to a liquid?

A. vaporizing

B. melting

C. freezing

D. condensation

30. The heat required to change a substance from the liquid to the vapor state is the heat of:

A. melting

B. condensation

C. vaporization

D. fusion

31. When a solid melts, what change occurs in the substance?

A. Heat energy dissipates

B. Heat energy enters

C. Temperature increases

D. Temperature decreases

32. When a liquid freezes, what change occurs in the substance?

    A. Heat energy dissipates

    B. Heat energy enters

    C. Temperature increases

    D. Temperature decreases

33. When a liquid evaporates, what change occurs in the substance?

    A. Heat energy dissipates

    B. Heat energy enters

    C. Temperature increases

    D. Temperature decreases

34. Why is it that when a swimmer gets out of a swimming pool and stands in a breeze dripping wet, he feels much colder than when he dries off?

    A. This is a physiological effect resulting from the skin's sensory nerves

    B. The water on his skin is colder than the surrounding air

    C. To evaporate a gram of water from his skin requires heat and most of this heat flows out of his body

    D. Water has a relatively small specific heat

35. A solid sample of a pure compound is contained in a closed, well-insulated container. Heat is added at a constant rate, and the sample temperature is recorded. The resulting data is shown in the graph. Which of the following statements is true?

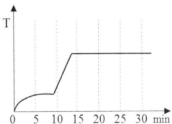

    A. After 5 minutes, the sample was a mixture of solid and liquid

    B. The heat capacity of the solid phase is greater than that of the liquid phase

    C. The sample never boiled

    D. The heat of fusion is greater than the heat of vaporization

36. Which of the following represents the breaking of a noncovalent interaction?

    A. Ionization of water

    B. Decomposition of hydrogen peroxide

    C. Hydrolysis of an ester

    D. Dissolving of salt crystals

37. Which transformation describes condensation?

    A. solid → gas

    B. solid → liquid

    C. liquid → gas

    D. gas → liquid

38. What is the name given to the transition of a compound from the gas phase directly to the solid phase?

    A. deposition

    B. sublimation

    C. freezing

    D. condensation

Notes for active learning

Chemical Reactions

1. Which of the following is an example of a chemical reaction?

   A. two solids mix to form a heterogeneous mixture
   B. two liquids mix to form a homogeneous mixture
   C. one or more new compounds are formed by rearranging atoms
   D. a new element is formed by rearranging nucleons

2. What is the term for a reaction that proceeds by absorbing heat energy?

   A. Isothermal reaction
   B. Exothermic reaction
   C. Endothermic reaction
   D. Spontaneous

3. Whether a reaction is endothermic or exothermic is determined by:

   A. energy difference between bond-breaking and bond-forming with a net loss or gain of energy
   B. the presence of a catalyst
   C. the activation energy
   D. the physical state of the reaction system

4. Which of the reactions is the most exothermic, assuming that the following energy profiles have the same scale? (Use the notation of R = reactants and P = products)

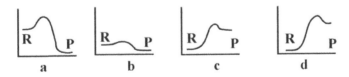

   A. a   **B.** b   **C.** c   **D.** d

5. What is the term for a reaction that proceeds by releasing heat energy?

   A. Endothermic reaction
   B. Isothermal reaction
   C. Exothermic reaction
   D. Nonspontaneous

6. If it takes energy to break bonds and energy is gained in forming bonds, how can some reactions be exothermic while others are endothermic?

    A. Some products have more energy than others and always require energy to be formed

    B. Some reactants have more energetic bonds than others and always release energy

    C. It is the total number of bonds that is determinative. Since bonds have the same amount of energy, the net gain or net loss of energy depends on the number of bonds

    D. It is the total amount of energy that is determinative, with some bonds stronger than others, so there is a net gain or loss of energy when formed

7. What can be deduced about the activation energy of a reaction that takes billions of years to go to completion and a reaction that takes a fraction of a millisecond?

    A. The slow reaction has high activation energy, while the fast reaction has a low activation energy

    B. The slow reaction has low activation energy, while the fast reaction has a high activation energy

    C. The activation energy of both reactions is low

    D. The activation energy of both reactions is high

8. What is the term for a substance that allows a reaction to proceed faster by lowering the energy of activation?

    A. catalyst   **C.** collision energy

    B. energy barrier   **D.** activation energy

9. What is the effect on the energy of the activated complex and on the rate of the reaction when a catalyst is added to a chemical reaction?

    A. Energy of the activated complex increases, and the reaction rate decreases

    B. Energy of the activated complex decreases, and the reaction rate increases

    C. Energy of the activated complex and the reaction rate increase

    D. Energy of the activated complex and the reaction rate decrease

10. Which of the following statements can be assumed to be true about how reactions occur?

    A. Reactant particles must collide with each other

    B. Energy must be released as the reaction proceeds

    C. Catalysts must be present in the reaction

    D. Energy must be absorbed as the reaction proceeds

11. The minimum combined kinetic energy reactants must possess for collisions to result in a reaction is:

    A. orientation energy   **C.** collision energy

    B. activation energy   **D.** dissociation energy

12. Which factors decrease the rate of a reaction?

      I. Lowering the temperature

      II. Increasing the concentration of reactants

      III. Adding a catalyst to the reaction vessel

  A. I only

  B. II only

  C. III only

  D. I and II only

13. Assuming vessels a, b and c are drawn to relative proportions, which of the following reactions proceeds the fastest? (Assume equal temperatures)

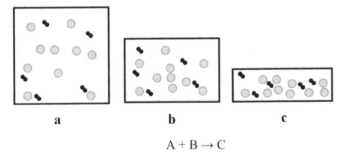

$$A + B \rightarrow C$$

  A. a

  B. b

  C. c

  D. All proceed at same rate

14. The reaction rate is:

  A. the ratio of the masses of products and reactants

  B. the ratio of the molecular masses of the elements in a given compound

  C. the speed at which reactants are consumed or product is formed

  D. the balanced chemical formula that relates the number of product molecules to reactant molecules

15. What is the term for a chemical reaction that involves electron transfer between two reacting substances?

  A. Reduction reaction

  B. Electrochemical reaction

  C. Oxidation reaction

  D. Redox reaction

16. When a substance loses electrons, it is [   ], while the substance itself is acting as [   ] agent.

  A. reduced… a reducing

  B. oxidized… a reducing

  C. reduced… an oxidizing

  D. oxidized… an oxidizing

17. Which equation is NOT correctly classified by the type of chemical reaction?

    A. $PbO + C \rightarrow Pb + CO$: single-replacement/non-redox

    B. $2\,Na + 2HCl \rightarrow 2\,NaCl + H_2$: single-replacement/redox

    C. $NaHCO_3 + HCl \rightarrow NaCl + H_2O + CO_2$: double-replacement/non-redox

    D. $2\,Na + H_2 \rightarrow 2\,NaH$: synthesis/redox

18. Which of the following is a *double-replacement* reaction?

    A. $2\,HI \rightarrow H_2 + I_2$ **C.** $HBr + KOH \rightarrow H_2O + KBr$

    B. $SO_2 + H_2O \rightarrow H_2SO_3$ **D.** $CuO + H_2 \rightarrow Cu + H_2O$

19. Which of the following reactions is NOT correctly classified?

    A. $AgNO_3\ (aq) + KOH\ (aq) \rightarrow KNO_3\ (aq) + AgOH\ (s)$: non-redox / double-replacement

    B. $2\,H_2O_2\ (s) \rightarrow 2\,H_2O\ (l) + O_2\ (g)$: non-redox / decomposition

    C. $Pb(NO_3)_2\ (aq) + 2\,Na\ (s) \rightarrow Pb\ (s) + 2\,NaNO_3\ (aq)$: redox / single-replacement

    D. $HNO_3\ (aq) + LiOH\ (aq) \rightarrow LiNO_3\ (aq) + H_2O\ (l)$: non-redox / double-replacement

20. What is the term for a reaction that represents separate oxidation or reduction processes?

    A. Reduction reaction   **C.** Oxidation reaction

    B. Redox reaction   **D.** Half-reaction

21. For the reaction $A + B \rightarrow C$, which proceeds the slowest? (Assume equal temperatures)

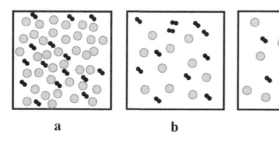

          a   **b**   **c**

    A. a   **C.** c

    B. b   **D.** All proceed at same rate

22. Which of the following reactions is NOT correctly classified?

    A. $AgNO_3 + KCl \rightarrow KNO_3 + AgCl$ (double-replacement)

    B. $CH_4 + 2\,O_2 \rightarrow CO_2 + 2\,H_2O$ (single-replacement)

    C. $Zn + H_2SO_4 \rightarrow ZnSO_4 + H_2$ (single-replacement)

    D. $2\,KClO_3 \rightarrow 2\,KCl + 3\,O_2$ (decomposition)

23. Which of the following balanced equations is a *decomposition* reaction?

A. $2\,Cr\,(s) + 3\,Cl_2\,(g) \rightarrow 2\,CrCl_3\,(s)$

B. $6\,Li\,(s) + N_2\,(g) \rightarrow 2\,Li_3N\,(s)$

C. $C_7H_8O_2\,(l) + 8\,O_2\,(g) \rightarrow 7\,CO_2\,(g) + 4\,H_2O\,(l)$

D. $2\,KClO_3\,(s) \rightarrow 2\,KCl\,(s) + 3\,O_2\,(g)$

24. Which statement(s) is/are true for an exothermic reaction?

I. There is a net absorption of energy from a reaction

II. The products have more energy than the reactants

III. Heat is a product of the reaction

A. I and II only

B. I and III only

C. III only

D. II and III only

25. Which of the following reaction is NOT classified correctly?

A. $BaCl_2 + H_2SO_4 \rightarrow BaSO_4 + 2\,HCl$ (single-replacement)

B. $F_2 + 2\,NaCl \rightarrow Cl_2 + 2\,NaF$ (single-replacement)

C. $Fe + CuSO_4 \rightarrow Cu + FeSO_4$ (single-replacement)

D. $2\,NO_2 + H_2O_2 \rightarrow 2\,HNO_3$ (synthesis)

26. For the reaction $D + E \rightarrow F$ illustrated below, which proceeds the slowest? (Assume each reaction is at STP and each vessel is drawn to scale)

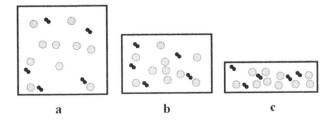

      a   b   c

A. a

B. b

C. c

D. All proceed at same rate

27. What conditions are required for a chemical reaction?

A. Sufficient energy of the collision only

B. Proper spatial orientation of the molecules only

C. Sufficient energy of the collision and proper spatial orientation of the molecules

D. Sufficient temperature and sufficient duration of molecular contact

28. For the following reaction of A + B → C, which proceeds at the fastest rate at STP? (Assume that each graph is drawn to proportion)

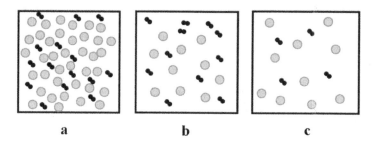

a   b   c

A. a

B. b

C. c

D. All proceed at the same rate

29. Which of the following statements is true regarding a chemical reaction?

A. The number of products is equal to the number of reactants

B. The number of atoms is equal on both sides of the reaction

C. The number of atoms in a reaction varies when the conditions change during the reaction

D. The number of molecules is equal on both sides of the reaction

30. Enzymes act by:

A. lowering the overall free energy change of the reaction

B. decreasing the distance reactants must diffuse to find each other

C. increasing the activation energy

D. decreasing the activation energy

Section III

Scientific Reasoning

Scientific Measurements and Laboratory Tools

Scientific Explanations Using Logic and Evidence

Relationships Among Events, Objects, and Processes

Analysis and Design of a Scientific Investigation

Scientific Measurements and Laboratory Tools

1. What is the term for a blotting method where proteins are transferred from a gel to membranes and probed by antibodies to specific proteins?

A. Eastern blotting

B. Western blotting

C. Northern blotting

D. Southern blotting

2. All of the following statements about PCR are correct, EXCEPT:

A. PCR can be used to obtain large quantities of a particular DNA sequence

B. PCR does not require knowledge of the terminal DNA sequences of the region to be amplified

C. PCR uses a DNA polymerase to synthesize DNA

D. PCR uses short synthetic oligonucleotide primers

3. Which of the following methods was NOT used by Mendel to study the genetics of the garden pea?

A. Maintenance of true-breeding lines

B. Cross-pollination

C. Microscopy

D. Production of hybrid plants

4. Hill coefficient measures cooperativity of hemoglobin, where Hill coefficient greater than 1 signifies positive cooperativity, less than 1 signifies negative cooperativity, and equal to 1 signifies the absence of cooperativity. What is the Hill coefficient of hemoglobin?

A. 2.3

B. 1

C. 0

D. −1.5

5. What is the numerical difference in $[H^+]$ between a liquid at pH 4 and 6?

A. 2 times

B. 10 times

C. 20 times

D. 100 times

6. A difference of 1 pH unit (e.g., pH of 6 *vs.* 7) corresponds to what change in the $[H^+]$?

A. 1

B. 2

C. 10

D. doubling

7. Among the following choices, how tall should a properly designed Torricelli mercury barometer be?

A. 100 in

B. 380 mm

C. 76 mm

D. 800 mm

8. Which of the following is NOT a unit used in measuring pressure?

A. kilometers Hg

B. millimeters Hg

C. atmosphere

D. Pascal

9. At what reading are degrees Celsius equivalent to degrees Fahrenheit?

A. 0

B. −10

C. −25

D. −40

10. Which statement about the boiling point of water is NOT correct?

A. At sea level and a pressure of 760 mmHg, the boiling point is 100 °C

B. The boiling point is greater than 100 °C for locations at low elevations

C. The boiling point is greater than 100 °C in a pressure cooker

D. The boiling point is less than 100 °C for locations at low elevations

11. To simplify comparisons, the energy value of fuels is expressed in units of:

A. kcal/g

B. kcal/L

C. J/kcal

D. kcal/mol

12. Which of the following solutions is the most concentrated?

A. One liter of water with 1 gram of sugar

B. One liter of water with 2 grams of sugar

C. One liter of water with 5 grams of sugar

D. One liter of water with 10 grams of sugar

13. Which of the following describes the solution for a vinegar sample at a pH of 5?

A. Weakly basic

B. Neutral

C. Weakly acidic

D. Strongly acidic

14. Relative to a pH of 7, a solution with a pH of 4 has:

A. 30 times less $[H^+]$

B. 300 times less $[H^+]$

C. 1,000 times greater $[H^+]$

D. 300 times greater $[H^+]$

15. The conditions known as standard temperature and pressure (STP) are:

A. 1 mmHg and 273.15 K

B. 1 atm and 273 °C

C. 760 mmHg and 25 °C

D. 10^5 Pa and 273.15 K

16. Which of the following indicators is/are orange at pH 5.2?

      I. phenolphthalein   II. methyl red   III. bromothymol blue

    A. I only   **C.** III only

    B. II only   **D.** I and II only

17. What is the color of phenolphthalein indicator at pH 6?

    A. pink   **C.** red

    B. colorless   **D.** blue

18. Molarity is defined as the number of:

    A. liters of solute per mole of solution   **C.** grams of solute per liter of solution

    B. moles of solute per liter of solvent   **D.** moles of solute per liter of solution

19. Which of the following best describe(s) temperature of matter?

      I. It is the measure of the heat of matter

      II. It is the measure of the average amount of kinetic energy in a substance

      III. It is the measure of the total amount of energy in a substance

    A. I only   **C.** III only

    B. II only   **D.** I and II only

20. What is heat a measure of?

    A. temperature   **C.** average kinetic energy

    B. internal thermal energy   **D.** potential energy

21. At sea level, what is the vapor pressure of water at 100 °C?

    A. 760 mmHg   **C.** 76 mmHg

    B. 100 mmHg   **D.** 1 mmHg

22. Which color does litmus paper turn when exposed to an acidic solution?

    A. Blue   **C.** Purple

    B. Red   **D.** White

Notes for active learning

Scientific Explanations Using Logic and Evidence

1. A small subpopulation of flies with a slightly advantageous modification in the structure was found extinct after a locally-isolated decimating fire. A geneticist would most likely attribute the loss of this advantageous gene to:

A. differential reproduction

B. natural selection

C. Hardy-Weinberg principle

D. genetic drift

2. A patient who has gained 35 lbs in the past 3 months visits her physician and complains of fatigue. She is diagnosed with a goiter and a decreased metabolic rate. Based on this, which hormone is most likely to be deficient in this patient?

A. estrogen

B. cortisol

C. thyroxine

D. aldosterone

3. A radio-labeled hormone was introduced to a culture of liver cells. After 5 hours of incubation, the cells were separated, and the radioactivity was observed primarily in the nucleus. Which of these conclusions about the hormone is the most consistent with the observations?

A. It is a steroid because it functions as a transcriptional activator by binding to DNA

B. It is a steroid because it contains hydrophilic regions that allow crossing the nuclear membrane

C. It is a peptide because it functions as a transcriptional activator by binding to DNA

D. It is a peptide because it contains hydrophilic amino acids that allow crossing the nuclear membrane

4. An unknown inheritance pattern has the following characteristics:

- 25% probability of having a homozygous unaffected child

- 25% probability of having a homozygous affected child

- 50% probability of having a heterozygous child

Which of these Mendel's inheritance patterns best matches the above observations?

A. autosomal recessive

B. autosomal dominant

C. X-linked recessive

D. X-linked dominant

5. Which of the following observations would support the theory of maternal inheritance for the spunky phenotype?

A. Spunky female × wild-type male → progeny all spunky

B. Wild-type female × spunky male → progeny all spunky

C. Wild-type female × spunky male → progeny 1/2 spunky, 1/2 wild-type

D. Spunky female × wild-type male → progeny 1/2 spunky, 1/2 wild-type

6. Hemophilia is a recessive X-linked trait. Knowing that females with Turner's syndrome have a high incidence of hemophilia, it can be concluded that these females have:

A. lost an X and gained a Y

B. lost an X

C. gained an X

D. gained a Y

7. Given that surfactant is produced by pneumocytes and is fully functional when it forms *micelles*, which of the following properties most likely describes a surfactant?

A. hydrophobic molecule

B. hydrophilic molecule

C. neutral molecule

D. basic molecule

8. Based on the diagram showing the relationship between lymph flow and interstitial (extracellular) fluid pressure, would an increase in interstitial fluid protein result in increased lymph flow?

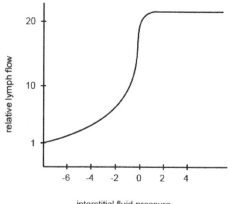

A. No, because fluid movement into the capillaries decreases interstitial fluid pressure

B. No, because the subsequent increase in interstitial fluid pressure reduces lymph flow

C. Yes, because fluid movement out of the capillaries increases interstitial fluid pressure

D. Yes, because the increased interstitial fluid protein reduces interstitial fluid volume

9. Which nutrient would be the most difficult to digest if a gallstone blocked the duct leading from the gallbladder?

A. fats

B. starch

C. amino acids

D. proteins

10. Which tissue would result in the LEAST amount of pain when surgically cut?

A. skin

B. smooth muscle

C. bone

D. cartilage

11. Which of these is expected to be observed in a patient with acromegaly, which is a condition from oversecretion of growth hormone, considering that growth hormone decreases cellular receptors' sensitivity to insulin?

A. decreased urine volume

B. decreased cardiac output

C. low blood glucose concentration

D. high blood glucose concentration

12. A presence of glucose in a patient's urine indicates that:

A. the proximal tubule is impervious to glucose

B. glucose is entering the filtrate at a higher rate than it is being reabsorbed

C. glucose transporters in the loop of Henle are defective

D. no clinical significance because glucose in the urine is normal

13. During a hydropathy analysis of a protein that has recently been sequenced, a researcher discovers that the protein has several regions that contain 20-25 hydrophobic amino acids. What conclusion would she draw from this finding?

A. Protein would be specifically localized in the mitochondrial inner membrane

B. Protein would be targeted to the mitochondrion

C. Protein is likely to be an integral protein

D. Protein is probably involved in glycolysis

14. When a female mouse with a defect in mitochondrial protein required for fatty acid oxidation is crossed with a wild-type male, all progeny (both male and female) have the wild-type phenotype. Which statement is most likely correct?

A. Mice do not exhibit maternal inheritance

B. The defect is a result of a nuclear gene mutation

C. The defect is a result of an X-linked recessive trait

D. The defect is a result of a recessive mitochondrial gene

Notes for active learning

With each topic, reinforce learning by reading review chapters in your *ATI TEAS Science Review* book.

Visit our Amazon store

Relationships Among Events, Objects, and Processes

1. If a hormone administered to mice intravenously accumulates rapidly inside renal cells without endocytosis, this hormone is most likely a:

A. neurotransmitter

B. second messenger

C. steroid

D. polypeptide

2. A neuroendocrine tumor of the adrenal glands releases epinephrine at abnormally high levels. Which of the following symptoms would be observed in a patient with such a tumor?

A. pupil constriction

B. abnormally low heart rate

C. reduced blood pressure

D. elevated blood pressure

3. If a thyroid tumor secreted an excessive amount of calcitonin, this would result in:

A. increase in blood calcium concentration

B. reduction in the rate of endochondral ossification

C. increase in the level of osteoblast activity

D. increase in the level of osteoclast activity

4. Which layer of the epidermis would be affected first by a drug that inhibits cell division (e.g., chemotherapy drug)?

A. stratum spinosum

B. stratum basale

C. stratum corneum

D. stratum lucidum

5. The surgical removal of the seminal vesicles would likely cause:

A. sterility, because sperm would not be produced

B. sterility, because sperm would not be able to exit the body

C. reduced volume of semen

D. enhanced fertilization potency of sperm

6. Which of these enzymes would be affected the most in a patient with a peptic ulcer after an overdose of antacid?

A. procarboxypeptidase

B. trypsin

C. pepsin

D. lipase

7. Tay-Sachs disease is a rare autosomal recessive genetic disorder. Suppose a male heterozygous carrier and a female heterozygous carrier have a homozygous first child. What is the chance that the second child develops Tay-Sachs?

A. 1/4

B. 1/2

C. 1/16

D. 1/8

8. T and B-cell abnormalities can be caused by severe combined immunodeficiency (SCID), which develops due to a genetic disease where adenosine deaminase is deficient. Which organs would be underdeveloped in an individual afflicted with SCID?

A. bone marrow only

B. bone marrow and thymus

C. thymus only

D. bone marrow and spleen

9. A patient has a blood clot forming in one of the large veins of his leg due to infection. If the clot dislodges and moves, what would be the most likely initial problem for this patient?

A. Cerebral stroke because the clot has moved to the brain

B. Coronary thrombosis because the clot has moved to the coronary circulation

C. Pulmonary embolism because the clot has moved to the pulmonary capillaries

D. Renal shut down because the clot has moved to the kidney

10. In an infant born with a congenital heart defect, which of the following is most likely to result from the mixing of blood between the right and left ventricles?

A. recurrent fever

B. hemoglobin deficiency

C. poor oxygenation of the tissues

D. low blood pressure

11. Hypovolemic shock occurs when a patient's blood volume falls abruptly and is likely the result of:

A. depleted Na^+ consumption

B. arterial bleeding

C. venous bleeding

D. high levels of aldosterone

12. Which of the following would be observed by a physician about her patient with type 1 diabetes and low blood insulin concentration?

A. decreased levels of blood glucose

B. increased insulin levels from thyroid stimulation

C. decreased levels of circulating erythrocytes

D. presence of glucose in the urine

13. Which of the following is likely to occur within several hours after the pancreatic duct is obstructed?

      I. diabetic crisis

      II. acromegaly

      III. impaired digestion

A. I only

B. I and III only

C. III only

D. II and III only

14. Which of the following would most likely occur if a diabetic patient accidentally overdoses with insulin?

A. increased urine excretion leading to dehydration

B. increased conversion of glycogen to glucose

C. decreased plasma glucose levels leading to convulsions

D. increased glucose concentration in urine

15. Why might an increase in the concentration of a set of reactants increase the reaction rate?

A. The rate of reaction depends only on the mass of the atoms and increases as the mass of the reactants increase

B. There is an increased probability that two reactant molecules collide and react

C. There is an increased ratio of reactants to products

D. The concentration of reactants is unrelated to the rate of reaction

Notes for active learning

Analysis and Design of a Scientific Investigation

1. Experiments designed by Avery, McLeod, and McCarty to identify the transforming principle were based on:

    I. purifying each of the macromolecule types from a cell-free extract

    II. removing each of the macromolecules from a cell, then testing its type

    III. selectively destroying the different macromolecules in a cell-free extract

    A. I only

    B. II only

    C. III only

    D. I, II and III

2. The Hershey–Chase experiment:

    A. proved that DNA replication is semiconservative

    B. used ^{32}P to label protein

    C. used ^{35}S to label DNA

    D. supported the hypothesis that DNA is the transforming molecule

3. For laboratory use, cellulose is a neutral polymer of glucose that can become either positive or negative by attaching cationic or anionic groups. What type of plasma compound is most likely to be filtered from blood during dialysis with anionic groups on the cellulose?

    A. negatively charged compounds

    B. positively charged compounds

    C. all compounds are filtered uniformly

    D. neutral charged compounds

4. Which of the following is a characteristic that makes an organism unsuitable for genetic studies?

    A. Large number of chromosomes

    B. Short generation time

    C. Ease of cultivation

    D. Ability to control crosses

5. Which is a good experimental method to distinguish between ordinary hydrogen and deuterium, the rare isotope of hydrogen?

    I. Measure the density of the gas at STP

    II. Measure the rate at which the gas effuses

    III. Infrared spectroscopy

    A. I only

    B. II only

    C. I and II only

    D. I, II, and III

6. A container is labeled "Ne, 5.0 moles" but has no pressure gauge. By measuring the temperature and determining the volume of the container, a chemist uses the ideal gas law to estimate the pressure inside the container. If the container were mislabeled and contained 5.0 moles of He, not Ne, how would this affect the scientist's estimate?

    A. The estimate is correct, but only because both gases are monatomic

    B. The estimate is too high

    C. The estimate is correct because the identity of the gas is irrelevant

    D. The estimate is significantly lower because of the large difference in molecular mass

7. For an isolated system, which of the following can NOT be exchanged between the system and its surroundings?

    I. Temperature   II. Matter   III. Energy

    A. I only   **C.** III only

    B. II only   **D.** I, II, and III

8. Heat is often added to chemical reactions performed in the laboratory to:

    A. compensate for the natural tendency of energy to disperse

    B. increase the rate at which reactants collide

    C. increase the energy of the reactant molecules

    D. all of the above

9. Increasing the temperature of a chemical reaction:

    A. increases the reaction rate by lowering the activation energy

    B. increases the reaction rate by increasing reactant collisions per unit time

    C. increases the activation energy, thus increasing the reaction rate

    D. raises the activation energy, thus decreasing the reaction rate

10. Most reactions are carried out in liquid solution or the gaseous phase because in such situations:

    A. kinetic energies of reactants are lower

    B. reactant collisions occur more frequently

    C. activation energies are higher

    D. reactant activation energies are lower

11. Which component of an insulated vessel design minimizes heat loss by convection?

    A. Heavy-duty aluminum construction   **C.** Tight-fitting, screw-on lid

    B. Reflective interior coating   **D.** Double-walled construction

12. What kind of system is represented when an investigator compresses gas within a hermetically sealed system by pushing down on the inside of a piston?

A. isolated

B. closed

C. open

D. endergonic

13. Which component of an insulated vessel design minimizes heat conduction?

A. Reflective interior coating

B. Heavy-duty plastic casing

C. Double-walled construction

D. Tight-fitting, screw-on lid

14. For a closed system, what can be exchanged between the system and its surroundings?

I. Heat II. Matter III. Energy

A. I only

B. II only

C. III only

D. I and III only

Notes for active learning

ATI TEAS
Science Questions

Part II

Answer Keys and
Detailed Explanations

Section I

Human Anatomy and Physiology

Anatomy & Physiology; Basic Biology

Respiratory System

Cardiovascular and Hematological Systems

Immune System

Digestive System

Nervous System

Skeletal System

Muscular System

Reproductive System

Integumentary System

Endocrine System

Genitourinary System

Anatomy & Physiology; Basic Biology – Explanations

Answer Key

1: B	11: D	21: B	31: B
2: A	12: B	22: D	32: D
3: D	13: C	23: C	
4: C	14: B	24: A	
5: D	15: C	25: A	
6: D	16: C	26: B	
7: A	17: A	27: B	
8: B	18: C	28: B	
9: A	19: B	29: A	
10: C	20: B	30: A	

1. B is correct.

Superior (or cranial) and inferior (or caudal) are relative and comparative directional terms describing a body part or anatomical structure above or below another body part or anatomical structure.

For example, the knee is superior to the ankle and inferior to the pelvis in the anatomical position.

2. A is correct.

Medial and lateral are relative and comparative directional terms describing a body part or anatomical structure towards or away from the center of the body, compared to another body part or anatomical structure.

For example, the nipple is medial to the shoulder and lateral to the sternum.

3. D is correct.

Proximal and distal are relative and comparative directional terms describing an anatomical structure (or body part) closer to the body core than another.

For example, the knee is distal to the hip and proximal to the ankle.

4. C is correct.

Anterior (or *ventral*) and posterior (or *dorsal*) are relative and comparative directional terms describing a body part or anatomical structure closer to or further from the front of the body compared to another body part or anatomical structure.

For example, the esophagus is anterior to the lungs and posterior to the sternum.

5. D is correct.

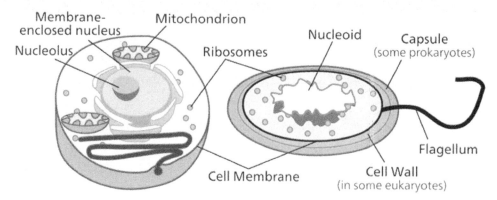

Structures within eukaryotic (left) and prokaryotic (right) cells

Earth formed approximately 4.6 billion years ago.

Prokaryotes are estimated to have arisen 3.7 billion to 4.2 years ago.

Eukaryotes are proposed to originate about 1.5 billion years ago (i.e., *endosymbiotic theory of evolution*).

Prokaryotic cells

The simplest cells are likely the first type of cells formed on Earth. These are *prokaryotic cells and* often have a cell wall surrounding the cell. The cytoplasm is where metabolic processes occur.

Ribosomes make proteins in the cytoplasm, and the cell contains a circular double-stranded DNA molecule.

The DNA is in a nucleoid region, where the genetic information (i.e., genome) is located.

Prokaryotic organisms are unicellular; the entire organism is one cell.

Prokaryotic organisms are asexual and do not need a partner to reproduce. Most reproduce through a process called binary fission, where the cell copies the circular DNA (i.e., genome) and divides.

Without mutations within the DNA, offspring are identical to their parent (compare with genetic variability introduced by sexual reproduction).

All organisms in the taxonomic domains Archaea and Bacteria are prokaryotic organisms.

Many of the species within the Archaea domain are found within hydrothermal vents. They may represent the first living organisms on Earth when life was first forming (i.e., 3.7 to 4.2 billion years ago).

Eukaryotic cells

The *eukaryotic cell* is complex. Like prokaryotic cells, eukaryotic cells have cell membranes, cytoplasm, ribosomes, and DNA. However, there are many more organelles within eukaryotic cells.

Organelles include a nucleus for the DNA, a nucleolus where ribosomes are synthesized, rough endoplasmic reticulum (RER) for protein assembly, smooth endoplasmic reticulum (SER) for lipid synthesis, Golgi apparatus for modifying, sorting, and exporting proteins, mitochondria for creating energy (i.e., ATP synthesis), a cytoskeleton for structure and transporting information, and vesicles to move biomolecules around the cell.

Some eukaryotic cells have lysosomes or peroxisomes to digest waste, vacuoles for storing water, chloroplasts for photosynthesis, and centrioles for dividing the cell during mitosis.

Cell walls often surround plans but not animal cells.

Most eukaryotic organisms are multicellular, with cells within the organism as specialized.

These cells take on characteristics and interact with other cell types to create an organism through *cellular differentiation* (i.e., morphology and function).

There are a few unicellular eukaryotes. These sometimes have tiny hair-like cilia projections to brush away debris and may have a long thread-like tail called a flagellum for locomotion.

The third taxonomic domain is the Eukarya Domain; this domain includes eukaryotic organisms.

The domain includes animals, plants, protists, and fungi. Eukaryotes may use asexual or sexual reproduction, depending on the organism's complexity.

Sexual reproduction allows for genetic diversity in offspring by mixing the parents' genes (e.g., egg and sperm) to form new genetic combinations. These random mutations are evolution and adaptations to the environment (i.e., selective advantage).

6. D is correct.

The intercellular space contains an acid-rich mucoprotein acting as a strong adhesive.

A hemidesmosome provides a secure connection between the cell and its underlying connective tissue.

A: not all junctions between cells produce cytoplasmic connections; instead, *tight junctions* create a watertight seal between two adjacent animal cells.

At the site of a tight junction, cells are held firmly against each other by many individual groups of tight junction proteins called *claudins*, each interacting with a partner group on another cell membrane.

The groups are arranged into strands forming a branching network, with many strands making for a tighter seal.

C: in vertebrates, *gap junctions* develop when a set of six membrane proteins called *connexins* form an elongated, donut-like structure.

When the pores, or "doughnut holes," of connexons in adjacent animal cells align, a channel forms between the cells. (Invertebrates form gap junctions but use a different set of proteins called innexins).

7. A is correct.

Animal cells do not have cell walls.

Cell walls are in plant cells, fungi, some protists, and prokaryotic cells. Cell walls act as a protection for cell contents and give cells strength and rigidity but do not interfere with the function of the plasma membrane.

The rigid cell wall permits plants to be erect without an endoskeleton (e.g., the internal skeleton of vertebrates) or an exoskeleton (e.g., the shell of insects).

8. B is correct.

Endosymbiotic theory states that mitochondria were once free-living aerobic prokaryotes consumed by a cell about 1.5 billion years ago.

The prokaryote (probably a proteobacterium) became an endosymbiont within the cell, providing the anaerobic host cell with ATP via aerobic respiration. In return, the host cell provided the endosymbiont with a stable environment and nutrients.

Over time, the endosymbiont transferred most of its genes to the host nucleus, to the point that it became obligate (i.e., could no longer survive outside the host cell) and evolved into a mitochondrion.

Biologists largely accept the endosymbiotic theory.

One compelling piece of evidence is that mitochondrial DNA does not encode for its proteins. Instead, many of its genes are in the nuclear DNA; therefore, many proteins must be imported into the mitochondria.

Furthermore, mitochondrial DNA, ribosomes, and enzymes are similar to bacterial forms, and mitochondria replicate a process similar to binary fission.

Additionally, some of the proteins within the plasma membrane of the mitochondria are similar to prokaryotes, which are different from proteins in the eukaryotic plasma membrane.

Chloroplasts are organelles performing photosynthesis. They exhibit strong evidence of an endosymbiotic origin, although they are hypothesized to have descended from cyanobacteria rather than proteobacteria (i.e., endosymbiotic theory).

Chloroplasts and other plastids can undergo secondary and even tertiary endosymbiosis, causing the development of additional membranes.

9. A is correct.

The Krebs cycle is the second phase of the cellular respiration mechanism and occurs in the fluid matrix of the cristae compartments of the mitochondria.

The cycle is named after Sir Hans Krebs (1900-1981), who received the 1953 Nobel Prize for identifying these reactions. It is also called the *citric acid cycle* or the *tricarboxylic acid cycle* (TCA).

One glucose molecule undergoes two turns of the Krebs cycle to produce ATP for cellular energy.

10. C is correct.

Transcription is the synthesis of RNA from a DNA template.

Messenger RNA (mRNA) is transcribed from a DNA template strand and then *translated* into a protein.

11. D is correct.

Unlike most other eukaryotic cells, mature red blood cells (i.e., erythrocytes) do not have nuclei.

When red blood cells first enter the bloodstream, they eject their nuclei and organelles to carry more hemoglobin and more oxygen.

Because they have no genetic material and no organelles, they cannot divide or synthesize proteins and have minimal repair abilities.

12. B is correct.

Ribosomes are organelles composed of proteins and ribosomal RNA (rRNA).

Ribosomes are 1) floating free in the cytoplasm, 2) attached to the surface of the rough ER, or 3) within mitochondria and chloroplasts. They translate messenger RNA (mRNA) to coordinate the assembly of amino acids into polypeptide chains, folding into functional proteins.

Each ribosome consists of a small subunit and a large subunit.

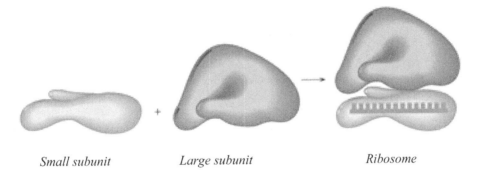

Small subunit   *Large subunit*   *Ribosome*

In ribosomes, the ribonucleotide sequence of mRNA is interpreted and synthesized into an amino acid sequence.

The mRNA strand fits into a groove on the small subunit, with the bases pointing toward the large subunit.

The ribosome acts as a "reader," and when it reaches a termination sequence in the mRNA, the link between the synthesized polypeptide chain and tRNA is broken.

Then, the completed polypeptide is released from the ribosome.

13. C is correct.

I: water relies on aquaporins to diffuse across a plasma membrane. Without aquaporins, a small fraction of water molecules can diffuse through the cell membrane per unit of time because of water molecules' polarity.

II: small hydrophobic molecules readily diffuse through the hydrophobic tails of the plasma membrane.

III: small ions rely on ion channel transport proteins to diffuse across the membrane.

IV: neutral gas molecules (e.g., O_2, CO_2) readily diffuse through the hydrophobic tails in the plasma membrane.

14. B is correct.

The lysosome is the digestive region of the cell and is a membrane-bound organelle with a low pH (around 5) that stores hydrolytic enzymes.

A: vacuoles and vesicles are membrane-bound sacs involved in the transport and storage of ingested materials secreted, processed, or digested by cells.

Vacuoles are larger than vesicles and are more likely in plant cells (e.g., central vacuole).

C: chloroplasts are sites for photosynthesis and are found in algae and plant cells.

Chloroplasts contain DNA and ribosomes and may have similarly evolved via endosymbiosis to the mitochondria.

D: phagosomes are vesicles that transport and store materials ingested by the cell through phagocytosis.

The vesicles form by fusion of the cell membrane around the particle.

A phagosome is a cellular compartment in which pathogenic microorganisms can be digested.

Phagosomes fuse with lysosomes in their maturation process to form phagolysosomes.

15. C is correct.

The two ribosomal subunits are produced in the nucleolus, a region within the nucleus. The ribosomes are the sites of protein production.

Prokaryotic ribosomes (30S small + 50S large subunit = 70S complete ribosome) are smaller than eukaryotic ribosomes (40S small + 60S large subunit = 80S complete ribosome).

A: Golgi apparatus is a membrane-bound organelle that modifies (e.g., glycosylation), sorts, and packages proteins synthesized by the ribosomes.

B: lysosomes have a low pH of about 5 and contain hydrolytic enzymes involved for digestion.

D: rough endoplasmic reticulum (RER) is a portion of the endomembrane system that extends from the nuclear envelope.

The RER has ribosomes associated with its membrane and is the site of the production and folding of proteins.

Misfolded proteins exit the rough ER and are sent to the proteasome for degradation.

16. C is correct.

Peroxisomes are organelles in most eukaryotic cells.

A significant function of the peroxisome is the breakdown of very-long-chain fatty acids through beta-oxidation.

In animal cells, the peroxisome converts the very-long-chain fatty acids to medium-chain fatty acids, subsequently shuttled to the mitochondria, where they are eventually broken down, via oxidation, into CO_2 and H_2O.

17. A is correct.

The cytoskeleton is integral in proper cell division because it forms the mitotic spindle and is responsible for separating sister chromatids during cell division.

The cytoskeleton is composed of microtubules and microfilaments for mechanical support, maintaining shape, and functioning in cell motility.

18. C is correct.

The Golgi apparatus (i.e., Golgi complex) is a eukaryotic cell organelle. It processes proteins via post-translational modifications. The proteins shuttled through the Golgi have three destinations: secreted out of the cell, transported into organelles, or targeted to the plasma membrane.

19. B is correct.

Most animal and plant cells range in size between 1 and 100 micrometers and are visible with a microscope.

Light microscopes visualize objects from 1 millimeter (10^{-3} m) to 0.2 micrometers (2×10^{-7} m).

Electron microscopes visualize objects as small as an atom (1 angstrom or 10^{-10} m).

The microscopic scale is from 1 millimeter (10^{-3} m) to a ten-millionth of a millimeter (10^{-10} m).

Even within the microscopic scale, there are immense variations in objects' size. 10^{-3} m is 10 million times larger than 10^{-10} m. By comparison, that is equivalent to the Earth's size *vs.* a beach ball.

Use the magnification to determine the size of the objects observed.

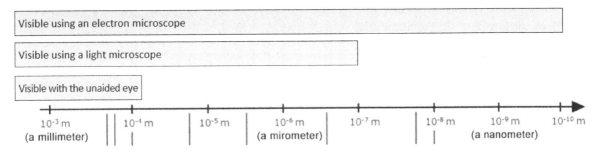

20. B is correct.

Ribosomes are composed of specific rRNA molecules and associated proteins.

The ribosome is identified by the sedimentation coefficients (i.e., S units for Svedberg units) for density.

Prokaryotes have a 30S small subunit and a 50S large subunit (i.e., complete ribosome = 70S).

Eukaryotes have a 40S small subunit and a 60S large subunit (i.e., complete ribosome = 80S).

A: peroxisomes are organelles involved in hydrogen peroxide (H_2O_2) synthesis and degradation.

Peroxisomes detoxify the cell and contain the enzyme catalase that decomposes H_2O_2 (peroxides) into H_2O and O_2.

C: Mitochondria are organelles that are the site of cellular respiration (i.e., oxidation of glucose to yield ATP) and are plentiful in cells with high demands for ATP (e.g., muscle cells).

The number of mitochondria within a cell varies widely by organism and tissue type. Many cells have a single mitochondrion, whereas others contain several thousand mitochondria.

D: The *nucleus* is the largest membrane-bound organelle in the center of most eukaryotic cells.

The nucleus contains the cell's genetic code (i.e., DNA).

The function of the nucleus is to direct the cell by storing and transmitting genetic information. Cells can contain multiple nuclei (e.g., skeletal muscle cells), one nucleus, or rarely, none (e.g., red blood cells).

21. B is correct.

Active transport involves a carrier protein and uses energy to move a substance across a membrane against (i.e., up) a concentration gradient: from low solute to a region of high solute concentration.

Donnan equilibrium refers to the fact that some ionic species can pass through the barrier while others cannot.

The presence of a different charged substance that cannot pass through the membrane creates an uneven electrical charge. The electric potential arising between the solutions is the *Donnan* potential.

22. D is correct.

Glycolysis occurs in the cytoplasm, while the oxidation of pyruvate to acetyl-CoA and the Krebs (TCA) cycle occurs in the matrix of the mitochondria.

The electron transport chain (ETC) occurs in the inner membrane (i.e., cytochromes) / intermembrane space (i.e., H^+ proton gradient) of the mitochondria.

A: pyruvate is oxidized to acetyl-CoA as a preliminary step before joining oxaloacetate in the Krebs cycle, which occurs in the mitochondrion.

B: the Krebs cycle is the second stage of cellular respiration and occurs in the mitochondrion matrix.

C: the electron transport chain is the final stage of cellular respiration occurring in the inner membrane (i.e., cytochromes) / intermembrane space (i.e., H^+ proton gradient) of the mitochondrion.

23. C is correct.

Centrioles are cylindrical structures composed mainly of tubulin in most eukaryotic cells (except flowering plants and fungi).

Centrioles are involved in the mitotic spindle organization and the completion of cytokinesis. Centrioles contribute to centrosomes' structure and organize microtubules in the cytoplasm.

The centriole position determines the location of the nucleus and is critical in the cell's spatial arrangement.

24. A is correct.

Centrioles are the organizational sites for microtubules (i.e., spindle fibers) that assemble during cell division (e.g., mitosis and meiosis).

The four phases of mitosis are prophase, metaphase, anaphase, and telophase, followed by cytokinesis, which physically divides the cell into two genetically identical daughter cells.

The condensed chromosomes are aligned along the equatorial plane in mitotic metaphase before the centromere (i.e., heterochromatin region on the DNA) splits. The two sister chromosomes begin their journey to the cell's respective poles.

25. A is correct.

Mitosis is cell division when new somatic (i.e., body) cells are added to multicellular organisms as they grow and when tissues are repaired or replaced.

Mitosis does not produce genetic variations. A daughter cell is identical in chromosome number and genetic makeup to the parent cell.

The purpose of mitosis is to distribute identical genetic material to two daughter cells. The fidelity of DNA transmission between generations without dilution is remarkable. Eukaryotes divide by mitosis.

26. B is correct.

Apoptosis is programmed cell death during fetal development and aging.

The synaptic cleft development, the formation of separate digits in the hand of a fetus, and tadpole tail reabsorption are examples of apoptosis during organismal development.

The uterine lining synthesis is an anabolic process that involves mitosis (i.e., cell division).

27. B is correct.

Bone and cartilage are connective tissues that function to connect and support tissues and organs and are related in their lineage and activities. Connective tissue functions to bind and support other tissues.

Connective tissue consists of loose connective tissue and dense connective tissue (subdivided into dense regular and dense irregular). Special connective tissue consists of reticular connective tissue, adipose tissue, blood, bone, and cartilage.

28. B is correct.

Mitochondria self-replicate autonomously, and the number of mitochondria in a cell varies widely by organism and tissue/type. Many cells have a single mitochondrion, while others contain several thousand mitochondria.

A and C: nucleus and nucleolus replicate and divide during mitosis and meiosis.

D: ribosomes are not self-replicating. They consist of rRNA (synthesized in the nucleolus) and associated proteins. Ribosomes are assembled by cellular machinery.

29. A is correct.

Organs are recognizable structures within the body (e.g., heart, lungs, liver) performing specific functions.

30. A is correct.

An organ is usually made of several types of tissue and, therefore, many types of cells.

31. B is correct.

The four primary tissue types are connective, muscle, nervous and epithelial.

32. D is correct.

Adipose tissue (along with cartilage, bone, and blood) is a particular connective tissue, mainly located beneath the skin and around internal organs. In adipose tissue, glucose is transformed and stored as fat.

Fatty acids are an essential energy source, ideal for an organism to store as fat in the adipose tissue when a large quantity of energy needs to be stored for later use (e.g., hibernating bear).

Notes for active learning

Notes for active learning

Respiratory System – Explanations

Answer Key

1: B	11: A	21: C	31: B
2: A	12: D	22: C	32: A
3: B	13: C	23: A	
4: B	14: D	24: D	
5: B	15: C	25: D	
6: D	16: C	26: D	
7: C	17: D	27: D	
8: D	18: C	28: D	
9: C	19: B	29: D	
10: B	20: C	30: C	

1. B is correct.

The transport of gases to and from tissues is the circulatory system's function. The respiratory system conducts the gas exchange in the lungs' alveoli, while the circulatory system carries the gases to and from tissues and cells.

2. A is correct.

The intensity of sound (i.e., loudness) is controlled primarily by the force with which air from the lungs can pass through the larynx.

The size of vocal folds affects the pitch of the voice.

3. B is correct.

When the pressure in the lungs exceeds atmospheric pressure, air moves out of the lungs by flowing down the pressure gradient.

4. B is correct.

The diaphragm is a sheet of internal skeletal muscle that extends across the bottom of the rib cage. It separates the thoracic cavity (heart, lungs, and ribs) from the abdominal cavity. The diaphragm performs the vital function in respiration – as the diaphragm contracts, the volume of the thoracic cavity increases, and air enters the lungs.

5. B is correct.

C-shaped cartilage rings form the trachea's foundation, allowing it to maintain openness.

6. D is correct.

Intrapulmonary pressure is the pressure within the lungs, which varies between inspiration and expiration. Intrapulmonary pressure must fall below atmospheric pressure to initiate inspiration.

For inspiration, an increase in lung volume decreases intrapulmonary pressure to sub-atmospheric levels, and air enters the lungs.

A decrease in lung volume raises intrapulmonary pressure above atmospheric pressure expelling air from the lungs for expiration.

7. C is correct.

The fenestrated (i.e., openings between cells) capillaries are endothelial cells of a single layer.

The blood (with the erythrocytes) moves under hydrostatic pressure for oxygen exchange.

8. D is correct.

The increased concentration of carbon dioxide (CO_2) in the blood is detected by respiratory centers in the brain's pons and medulla, which stimulate the body to breathe more deeply and frequently.

Conversely, decreased levels of CO_2 lead to a decrease in frequency and depth of breathing.

9. C is correct.

In respiration, inhalation stretches the lungs, and *elastic recoil* refers to the ease with which the lungs rebound.

During inhalation, the intrapleural pressure (i.e., the pressure within the pleural cavity) decreases.

During expiration, the diaphragm relaxes, the lungs recoil, and the intrapleural pressure restores.

Lung compliance (i.e., a measure of the lung's ability to stretch and expand) is inversely related to elastic recoil.

Elastic recoil of the lungs occurs because 1) the elastic fibers in the connective tissue of the lungs, and 2) the surface tension of the fluid that lines the alveoli.

Due to cohesion, water molecules bond together (via hydrogen bonding), which pulls on the alveolar walls and causes the alveoli to recoil and become smaller.

The two factors that prevent the lungs from collapsing are 1) surfactant as a surface-active lipoprotein complex formed by type II alveolar cells and 2) intrapleural pressure.

10. B is correct.

Chemoreceptors are in the medulla oblongata, the carotid arteries, and the aorta. They detect and signal the respiratory centers in the medulla to modify the breathing rate when the respiratory gases' partial pressure is too low or high.

The chemoreceptors are most responsive to changes in $[CO_2]$ and $[H^+]$, while extreme changes in $[O_2]$ are relayed to the medulla oblongata.

The $[H^+]$ of the blood is directly proportional to the partial pressure of CO_2. In erythrocytes, CO_2 combines with H_2O to form H_2CO_3, dissociating into HCO_3^- and H^+. An increase in $[H^+]$ decreases the pH of the blood. When chemoreceptors detect an increase in the partial pressure of CO_2 or an increase in $[H^+]$, the rate of breathing increases.

The high partial pressure of O_2 in the blood triggers a decrease, not an increase, in the rate of breathing.

11. A is correct.

Lung compliance measures the lung's ability to stretch and expand.

The surface tension of alveolar fluid is the force created by films of molecules that can reduce surface area, affecting lung compliance.

12. D is correct.

Tidal volume is the amount of air that enters the lungs during normal inhalation at rest; the same amount leaves the lungs during exhalation. The average tidal volume is 500ml.

Inspiratory reserve volume is the amount of air inhaled above tidal volume during a deep breath.

Expiratory reserve volume is the amount of air exhaled above tidal volume during a forceful breath out.

Residual volume is the amount of air remaining in the lungs after a maximal exhalation; some air is left to prevent the lungs from collapsing.

Vital capacity is the most air exhaled after taking the deepest possible breath; this amount can be up to ten times more than customarily exhaled.

Total lung capacity is the vital lung capacity plus the residual volume and equals the total amount of air the lungs can hold. The average total lung capacity is 6000ml; however, this value varies with age, height, gender, and health status.

13. C is correct.

Hypoxia is a pathological condition whereby tissue is deprived of adequate oxygen supply.

14. D is correct.

The lower respiratory tract begins at the trachea and extends into the primary bronchi and the lungs.

15. C is correct.

Sensory organs of the brain and those in the aorta and carotid arteries monitor oxygen and carbon dioxide levels in the blood. Carbon dioxide must continuously be eliminated from the blood to maintain the body's acid-base balance.

Chemoreceptors near the respiratory center in the brain control acid-base balance by sensing the pH of cerebrospinal fluid.

Typically, an increased concentration of CO_2 is the most potent stimulus to breathe more deeply and more frequently to remove excess CO_2.

In chronic hypoventilation (e.g., patients with chronic obstructive pulmonary disease), when chemoreceptors lose their sensitivity and inadequately respond to increases in CO_2, peripheral chemoreceptors attempt to regulate respiratory function to restore the acid-base balance. These peripheral chemoreceptors are sensitive to the concentration of oxygen in peripheral blood.

Therefore, the stimulus to breathe is now low oxygen levels rather than increased carbon dioxide levels. If the oxygen level is significantly increased by administering supplemental oxygen, the peripheral chemoreceptors will not stimulate breathing, resulting in apnea. This is why supplemental oxygen must be given at low levels to patients with chronic obstructive pulmonary disease.

Elevated blood pressure does not encourage breathing or cause external symptoms.

16. C is correct.

The esophagus is part of the digestive system and is not a part of the respiratory tract.

The respiratory tract begins with the trachea and divides into the two main bronchi.

The main bronchi further subdivide into branching bronchioles, which lead to alveoli (site of gas exchange in the lungs).

17. D is correct.

Respiratory centers are in the medulla oblongata and pons (i.e., brain stem structures). The respiratory centers have receptors that receive neural, chemical, and hormonal signals to control the depth and rate of breathing via movements of the diaphragm and other respiratory muscles.

18. C is correct.

The exhalation process begins in the alveoli of the lungs, then air moves through the bronchioles to the bronchi, then passes through the trachea towards the larynx and finally the pharynx.

19. B is correct.

Nasal conchae (concha *singular*) are long, spongy curled shelves of bone protruding into the breathing passage of the nose.

20. C is correct.

Diffusion is how oxygen (O_2) and carbon dioxide (CO_2) are exchanged in the lungs and through cell membranes.

21. C is correct.

I: gas exchange is a passive process whereby gases diffuse down their partial pressure gradients.

II: inhalation is an active process requiring contraction of the diaphragm and the external intercostals muscles.

III: exhalation is a passive process from the lungs' elastic recoil and relaxation of the diaphragm and the external intercostal muscles. However, during vigorous exercise, active muscle contraction assists in exhalation.

22. C is correct.

The carina is a ridge of cartilage in the lower part of the trachea that divides the two main bronchi.

23. A is correct.

When air pressure within the lungs is less than the atmospheric pressure, air rushes into the lungs.

B: thoracic cavity enlargement causes air pressure within the lungs to fall.

C: low pressure inside the thoracic cavity is due to the expansion of the thoracic volume when the diaphragm contracts.

D: when the pressure drops, air rushes in, and the ciliated membranes warm, moisten, and filter the inspired air. Air then travels through the bronchi, into the bronchioles, and then into the alveoli, where diffusion occurs to oxygenate the blood and release CO_2.

24. D is correct.

Mucus in the nose traps dust and microbes, carried away by cilia (tiny hairs that line nasal passages).

25. D is correct.

The larynx is the organ that connects the lower portion of the pharynx and the trachea. It functions as a valve to close the air passages during swallowing. It maintains a patent airway and for vocalization.

The human pharynx is divided into nasopharynx, oropharynx, and laryngopharynx.

The pharynx is part of the digestive and respiratory systems and plays an essential role in vocalization.

A: laryngopharynx (hypopharynx) is the part of the throat that connects to the esophagus. It lies inferior to (below) the epiglottis and extends to the location where the pharynx diverges into the respiratory (larynx) and digestive (esophagus) pathways. Like the oropharynx above it, the laryngopharynx serves as a passageway for food and air.

B: oropharynx (mesopharynx) lies behind the oral cavity, extending from the uvula to the level of the hyoid bone. Food and air pass through the oropharynx, and a flap of connective tissue (i.e., the epiglottis) closes over the glottis when food is swallowed to prevent aspiration.

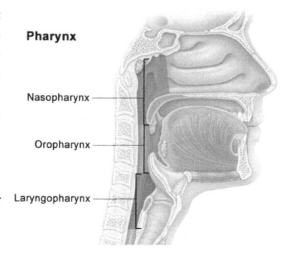

C: nasopharynx (epipharynx) is the higher portion of the pharynx that extends from the skull base to the soft palate's upper surface and lies above the oral cavity. The pharyngeal tonsils (adenoids) are lymphoid tissue structures in the nasopharynx's posterior wall.

26. D is correct.

During normal inhalation, the air is warmed and humidified by the nasal passageway's extensive surface, and particles are filtered from the air by nasal mechanisms.

When a patient undergoes a tracheotomy, the air entering the respiratory system bypasses the nasal cavities and is not warmed or moistened.

A: air does bypass the larynx, but this does not account for its effects.

B: filtering the air as it enters the lungs is a separate process from making it warm and moist.

C: air does bypass the mouth and tongue, but this does not account for its effects.

27. D is correct.

The upper respiratory tract consists of the passage from the nose into the larynx and trachea.

28. D is correct.

Respiratory bronchioles are the smallest bronchioles that connect terminal bronchioles to alveolar ducts. The ciliated epithelium lines the passageway from the terminal bronchiole to the alveoli.

29. D is correct.

Voluntary cortical control allows breathing to be controlled consciously and unconsciously. It allows the rate and depth of breathing to be influenced by the cerebral cortex.

30. C is correct.

The epiglottis is an elastic flap at the larynx entrance open during breathing and closed during swallowing, directing food down the esophagus.

31. B is correct.

Hyaline cartilage rings help support the trachea while simultaneously allowing it to be flexible during breathing.

32. A is correct.

CO_2 is carried in blood in three ways, and the percent concentration varies between venous or arterial blood.

70-80% of CO_2 is converted to bicarbonate ions HCO_3^- by the carbonic anhydrase in the red blood cells via reaction $CO_2 + H_2O \rightarrow H_2CO_3 \rightarrow H^+ + HCO_3^-$

5-10% is dissolved in blood plasma.

5-10% is bound to hemoglobin as carbamino compounds.

Hemoglobin is the primary oxygen-carrying molecule in the RCB and carries carbon dioxide. Carbon dioxide does not bind to the same site as oxygen; it combines with the N-terminal groups on the four chains of globin.

However, due to the allosteric effect (i.e., preferential binding) on the hemoglobin, the binding of CO_2 lowers the amount of oxygen bound for a given partial pressure of oxygen.

Deoxygenation of the blood increases its ability to carry carbon dioxide – this is the *Haldane effect*.

Conversely, oxygenated blood has a reduced capacity for carbon dioxide, affecting blood's ability to transport carbon dioxide from the tissues to the lungs.

A rise in the partial pressure of CO_2 causes an offloading of oxygen from the hemoglobin (Bohr Effect).

Notes for active learning

Cardiovascular and Hematological Systems – Explanations

Answer Key

1: B	11: C	21: C	31: C
2: A	12: A	22: C	
3: C	13: A	23: D	
4: A	14: C	24: A	
5: D	15: D	25: B	
6: C	16: B	26: D	
7: C	17: D	27: A	
8: D	18: C	28: A	
9: C	19: C	29: C	
10: D	20: B	30: A	

1. B is correct.

The capillaries are the most extensive capillary network of blood vessels, having the greatest cross-sectional area and blood flow resistance.

Blood pressure is highest in the aorta and drops until the blood returns to the heart via the inferior and superior venae cavae.

2. A is correct.

Ventricles are the heart's pumping chambers, while the atria are collecting chambers.

Oxygenated blood returns from the lungs (i.e., pulmonary circulation) and feeds into the heart's left atrium.

From the left atrium, the oxygenated blood flows into the left ventricle that pumps it through the systemic (i.e., body) circulation.

The right atrium receives deoxygenated blood via the inferior and superior vena cava.

The blood is pumped from the right ventricle to the lungs.

3. C is correct.

At the arteriole end of the capillary bed, the hydrostatic pressure is approximately 30-36 mmHg, while the opposing osmotic pressure is approximately 25-27 mmHg.

The higher hydrostatic pressure forces fluid out of the capillaries and into the interstitial space.

At the venule end of the capillary bed, the osmotic pressure is higher than the hydrostatic pressure, which has dropped to 12-15 mmHg.

The higher osmotic pressure draws fluid into the capillaries from the interstitial space and permits the liquid to return to the heart.

Most of the fluid (blood) is forced from the capillaries to the interstitial space at the arteriole end (via hydrostatic pressure). The capillaries reabsorb it at the venule end (via osmotic pressure).

4. A is correct.

Veins are thin-walled inelastic vessels that usually transport deoxygenated blood (pulmonary vein is the exception) *toward* the heart.

Veins do not have a steady pulse because of the fluid exchange that occurs in the capillaries. Because of their low pressure, blood flow along veins depends on compression by skeletal muscles rather than on the elastic, smooth muscles that line the arteries.

B: arteries transport blood *away* from the heart and are thick-walled, muscular elastic circulatory vessels.

Blood in the arteries is usually oxygenated. The pulmonary arteries are the exception whereby deoxygenated blood from the heart, returning from the body, is pumped to the lungs.

C: mammals have a four-chambered heart.

D: lymphatic system is an open circulatory system that transports excess interstitial fluid (lymph) to the cardiovascular system and maintains constant fluid levels.

Lymph enters the bloodstream at the thoracic duct that connects to the superior vena cava.

5. D is correct.

Blood enters the heart through the inferior and superior vena cava.

The right atrium receives the oxygen-poor blood and contracts, bringing the blood to the right ventricle.

When the ventricle contracts, blood enters the pulmonary artery and lungs, where it is oxygenated.

The pulmonary vein empties the blood into the left atrium, after which it flows into the left ventricle.

Finally, the ventricle contracts and the blood leaves through the aortic valve into the aorta.

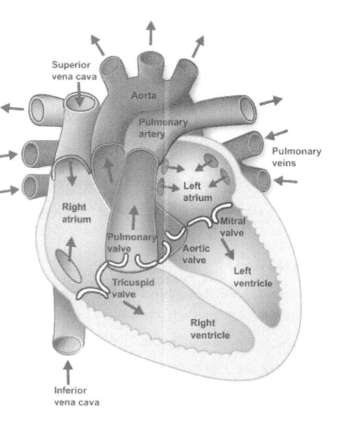

6. C is correct.

Blood has three leading roles in the body: transport, protection, and regulation.

In its transport role, blood transports the following substances:

- Gases (oxygen and carbon dioxide) between the lungs and tissues

- Nutrients from the digestive tract and storage sites to the cells

- Waste products to be removed by the liver and kidneys

- Hormones from where they are secreted to their target cells

Blood's protective role includes:

- Leukocytes (i.e., white blood cells) destroy invading microorganisms and cancer cells

- Antibodies and other proteins destroy pathogenic substances

- Platelet factors initiate blood clotting and minimize blood loss

Blood helps regulate:

- pH by interacting with acids and bases

- Water balance by transferring water to and from tissues

7. C is correct.

Platelets are cell fragments that lack nuclei and are involved in clot formation.

Platelets (i.e., thrombocytes) are small, disk-shaped clear cell fragments (i.e., do not have a nucleus), 2–3 μm in diameter, derived from the fragmentation of precursor megakaryocytes.

The lifespan of a typical platelet is 5 to 9 days.

Platelets are a natural source of growth factors circulating in the blood and are involved in hemostasis (formation of blood clots to stop bleeding).

A low platelet count may result in excessive bleeding, while too high of a number may result in the formation of blood clots (thrombosis), which may obstruct blood vessels and result in stroke, myocardial infarction, pulmonary embolism or the blockage of blood vessels, for example, in the extremities of the arms or legs.

A: erythrocytes (i.e., red blood cells) are the blood's oxygen-carrying components and contain hemoglobin that binds up to four molecules of oxygen.

B: macrophages perform phagocytosis of foreign particles and bacteria by engulfing them, digesting the material, and then presenting the fragments on their cell surface.

D: T cells lyse virally infected cells or secrete proteins that stimulate B cells' development or other T cell types.

8. D is correct.

Capillaries have higher hydrostatic pressure at the arteriole end and lower pressure at the venule end.

As blood flows from arterioles to capillaries, blood pressure gradually drops due to friction between the blood and the walls of the vessels and the increase in cross-sectional areas provided by numerous capillary beds.

Blood plasma in the capillaries has a higher osmotic pressure than interstitial fluid pressure. This results from the higher number of dissolved solutes in the capillaries' blood plasma.

Hydrostatic pressure is defined as the force per area that blood exerts on the blood vessels' walls.

The pumping force of the heart through the blood vessels creates hydrostatic pressure.

9. C is correct.

In an adult, hematopoiesis (i.e., the formation of blood cellular components) occurs in the bone marrow.

In the fetus, hematopoiesis occurs in the fetal liver.

The spleen acts as a reservoir for red blood cells (red blood cells) and filters the blood.

Erythrocytes are produced in the bone marrow to replace erythrocytes during their 120-day life span.

A: erythrocytes (mature red blood cells) are not nucleated to create more space for hemoglobin.

B: blood platelets are crucial for the clotting of blood.

D: leukocytes (white blood cells) such as macrophages and neutrophils engulf foreign matter.

Neutrophils are the most abundant white blood cells and account for approximately 50-70% of white blood cells.

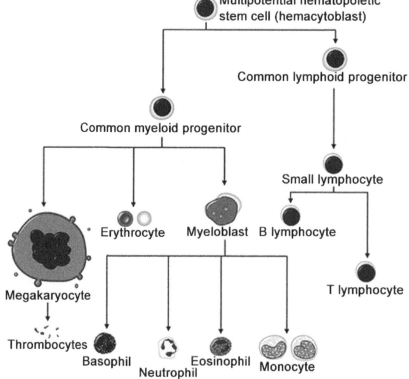

10. D is correct.

Blood traveling from the left ventricle enters the aorta and then flows to the body areas (i.e., systemic circulation) except the lungs (i.e., pulmonary circulation).

Examples of systemic circulation include blood in the brachiocephalic artery (travels to the head and the shoulders) and blood in the renal artery (travels to the kidney to be filtered).

Superior/inferior vena cava → right atrium → right ventricle → pulmonary artery (*pulmonary circulation*) → lungs → pulmonary vein → left atrium → left ventricle → aorta (*systemic circulation*) → superior/inferior vena cava

For systemic circulation, blood moves from arteries into arterioles, then capillaries, where nutrients, waste, and energy are exchanged.

Blood then enters venules, collects in veins, is transported to the superior and inferior venae cavae, and then enters the right atrium and flows into the right ventricle.

For pulmonary circulation, blood is transported to the lungs via the pulmonary artery.

Capillary beds around the alveoli exchange gas (O_2 into the blood and CO_2 from the blood) in the lungs.

The pulmonary veins bring blood back to the left atrium to start the systemic circulation.

11. C is correct.

The right atrium is the upper chamber of the heart's right side. The blood returned to the right atrium by the superior, and inferior vena cava is deoxygenated (low in O_2) and passes into the right ventricle to be pumped through the lungs' pulmonary artery for O_2 and removal of CO_2.

The left atrium receives newly oxygenated blood from the lungs by the pulmonary vein. The blood is passed into the muscular left ventricle to be pumped through the aorta to the body's organs.

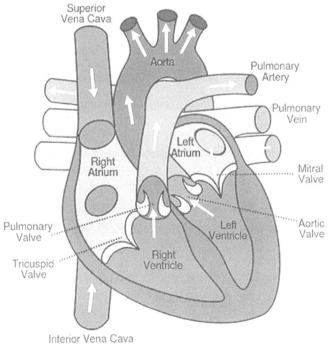

In a healthy heart, the right ventricle pumps blood through the pulmonary arteries to the lungs during pulmonary circulation. The left ventricle pumps blood through the aorta to the body by systemic circulation.

If blood mixes between the ventricles, some deoxygenated blood in the right ventricle mixes with the left ventricle's oxygenated blood for systemic circulation. This mixing lowers the O_2 supplied to the tissues.

12. A is correct.

Blood plasma is the liquid part of blood, consisting primarily of water (up to 95%), suspending blood cells and acting as the extracellular matrix.

13. A is correct.

The aorta carries oxygenated blood from the heart through the systemic (i.e., body) circulation and (like the pulmonary vein) has the highest partial pressure of O_2.

B: coronary veins carry deoxygenated blood to the heart's right side.

C: the superior vena cava carries deoxygenated blood from the body's upper regions to the heart. The inferior vena cava carries deoxygenated blood from the lower half of the body into the right atrium.

D: pulmonary arteries carry deoxygenated blood *away* from the heart towards the lungs. The pulmonary artery is the only artery in the adult carrying deoxygenated blood.

14. C is correct.

Deoxygenated blood returns from the systemic circulation and drains into the right atrium from the inferior and superior vena cava.

From the right atrium, blood is pumped through the tricuspid valve into the right ventricle, pumps blood to the lungs via the pulmonary arteries.

CO_2 is exchanged for O_2 in the alveoli of the lungs.

Oxygenated blood is returned to the left atrium via the pulmonary veins.

The left atrium pumps the blood through the mitral valve into the left ventricle, which ejects it into the aorta for systemic circulation.

If a tracer substance were injected into the superior vena cava, it would take the longest time to reach the left ventricle.

A: the tricuspid valve separates the right atrium from the right ventricle. It prevents blood's backflow into the right atrium when the right ventricle contracts, forcing blood into the pulmonary artery.

B: blood with the tracer would travel from the right ventricle to the lungs via the pulmonary arteries and return through the pulmonary veins to the left atrium.

D: from the systemic circulation, the tracer first enters the right atrium and then passes through the tricuspid valve as it is pumped into the right ventricle.

15. D is correct.

Semi-lunar valves prevent blood backflow as it leaves the heart via the aorta (systemic circulation to the body) and pulmonary arteries (pulmonary circulation to the lungs).

The ventricles have negative pressure once they start to relax before receiving blood from the atria.

16. B is correct.

The atrioventricular (AV) node is located at the junction between the atria and the ventricles and functions to delay the ventricles' conduction impulse for a fraction of a second.

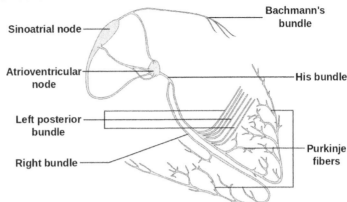

A wave of excitation spreads out from the sinoatrial (SA) node through the atria along specialized conduction channels.

This activates the AV node, which delays conduction impulses by approximately 0.12s.

This delay in the cardiac pulse ensures that the atria have ejected their blood into the ventricles before the ventricles contract.

17. D is correct.

The mitral valve is between the left atrium and the left ventricle and prevents the backflow of blood into the left atrium during the contraction of the left ventricle.

A patient suffering from stenosis of the mitral valve has impeded blood flow from the left atrium into the left ventricle.

Therefore, the effect is an increase in blood volume in the left atrium and a reduced net movement of blood from the left atrium into the left ventricle, which results in increased left atrial pressure and decreased left ventricular pressure.

A: the right atrium receives deoxygenated blood by venous circulation and is too removed for the circulatory process to be affected by mitral valve stenosis.

B: the left ventricle ejects blood into the aorta as it begins systemic circulation.

Since volume/pressure in the left ventricle is reduced due to impeded flow from the left atrium, the patient experiences decreased pressure in the aorta.

18. C is correct.

A hemorrhage is a loss of blood from the circulatory system.

Hemorrhage can be external (i.e., when blood is lost to the outside of the body through a wound or a natural opening) or internal (i.e., when blood escapes from the blood vessels into other structures within the body).

Moderate blood loss results in decreased cardiac output (volume of blood pumped by the heart each minute).

19. C is correct.

The cardiac conduction pathway begins with the SA node in the right atrium.

The conduction signal then travels to the AV node located between the atria and the ventricles before moving down the bundle of His, which then splits into the right/left Purkinje fibers.

The Purkinje fibers spread the conduction signal to the two ventricles, which contract simultaneously to eject blood.

The blood from the right ventricle enters the pulmonary artery. Blood from the left ventricle enters the aorta.

SA node → AV node → bundle of His → Purkinje fibers

20. B is correct.

Blood in the left ventricle returned via the pulmonary vein from the lungs, where it was oxygenated.

The pulmonary vein is the only vein in the adult that carries oxygenated blood.

The superior vena cava returns deoxygenated blood to the heart from the body's upper regions.

A: the right atrium receives blood via the inferior and superior venae cavae returning from systemic circulation.

Blood returning from the body has low O_2 content as it is transported to the lungs.

C: pulmonary artery blood is pumped to the lungs to be oxygenated and is the least oxygenated blood in the circulatory system.

D: lymph vessels, such as the thoracic duct, return lymphatic fluid to the venous circulation.

The lymph fluid has low O_2_partial pressure.

21. C is correct.

The pulmonary artery's blood is pumped to the lungs to be oxygenated and is the least oxygenated blood in the circulatory system.

A: lymph vessels, such as the thoracic duct, return lymphatic fluid to the venous circulation. The lymph fluid has a low O_2 partial pressure.

B: left ventricle blood returned via the pulmonary vein from the lungs, which was oxygenated.

The pulmonary vein is the only vein in the adult that carries oxygenated blood.

D: the inferior vena cava returns deoxygenated blood to the right atrium from the body's lower regions.

22. C is correct.

The afferent arteriole supplies blood to the kidney at the glomerulus.

Protein does not typically enter the kidney in the filtrate (fluid destined to become excreted as urine).

The loss of blood plasma into the kidney increases the protein concentration (relative to plasma).

The presence of proteins in the filtrate is a clinical indication of kidney abnormalities.

D: vasa recta form a series of straight capillaries of the kidney in the medulla and are parallel to the loop of Henle.

These vessels branch from the efferent arterioles of juxtamedullary nephrons (nephrons closest to the medulla), enter the medulla and surround the loop of Henle.

Each vasa recta has a hairpin turn in the medulla and carries blood at a slow rate, crucial for the support of countercurrent exchange that maintains the concentration gradients established in the renal medulla.

The maintenance of this concentration gradient is one of the components responsible for the kidney's ability to produce concentrated urine.

NaCl and urea are reabsorbed into the blood on the *descending* portion of the vasa recta while H_2O is secreted.

NaCl and urea are secreted into the interstitium on the *ascending* portion of the vasa recta while H_2O is reabsorbed.

23. D is correct.

Platelets are small pieces of large megakaryocyte cells.

When a wound occurs, platelets are activated to stick to the wound's edge and release their contents that stimulate the clotting reaction.

Platelets release several growth factors, including platelet-derived growth factor (PDGF), a potent chemotactic agent (direct movement from chemical stimuli), and TGF beta, which stimulates the extracellular matrix deposits.

Both growth factors play a significant role in the repair and regeneration of connective tissues.

A: leukocytes (i.e., white blood cells) are immune system cells defending against infectious disease.

There are five types of leukocytes.

Leukocytes are produced and derived from hematopoietic stem cells in the bone marrow. They survive for about three to four days in the human body and are throughout the body, including the blood and lymphatic system.

The name "white blood cell" derives from a blood sample's physical appearance after centrifugation.

White cells are in the *buffy coat* (a thin, typically white layer of nucleated cells between the sedimented red blood cells and the blood plasma).

Leukocytes have common traits, but each is distinct in form and function.

A significant distinction is the presence or absence of granules (i.e., granulocytes or agranulocytes).

Granulocytes (polymorphonuclear leukocytes) are characterized by the presence of differently staining granules in their cytoplasm.

These granules (lysozymes) are membrane-bound enzymes acting primarily to digest endocytosed particles.

There are three granulocytes: *neutrophils, basophils,* and *eosinophils,* named according to their staining properties.

Agranulocytes (mononuclear leukocytes) are characterized by the absence of granules in their cytoplasm.

The cells include *lymphocytes, monocytes,* and *macrophages.*

B: erythrocytes (i.e., red blood cells) are the most common type of blood cell and the principal means of delivering oxygen (O_2) to the body.

C: lymphocytes are a type of white blood cell in the immune system, a landmark of adaptive immunity.

Lymphocytes are categorized into large or small lymphocytes.

Large granular lymphocytes include natural killer cells (NK cells), while small lymphocytes consist of T cells and B cells.

24. A is correct.

The hepatic portal system directs blood from parts of the gastrointestinal tract to the liver.

The inferior vena cava is a large vein responsible for carrying deoxygenated blood into the heart.

25. B is correct.

The movement of fluids occurs between the capillaries and the tissues.

Blood enters the arterial end of the capillary bed as it passes to the venule end.

In the capillary bed, gases, nutrients, wastes, and fluids exchange with tissue cells in the interstitial space.

Two opposing forces affect the movement of fluids between the capillaries and the interstitial space.

At the arteriole end, hydrostatic pressure (i.e., blood pressure) is higher than the osmotic pressure, which forces fluids out of the capillaries and into the interstitial spaces.

Osmotic pressure is higher than the hydrostatic pressure at the venule end, which forces fluids back into the capillaries and returns the interstitial fluid into the circulatory system.

Starling's hypothesis proposes that not all fluid can be returned to the capillary.

Some fluid travels through the interstitial spaces towards the lymphatic system, where the lymph nodes filter it and then, via the thoracic duct, return to the circulatory system.

26. D is correct.

Hemoglobin exhibits positive cooperative binding (i.e., the sigmoid shape of the O_2 binding curve).

When O_2 binds to the first of four hemoglobin subunits, this initial binding of O_2 changes the shape of Hb and increases the affinity of the three remaining subunits for O_2.

Conversely, as the first O_2 molecule is unloaded, the other O_2 molecules dissociate more easily.

Cooperative binding is necessary for the hemoglobin transport of O_2 to the tissues.

A: hemoglobin reversibly binds carbon dioxide (CO_2) and transports it to the lungs.

In the alveoli of the lungs, CO_2 dissociates from the hemoglobin and is expired (i.e., exhaled) by the body.

B: fetal hemoglobin acquires O_2 from the maternal circulation, so it has a higher O_2 affinity than adult hemoglobin.

C: CO poisoning occurs because this odorless gas has a high hemoglobin affinity and binds tightly to hemoglobin, preventing oxygen from binding to the occupied site of the hemoglobin.

27. A is correct.

Blood volume depends on 1) the amounts of water and sodium ingested and 2) excreted in urine and the gastrointestinal tract, lungs, and skin.

These amounts are highly variable, and it is the function of kidneys to maintain blood volume within a normal range (i.e., homeostasis) by excreting water and sodium into the urine.

When there is an excess of ingested water and sodium, the kidneys respond by excreting more water and sodium in the urine.

28. A is correct.

Blood does not carry cells for injury repair. However, blood is essential for wound healing.

Special blood cells called platelets create clots to stop the bleeding.

Another blood cell called a macrophage acts as a wound protector by fighting infection and assisting in the repair process by producing chemical messengers (i.e., growth factors) helping repair the wound.

Oxygen-rich red blood cells help build new tissue.

Chemical signals prompt the cells to create collagen, which serves as a "scaffolding."

The result is a scar that starts red and dulls eventually.

29. C is correct.

Like O_2, CO binds to hemoglobin but more firmly than O_2, and its binding is almost irreversible.

Carbon monoxide is formed by incomplete combustion of fuels (i.e., hydrocarbons) resulting from natural gas or propane devices (e.g., space heaters, barbecue grills).

A: CO is not irritating, as it is odorless and colorless.

B: CO does not affect the cytochrome chain.

D: CO does not form complexes in blood.

30. A is correct.

Alveoli are thin air sacs and are the sites of gas (e.g., O_2 and CO_2) exchange via passive diffusion in the lungs between the air and blood.

B: pleura is the lungs' outer lining filled with pleural fluid that lubricates the lungs.

C: bronchi are the two main branches of the air intake pathway, with one bronchus for each lung.

D: bronchioles are smaller subdivisions of the bronchi.

31. C is correct.

Cardiac muscle, unlike the other two muscle types, is capable of spontaneous depolarization resulting in contraction.

Smooth and skeletal muscle requires stimulation (e.g., neurotransmitter) to initiate depolarization and contraction.

A: cardiac muscle cells (i.e., cardiomyocytes) are generally single-nucleated but can have up to four centrally located nuclei.

B: cardiac muscle is striated.

D: the autonomic nervous system innervates the cardiac muscle.

The somatic motor system innervates skeletal muscle and controls voluntary actions (e.g., walking, standing).

Notes for active learning

Notes for active learning

Immune System – Explanations

Answer Key

1: D	11: D	21: A
2: C	12: C	22: B
3: C	13: C	23: B
4: B	14: C	24: B
5: B	15: D	
6: B	16: A	
7: D	17: A	
8: B	18: D	
9: D	19: D	
10: B	20: B	

1. D is correct.

Gamma globulins, also known as immunoglobulins (Ig), are Y-shaped protein antibodies.

Gamma globulins are produced by B cells and used by the immune system to identify and neutralize foreign objects, such as bacteria and viruses.

Antibodies are secreted by white blood cells called plasma cells and recognize a unique part of the foreign target (i.e., antigen).

2. C is correct.

Humoral immunity is the antibody-mediated system (as opposed to cell-mediated immunity) because of macromolecules in the extracellular fluids (e.g., secreted antibodies, complement proteins, specific antimicrobial peptides).

Humoral immunity is so named because it involves substances in the humour (i.e., body fluids).

The immune system divides into a more primitive innate immune system and adaptive immune system (i.e., acquired), each of which contains humoral and cellular components (e.g., phagocytes, antigen-specific cytotoxic T-lymphocytes, cytokines).

The terms *antibody* and *immunoglobulin* are used interchangeably.

Immunoglobulins are glycoproteins that function as antibodies.

Antibodies are synthesized and secreted by plasma cells derived from the immune system's B cells.

Immunoglobulins (antibodies) are in the blood, tissue fluids, and many secretions.

Immunoglobulins are large Y-shaped globular proteins.

In mammals, there are five types of antibodies: IgA, IgD, IgE, IgG, and IgM.

Each immunoglobulin class differs in its biological properties and has evolved to target different antigens.

The acquired immune system uses an antibody to identify and neutralize foreign objects like bacteria and viruses.

Each antibody recognizes a specific antigen unique to its target.

By binding, antibodies cause agglutination and precipitation of antibody-antigen products, prime for phagocytosis by macrophages and other cells, block viral receptors, and stimulate other immune responses (i.e., complement pathway).

B: cytotoxic T cells (also known as cytotoxic T lymphocytes, T-killer cells, cytolytic T cells, CD8, or killer T cells) function in cell-mediated immunity.

Cytotoxic T cells are a type of white blood cell that destroy cancer cells, virally infected cells, or damaged cells.

Most cytotoxic T cells express T-cell receptors (TCRs) that recognize specific antigen molecules capable of stimulating an immune response, often produced by viruses or cancer cells.

3. C is correct.

Antibodies are produced in response to antigens (e.g., viral coat proteins, bacterial cell walls) detected by T cells.

T cells stimulate B cells to become plasma cells and secrete antibodies.

B cells mature into memory cells, or antibody-producing cells, during immune responses.

B cells are stimulated to become memory cells, which remain dormant in the interstitial fluid and lymphatics until the same antigens are detected and provide a rapid humoral response.

A: neurons are not involved in the immune response.

B: T cells are the immune response organizers and can become cytotoxic cells (i.e., kill invading cells), helper T cells (i.e., recruit other T and B cells), and suppressor T cells (i.e., inactivate the immune response when the antigen has been cleared).

D: macrophages are phagocytic cells that engulf and digest bacterial cells and foreign material.

4. B is correct.

Phagocytes are cells that function to eliminate foreign invaders (e.g., particles, microorganisms, dying cells) in the body by phagocyting (i.e., digesting) them.

Macrophages and neutrophils play an essential role in the inflammatory response by releasing proteins and other substances that control infection and damage the host tissue.

5. B is correct.

The innate immune system responds to foreign invaders with white blood cells (i.e., granulocytes) and inflammation.

Granulocytes include neutrophils, eosinophils, and basophils because of granules' presence in their cytoplasm.

They are referred to as polymorphonuclear cells (PMNs) due to their distinctive lobed nuclei.

Neutrophil granules contain toxic substances that kill or inhibit the growth of bacteria and fungi.

Like macrophages, neutrophils attack pathogens by activating a respiratory burst of potent oxidizing agents (e.g., hydrogen peroxide, free oxygen radicals, and hypochlorite).

Neutrophils are the most abundant type of phagocyte (i.e., 50 to 60% of the total circulating leukocytes) and are usually the first cells to arrive at the site of an infection.

Innate immunity does not involve humoral immunity (B cell) or cell-mediated immunity (T cell).

6. B is correct.

CD4$^+$ cells (also known as T helper cells) are white blood cells that are an essential part of the human immune system.

They are called helper cells because one of their primary roles is to send signals to other types of immune cells, including CD8 killer cells that destroy the infection or virus.

If CD4$^+$ cells become depleted (for example, in an untreated HIV infection or following immune suppression before a transplant), the body is left vulnerable to a wide range of infections that it would otherwise be able to fight.

CD4$^+$ cells are activators of cell-mediated and humoral responses.

AIDS is a form of *severe combined immunodeficiency* (SCID) since the loss of an adequate CD4$^+$ suppresses humoral and cell-mediated responses.

The immune system can be subdivided into non-specific (innate) and adaptive (i.e., acquired) immunity.

The innate immune system consists of physical barriers (e.g., skin and mucous membranes) and cells that non-specifically remove invaders (e.g., mast cells, macrophages, neutrophils).

The adaptive immune system synthesizes cells directed against specific pathogens and responds rapidly if a similar pathogen is encountered.

The innate system responds with the same mechanisms (and efficiency) to every infection.

7. D is correct.

Antigens are foreign substances (e.g., bacteria, virus) that enter the body and induce an immune response, specifically the production of antibodies to destroy the antigen.

8. B is correct.

The effectiveness of a vaccine depends on the organism's immune system.

Plasma cells (a differentiated form of a B cell) secrete antibodies (i.e., immunoglobulin).

The acquired immune system consists of humoral (i.e., antibodies) and cell-mediated (i.e., T cells) responses.

The humoral response is mediated by B cells synthesized and matured in the bone marrow.

When stimulated by antigens, B cells differentiate into several cells, including memory B cells, and plasma B cells secrete antibodies.

A: cell-mediated immunity involves T cells that originate in the bone marrow (as B cells do) but then migrate to and mature in the thymus.

T-helper cells regulate the activity of other T and B cells.

C: macrophages are non-specific immune cells released by the bone marrow and are involved in phagocytosis but do not synthesize or release immunoglobulin (i.e., antibodies).

D: the thymus is the structure where T cells mature.

T cells start as hematopoietic precursors and migrate from the bone marrow to the thymus.

T cells undergo maturation, which involves ensuring that the cells react against antigens (i.e., *positive selection*) and do not react against antigens on body tissues (i.e., *negative selection*).

Once mature, T cells leave the thymus to perform their vital functions in the immune system.

9. D is correct.

T cells are categorized as helper, cytotoxic (i.e., killer), memory, regulatory (i.e., suppressor), and natural killer T cells.

10. B is correct.

B-lymphocytes (B-cells) are a type of white blood cell that creates antibodies.

B-lymphocytes develop from stem cells in the bone marrow.

11. D is correct.

Tissue repair after an injury is not part of the inflammatory response—the restoration of tissue structure and function via two separate processes: regeneration and replacement.

For regeneration, the cell type destroyed must be replicated.

Replacement is when tissue is replaced with scar tissue.

12. C is correct.

When exposed to a specific antigen, B lymphocytes (B cells) differentiate and divide into memory or plasma cells.

The plasma cells produce antibodies that recognize and bind the specific antigen that activated the precursor B lymphocytes.

A: cytotoxic T cells originate from T cells (T lymphocytes), not B lymphocytes, and bind to and destroy the antigen directly.

B: lymphokines originate from T cells (T lymphocytes), not B lymphocytes, and are secreted by helper T cells that activate other T cells, B cells, and macrophages.

D: macrophages are highly specialized for removing dying/dead cells and cellular debris.

Macrophages do not originate from lymphocytes.

When a monocyte enters damaged tissue through the endothelium of a blood vessel (i.e., leukocyte extravasation), it undergoes a series of changes to become a macrophage.

Monocytes are attracted to a damaged site by chemotaxis (i.e., chemical signals) triggered by stimuli such as damaged cells, pathogens, and cytokines released by macrophages already at the site.

13. C is correct.

Memory B cells are formed after primary infection and differentiate into plasma cells (i.e., B lymphocytes) when exposed to a specific antigen.

A: phagocytosis is an example of nonspecific (innate) immunity.

Phagocytes include monocytes (large white blood cells), macrophages (which stimulate lymphocytes and other immune cells to respond to pathogens), neutrophils (one of the first-responders of inflammatory cells to migrate towards the site of inflammation), mast cells (involved in wound healing and defense against pathogens – prominent in allergy and anaphylaxis) and dendritic cells (antigen-presenting cells that function as a bridge between the innate and adaptive immune systems).

B: stomach acid is an example of innate (i.e., nonspecific) immunity.

D: skin is an example of innate (i.e., nonspecific) immunity.

14. C is correct.

Interferons are signaling proteins developed in response to pathogens (i.e., viruses, bacteria, parasites, tumor cells).

Interferons are named for their ability to interfere with replicating viral RNA and DNA.

15. D is correct.

Within the first few minutes after the injury, platelets (i.e., thrombocytes) aggregate at the injury site to form a fibrin clot that reduces active bleeding.

The speed of wound healing depends on bloodstream levels of platelets, fibrin, and hormones, such as oxytocin.

During the inflammation phase, bacteria and cell debris are removed via phagocytosis by white blood cells.

The proliferation phase is characterized by the release of blood factors into the wound that causes the migration and division of cells, angiogenesis (i.e., new vascular tissue growth), collagen deposition, granulation tissue formation, and wound contraction.

Fibrin is a fibrous protein involved in the clotting of blood. It is formed from fibrinogen by the protease thrombin.

Fibrin form a "mesh" that plugs or clots (in conjunction with platelets) over a wound site.

Fibrin is involved in signal transduction, blood coagulation, and platelet activation.

16. A is correct.

AB blood has neither anti-A nor anti-B antibodies, so there is no agglutination reaction when any type of blood is transfused into an AB recipient.

17. A is correct.

O type blood contains neither A nor B antigens, so there is no agglutination reaction when O type blood is infused into a patient with any other blood type.

18. D is correct.

Plasma cells are white blood cells that secrete antibodies that target and bind to antigens (foreign substances).

19. D is correct.

B cells (also called B lymphocytes) are a type of lymphocyte.

B cells participate in the humoral immunity of the adaptive immune system. B cells mature in the bone marrow.

Activated B cells go through a two-step differentiation process producing short-lived plasmablasts (for immediate immune response) and long-lived plasma cells and memory B cells (for persistent protection).

Plasma cells release into the blood and lymph antibody molecules closely modeled after the precursor B cell receptors.

When released, they bind to the target antigen (i.e., foreign substance) and initiate its destruction.

20. B is correct.

Lymph nodes are linked by lymph vessels and contain phagocytic cells (leukocytes) that filter the lymph, remove and destroy foreign particles/pathogens.

The lymphatic fluid absorbs fat and fat-soluble vitamins.

A: the liver breaks down hemoglobin and uses its components to produce bile salts.

C: amino acids are not absorbed from the digestive tract by the lymphatic system or lymph nodes.

D: glucagon is produced by the pancreas and increases the blood concentration of glucose.

21. A is correct.

The lymphatic system transports excess fluid and proteins from the interstitial space into the circulatory system.

The lymphatic system does not regulate erythropoiesis.

Erythropoiesis is the process of red blood cell production and occurs in the bone marrow. Erythropoiesis is stimulated by decreased oxygen detected by the kidneys, which secrete the hormone erythropoietin.

B: macrophages in lymph nodes engulf bacteria and other foreign particles.

C: the lymphatic system functions to remove proteins from interstitial spaces.

D: the lymphatic system is essential in absorbing nutrients (particularly lipids) from the small intestine via lacteals (i.e., specialized lymph vessels).

22. B is correct.

Antibodies bind to antigens through interactions between the antibody's variable region and the antigen.

The fragment antigen-binding (Fab fragment) is a region on an antibody that binds to antigens.

It is composed of one constant and one variable domain of each heavy and light chain at the monomer's amino-terminal end. The two variable domains bind the epitope on their specific antigens.

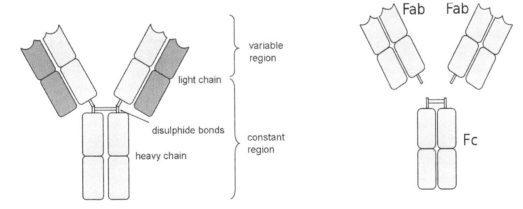

A: antibodies do not assist in the phagocytosis of cells.

D: antibodies are produced by plasma cells derived from stem cells in the bone marrow.

23. B is correct.

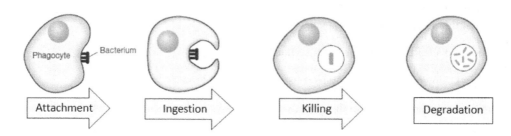

Stages of phagocytosis from attachment to degradation

24. B is correct.

Humans have approximately 500-600 lymph nodes distributed throughout the body, with clusters in the underarms, groin, neck, chest, and abdomen.

Enlargement of the lymph nodes is a common indicator of infection, malignancy, or autoimmune disease.

C: inflammatory responses draw fluid into the affected area.

Notes for active learning

Notes for active learning

Digestive System - Explanations

Answer Key

1: C	11: A	21: C
2: D	12: C	22: B
3: D	13: A	23: A
4: C	14: A	24: D
5: D	15: C	25: D
6: C	16: C	26: A
7: A	17: A	27: B
8: B	18: C	28: B
9: D	19: D	29: A
10: B	20: C	

1. C is correct.

The liver is a multi-function organ and is necessary for proper physiology within humans.

The liver does not synthesize red blood cells in the adult, although it is a source of red blood cells in the developing fetus. In the adult, red blood cells are formed primarily in the red bone marrow.

The liver regulates blood sugar levels by removing glucose from the blood and storing it as glycogen.

Conversely, the liver releases glycogen to increase plasma glucose when levels are low.

A: glycogen is stored in the liver and muscle cells for release when blood glucose levels are low.

B: liver detoxifies many compounds such as alcohol, drugs, and other metabolites.

For example, the liver hydrolyzes pharmaceutical compounds and prepares them for excretion by the kidneys.

D: liver forms urea from the metabolism of excess dietary amino acids.

Deamination removes amino groups combined with CO_2 via reactions forming urea as moderately toxic waste.

2. D is correct.

The epiglottis is the cartilaginous structure diverting food into the esophagus and preventing food from entering the trachea. The epiglottis closes off the respiratory tract (i.e., trachea) and covers the glottis (i.e., opening at the top of the trachea).

A: the tongue is a muscle that manipulates food for mastication but does not close off the trachea.

B: larynx is the voice box and is located below the glottis.

C: glottis is the opening at the top of the trachea (i.e., windpipe), between the vocal cords, and is covered by the epiglottis.

3. D is correct.

The process of digestion is aided by a variety of mechanical and chemical stimuli.

Mechanoreceptors and chemoreceptors embedded in the GI tract's lining respond to stimuli (e.g., stretching of the organ, osmolarity, pH, presence of substrates, end products of digestion) and initiate reflexes.

These reflexes may activate or inhibit glands from secreting substances (e.g., digestive juices, hormones) into the blood or mixing contents and move them along the length of the GI tract.

The walls of the alimentary canal (digestive system; the esophagus, stomach, and intestines) have sensors that help regulate digestion.

4. C is correct.

Chylomicrons are lipoprotein particles that consist of triglycerides (85-92%), phospholipids (6-12%), cholesterol (1-3%) and proteins (1-2%).

Chylomicrons are among the five major groups of lipoproteins (chylomicrons, VLDL, IDL, LDL, and HDL), enabling cholesterol and fats to move through the hydrophilic blood plasma.

They transport dietary lipids from the intestines to the liver, adipose, cardiac, and skeletal muscle tissue, where the activity of lipoprotein lipase unloads their triglyceride components.

The liver takes up chylomicron remnants.

Lipids are hydrophobic and require carrier proteins for transport within the hydrophilic blood plasma.

The chylomicrons are the carrier molecules, but they are too large to pass into the small arterioles.

Therefore, absorbed lipids are initially passed into lacteals (in the small intestine) of the lymphatic system, which then transports lipids into the cardiovascular system's large veins.

5. D is correct.

Lipid production and deposition depend on hormones and genetic predisposition.

The liver is the largest organ (i.e., with glandular functions).

The liver is involved in detoxification (e.g., drugs, alcohol), bile production for emulsification of dietary lipids, and storage of fat-soluble vitamins (A, D, E & K), synthesis of lipids, metabolism of cholesterol, and production of urea.

6. C is correct.

The liver produces bile stored in the gallbladder before its release into the small intestine duodenum.

Bile contains no enzymes but emulsifies fats, breaking down large globules into tiny fat droplets.

A: the large intestine absorbs water and vitamins K, B_1 (i.e., thiamine), B_2 (i.e., riboflavin), and B_{12} (i.e., cobalamin).

B: the small intestine completes chemical digestion and is where individual nutrients (i.e., monomers of proteins, carbohydrates, and lipids) are absorbed.

D: the gallbladder receives bile from the liver and stores it for release into the small intestine.

Bile is released upon stimulation from the hormone cholecystokinin (CCK), which I-cells synthesize in the small intestine's mucosal epithelium.

7. A is correct.

The alimentary canal is the digestive tract through which food enters the body and wastes are expelled.

The alimentary canal has the same structure throughout – a wall consisting of four main layers.

The mucosa is the layer closest to the lumen (tubular space), followed by submucosa, muscularis externa, and serosa. The mucosa's function is absorption and secretion.

The internalized elements are absorbed from the blood vessels of the submucosa.

The muscularis externa is responsible for gut movement and causes food to travel down the gastrointestinal tract.

The outside layer, serosa, secretes a fluid that reduces muscle movement friction.

8. B is correct.

The large intestine functions to absorb water from the remaining indigestible food matter and then passes waste material from the body.

Some salts and minerals are reabsorbed with this water.

Bacteria within the large intestine produce vitamin K.

The large intestine consists of the cecum, appendix, colon, rectum, and anal canal.

The large intestine takes about 16 hours to finish the digestion of food.

The large intestine removes water and remaining absorbable nutrients from food before sending the indigestible matter to the rectum.

The colon absorbs vitamins created by the colonic bacteria, such as vitamin K (especially important, as the daily ingestion of vitamin K is not usually enough to maintain adequate blood coagulation), vitamin B_{12}, thiamine, and riboflavin.

The large intestine secretes K^+ and Cl^-.

Chloride secretion increases in cystic fibrosis.

Recycling nutrients occurs in the colon, such as fermentation of carbohydrates, short-chain fatty acids, and urea cycling.

A: duodenum is the small intestine's anterior section, which connects to the posterior end of the stomach and precedes the jejunum and ileum. It is the shortest part of the small intestine, where most chemical digestion occurs.

The duodenum is mainly responsible for the enzymatic breakdown of food in the small intestine. The duodenum's villi have a leafy-looking appearance and secrete mucus (in the duodenum).

The duodenum regulates the rate of emptying of the stomach via hormonal pathways.

Secretin and cholecystokinin are released from cells in the duodenal epithelium in response to acidic and fatty stimuli present when the pylorus (from the stomach) opens and releases gastric chyme (i.e., food products) into the duodenum for further digestion.

These cause the liver and gallbladder to release bile and the pancreas to release bicarbonate and digestive enzymes such as trypsin, amylase, and lipase into the duodenum.

C: jejunum is the second section of the small intestine, which connects to the duodenum (anterior end) and the ileum (posterior end).

The lining (i.e., enterocytes) of the jejunum specializes in absorbing small nutrient particles, which enzymes have previously digested in the duodenum.

Once absorbed, nutrients (except for fat, which goes to the lymph) pass from the enterocytes into the enterohepatic circulation and enter the liver via the hepatic portal vein, where the blood is processed.

D: ileum mainly absorbs vitamin B_{12} and bile salts, and the products of digestion not absorbed by the jejunum.

The wall itself comprises folds, each of which has many tiny finger-like projections, known as villi, on its surface.

The epithelial cells that line these villi possess even more significant numbers of microvilli.

The lining of the ileum secretes the proteases and carbohydrases responsible for the final stages of protein and carbohydrate digestion.

The mouth does not absorb water but masticates (chews) and moistens food.

It converts a small amount of starch into maltose using the salivary amylase enzyme.

9. D is correct.

The oral cavity begins mechanical (i.e., mastication) and chemical digestion (i.e., salivary amylase and lingual lipase) of food (i.e., bolus).

Mechanical digestion (i.e., mastication) breaks down large particles into smaller particles through the searing action of teeth, thus increasing the total surface area of the ingested food.

Chemical digestion begins in the mouth when the salivary glands secrete saliva that contains salivary amylase, which hydrolyzes starch into simple sugars.

Saliva lubricates the bolus (ingested food) to facilitate swallowing and provides a solvent for food particles.

The muscular tongue manipulates the food during chewing and pushes the bolus into the pharynx.

10. B is correct.

Bile does not contain digestive enzymes.

Bile is an emulsifying agent released by the gallbladder that increases the surface area of dietary fats, allowing more contact with lipase to break down fats into smaller particles.

11. A is correct.

Muscular sphincters subdivide the digestive tract: the esophagus-stomach (lower esophageal sphincter), stomach-duodenum (pyloric sphincter) and ileum-colon (ileocecal sphincter).

B: the small intestine is the only organ with a high concentration of villi.

C: Peyer's patches are organized lymphoid follicles in the submucosa and the mucosa layers of the lowest portion of the small intestine, primarily in the distal jejunum and the ileum, though they can be in the duodenum.

Peyer's patches are essential in the immune system of the intestinal lumen and the generation of the immune response within the mucosa.

D: peristalsis is the process of wave-like contractions that move food along the gastrointestinal (GI) tract. It takes place along the entire length of the digestive system.

12. C is correct.

The low pH of the stomach (~2 to 3) is essential for the function of the protease enzymes (e.g., pepsin) that hydrolyze proteins into their amino acids.

A: peristalsis propels food (i.e., chyme) and indigestible waste (i.e., feces) through the system.

B: amylases, lipases, and bicarbonate are released through the pancreatic duct.

D: glucose and amino acids are absorbed into the blood, while dietary lipids, separated into glycerol and free fatty acids, are absorbed by lacteals (specialized vessels within the villi of the small intestine) that transport the ingested components into the lymphatic system.

13. A is correct.

Hydrochloric (HCl) acid released in the stomach denatures the proteins, unfolding them out of their three-dimensional shapes.

The enzyme pepsin hydrolyzes proteins into fragments of various sizes called peptides.

14. A is correct.

Carbohydrates absorbed into the bloodstream via the small intestine must be hydrolyzed to monosaccharides before absorption.

The digestion of starch (i.e., plant polymer of glucose) begins with salivary alpha-amylase/ptyalin (its activity is minimal compared with pancreatic amylase in the small intestine).

Amylase hydrolyzes starch to alpha-dextrin that is digested to maltose.

The products of digestion of alpha-amylase, along with dietary disaccharides, are hydrolyzed to their corresponding monosaccharides by enzymes (e.g., maltase, isomaltase, sucrase, lactase) present in the brush border of the small intestine.

Maltose is the disaccharide produced when amylase breaks down starch.

15. C is correct.

Gastrin is a digestive hormone responsible for the stimulation of acid secretions in the stomach in response to the presence of peptides and proteins.

16. C is correct.

The gastrointestinal (GI) tract is lined with involuntary smooth muscle controlled by the autonomic nervous system.

The esophagus is the exception; the upper 1/3 consists of voluntary skeletal muscle (e.g., swallowing), the middle 1/3 of a mixture of skeletal and smooth muscle, and the lower 1/3 of smooth muscle.

17. A is correct.

Hepatocytes make up the primary tissue of the liver and are 70-85% of the liver's cytoplasm.

Hepatocytes are involved in protein synthesis, protein storage, modification of carbohydrates, synthesis of cholesterol, bile salts and phospholipids, detoxification, modification, and excretion of substances.

The hepatocyte initiates the formation and secretion of bile.

18. C is correct.

Acinar cells synthesize and secrete pancreatic enzymes.

Pepsinogen and pancreatic proteases (e.g., trypsinogen) are secreted as zymogens (i.e., inactive precursors).

Proteases must be inactive while being secreted because they would digest the pancreas and the GI tract before reaching their target location.

A: protease is a general term for enzymes that digest proteins.

B: salivary amylase digests carbohydrates in the mouth and is secreted in its active form.

D: bicarbonate is not an enzyme but buffers the pH of the gastrointestinal system and blood.

The centroacinar cells of the exocrine pancreas secrete bicarbonate, secretin, and mucin.

19. D is correct.

The small intestine is where enzymatic digestion is completed and where the food monomers (i.e., amino acids, sugars, glycerol, and fatty acids) are absorbed.

The small intestine is highly adapted for absorption because of its large surface area formed by villi (i.e., finger-like projections).

Amino acids and monosaccharides pass through the villi walls and enter into the capillary system.

In contrast, after hydrolysis into glycerol and free fatty acids, dietary lipids are absorbed by lacteals within the villi of the small intestine that connect with the lymphatic system.

A: stomach is a large muscular organ that stores, mixes, and partially digest dietary proteins.

B: gallbladder stores bile before its release in the small intestine.

C: the large intestine functions in the absorption of salts and water.

20. C is correct.

Bicarbonate (HCO_3^-) is not a digestive enzyme but is an important compound that buffers (i.e., resists changes in pH) the blood and fluids of the gastrointestinal tract.

HCO_3^- is released into the duodenum as a weak base that increases the pH of the chyme entering the small intestine.

If the small intestine is too acidic, the small intestine's protein lining (i.e., mucus of the stomach lining is absent in the small intestine) would be digested; pancreatic enzymes would denature and be unable to digest the food in the small intestine.

21. C is correct.

Goblet cells are glandular simple columnar epithelial cells that secrete mucin, which forms mucus when dissolved in water.

Goblet cells use apocrine (i.e., bud secretions) and merocrine (i.e., exocytosis via a duct) methods for secretion.

Goblet cells are scattered among the epithelial lining of organs (i.e., intestinal and respiratory tracts) and inside the trachea, bronchus, and larger bronchioles in the respiratory tract, small intestines, the colon, and conjunctiva in the upper eyelid (i.e., goblet cells supply the mucus tears).

22. B is correct.

The proper digestion of macromolecules is required for adequate absorption of nutrients out of the small intestine.

Carbohydrates must be broken down into monosaccharides like glucose, fructose, and galactose.

Lactose is a disaccharide of glucose and galactose; sucrose is a disaccharide of glucose and fructose; maltose is a disaccharide of two glucose units.

Disaccharide digestion into monomers occurs at the intestinal brush border of the small intestine via enzymes like lactase, sucrase, and maltase.

A: amino acids are the monomers of proteins.

Proteins must be hydrolyzed into mono-peptides, di-peptides, or tripeptides for absorption in the duodenum of the small intestine.

D: lipids are degraded into free fatty acids and glycerol for absorption in the small intestine.

23. A is correct.

The large intestine (i.e., colon) absorbs vitamins created by bacteria, such as vitamin K, vitamin B_{12}, thiamine, and riboflavin.

B: many plants and animals synthesize vitamin C from carbohydrate precursors, including glucose and galactose.

Ascorbic acid is synthesized within tissues of mammals, except primates (including humans) and guinea pigs, who lack an enzyme necessary for the last step of vitamin C biosynthesis.

While some bacteria residing in the gut of people with Chron's disease can gain the ability to produce vitamin C to reduce inflammation, this is not a normal biological process for most healthy individuals.

C: while bacteria in the large intestine do produce gas, this role is not essential.

D: Bilirubin is the yellow breakdown product of normal heme catabolism.

Heme is in hemoglobin as the principal component of red blood cells; bilirubin is excreted in bile and urine, and elevated levels may indicate certain diseases.

It is responsible for the yellow color of bruises, the background straw-yellow color of urine, the brown color of feces, and the yellow discoloration in jaundice (i.e., resulting from liver disease).

24. D is correct.

The cardiac sphincter (also known as the lower esophageal sphincter) regulates the flow of material (i.e., bolus) from the esophagus into the stomach.

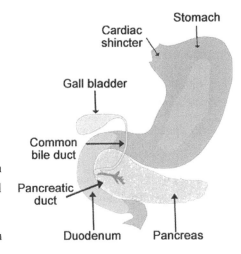

The food substance that was termed bolus in the mouth and esophagus is, upon entry into the stomach, referred to as chyme.

A: gallbladder is a small storage organ for bile (digestive secretion of the liver) before it is released into the duodenum of the small intestine via CCK for the emulsification of dietary fats.

B: pyloric sphincter regulates the flow of chyme from the stomach into the small intestine.

C: epiglottis is the structure that blocks the opening to the trachea (i.e., windpipe) during swallowing.

25. D is correct.

The intrinsic factor is secreted as a glycoprotein produced by the parietal cells of the stomach and is required for the absorption of vitamin B_{12} (cobalamin) in the small intestine.

The stomach secretes two other hormones: gastrin is a peptide hormone that stimulates the secretion of gastric acid (HCl) by the parietal cells of the stomach; pepsin is produced by the chief cells in the stomach to digest dietary proteins.

The stomach absorbs caffeine and ethanol (i.e., alcohol).

B: the pancreas produces several digestive enzymes, including the proteases (e.g., trypsin and chymotrypsin) and fat-digesting enzymes (e.g., pancreatic lipase and pancreatic amylase).

Pancreatic enzymes function within the small intestine and not within the pancreas itself.

26. A is correct.

Bile is an emulsifying agent that increases the surface area of dietary lipids (i.e., fats), allowing an increase in contact with lipase (i.e., enzyme) to dissociate fats into smaller particles.

Bile is not an enzyme and does not catalyze a chemical change of fats.

The lipids are separated into smaller micelles after interaction with bile.

Bile is made up of bile salts that are cholesterol derivatives and pigments from the breakdown of hemoglobin.

B: proteins are large polymers of amino acids linked by peptide bonds.

C: enzymes catalyze chemical reactions by lowering the energy of activation.

D: hormones are chemical messengers released into the blood that signal target cells.

27. B is correct.

Most chemical (i.e., enzymatic) digestion occurs in the small intestine.

Most digestion of starch/ disaccharide, lipid (fat) digestion, most protein digestion, and absorption of monomers occurs within the small intestine.

Before the small intestine, some starch is digested in the mouth by salivary amylase into the disaccharide maltose.

There is within the stomach a small amount of protein digestion, in which the stomach enzyme pepsin splits proteins into smaller chains of amino acids (i.e., peptides).

However, the digestion occurring before the small intestine is incomplete, and most of the digestive process occurs within the small intestine.

A: liver is not part of the alimentary (i.e., gastrointestinal) canal, and food does not pass through the liver.

The liver does produce bile (i.e., an emulsifying agent), which increases the surface area of fats and mixes them within the watery enzyme environment of the small intestine.

28. B is correct.

The liver is the largest and most metabolically complex organ in the body.

The liver performs detoxification by hydrolyzing and then excreting harmful materials (e.g., alcohol, toxins) or decomposing materials destined for excretion (e.g., hemoglobin) from the blood.

29. A is correct.

Carbohydrates (e.g., glucose, fructose, lactose, maltose) and proteins provide 4 calories per gram (i.e.,4 kcal/gram).

Fats (lipids) are energy-dense and provide 9 calories per gram.

Notes for active learning

Notes for active learning

Nervous System – Explanations

Answer Key

1: C	11: C	21: D
2: D	12: D	22: C
3: B	13: D	23: B
4: A	14: C	24: A
5: D	15: B	25: D
6: A	16: B	26: C
7: A	17: D	27: D
8: D	18: D	28: C
9: B	19: D	29: B
10: C	20: A	30: C

1. C is correct.

The parasympathetic nervous system maintains homeostasis (*rest and digest*), increasing gut motility, modulates heart rate, constricts the bronchi and the pupils.

The sympathetic nervous system prepares the body for action (*fight or flight*), decreasing digestive tract activity, increases heart rate, dilates the pupils, and relaxes the bronchi.

2. D is correct.

The autonomic nervous system (ANS) consists of motor neurons that: innervate smooth and cardiac muscle and glands, adjust to ensure optimal support for body activities, operate via subconscious control (involuntary nervous system or general visceral motor system), and have viscera as most of their effectors.

The effectors of the ANS are cardiac muscle, smooth muscle, and glands. The ANS uses a 2-neuron chain to its effectors.

The cell body of the first neuron (i.e., preganglionic neuron) resides in the brain or spinal cord.

The axon of the first neuron (i.e., preganglionic axon) synapses with the second motor neuron (i.e., ganglionic neuron) in an autonomic ganglion outside of the central nervous system.

The axon of the ganglionic neuron (i.e., postsynaptic axon) extends to the effector organ.

3. B is correct.

The frequency of action potentials is directly related to the intensity of the stimulus.

The strength of the stimulus is coded into the frequency of the action potentials generated.

The stronger the stimulus, the higher the frequency at which action potentials are generated.

Thus, the nervous system is frequency-modulated and not amplitude-modulated.

4. A is correct.

Unlike other body cells, neurons do not undergo mitosis (the splitting of cells) because they lack centrioles, essential in cell division.

This makes diseases affecting the brain and the nervous system particularly crippling.

However, some new neurons can be generated in adults from neural stem cells preserved in the subventricular zone during development.

Neural stem cells are presumed to play a role in adult brain plasticity.

5. D is correct.

The autonomic nervous system (ANS) is composed of sympathetic and parasympathetic divisions.

Both divisions rely on a two-neuron motor pathway away from the spinal cord and a two-neuron sensory pathway toward the spinal cord.

The ANS is unique as it requires a sequential two-neuron efferent pathway; the preganglionic (first) neuron must first synapse onto a postganglionic (second) neuron before innervating the target organ.

The preganglionic neuron begins at the *outflow* and synapses at the postganglionic neuron's cell body.

The postganglionic neuron then synapses at the target organ.

The sympathetic nervous system has a short preganglionic neuron and a long postganglionic neuron.

6. A is correct.

The cerebellum, along with the pons and medulla oblongata, is in the hindbrain.

Higher brain sensory neurons and motor neurons pass through the hindbrain.

The primary function of the cerebellum is coordinating unconscious movement.

Hand-eye coordination, posture, and balance are controlled by the cerebellum.

Therefore, damage to the cerebellum would most likely result in loss of muscle coordination.

The cerebrum is divided into left and right hemispheres that are further subdivided into four lobes.

The cerebrum is responsible for coordinating most voluntary activities, sensations, and *higher functions* (including speech and cognition).

The spinal cord controls the extremities.

7. A is correct.

The somatic nervous system controls skeletal muscles and consists of sensory and motor nerves.

8. D is correct.

The cerebral cortex is the outer layer of the brain, made up of gray matter.

White matter is a different type of nerve fiber in the brain's inner layer.

9. B is correct.

The cerebellum is part of the hindbrain (i.e., posterior part of brain), consisting of the pons and medulla oblongata.

The cerebellum receives sensory information from the visual and auditory systems and information about the orientation of joints and muscles.

The cerebellum's primary function is hand-eye coordination.

It receives information about the motor signals being initiated by the cerebrum and integrates the inputs to produce balance and unconscious coordinated movement.

Damage to the cerebellum could damage one of these functions, while destruction seriously impairs coordinated movement.

A: thermoregulation is a function of the hypothalamus (a part of the cerebrum).

C: the sense of smell (i.e., olfaction) is a function of the cerebrum.

D: urine formation is the primary function of the kidneys, along with some hormonal regulation.

10. C is correct.

The nervous system is divided into the peripheral nervous system and the central nervous system.

The peripheral nervous system (PNS) is divided into the autonomic nervous system (ANS) and the somatic nervous system (SNS).

The autonomic nervous system regulates the internal environment by way of involuntary nervous pathways.

The ANS innervates smooth muscle in blood vessels and the digestive tract and innervates the heart, the respiratory system, the endocrine system, the excretory system, and the reproductive system.

The autonomic nervous system is divided into sympathetic, parasympathetic, and enteric nervous systems.

The functions of ANS can be divided into sensory and motor subsystems.

The sensory subsystem consists of those receptors and neurons that transmit signals to the central nervous system.

The motor subsystem transmits signals from the central nervous system to effectors.

The sympathetic division innervates those pathways that prepare the body for immediate action, known as the "fight-or-flight" response.

Heart rate and blood pressure increase, blood vessels in the skin constrict, and those in the heart dilate (i.e., vasoconstriction and vasodilation).

Pathways innervating the digestive tract are inhibited, and epinephrine (i.e., adrenaline) is secreted by the adrenal medulla, increasing the conversion of glycogen into glucose and therefore increasing blood glucose concentration.

A: the central nervous system (CNS) consists of the brain and the spinal cord.

B: the somatic system innervates skeletal muscle, and its nervous pathways are typically under voluntary control.

D: the parasympathetic system innervates nervous pathways that return the body to homeostatic conditions following exertion.

Heart rate, blood pressure, and blood glucose concentration decrease from parasympathetic exertion.

The blood vessels in the skin dilate, and those in the heart constrict, and the digestive process is no longer inhibited.

11. C is correct.

The brain stem is the posterior part of the brain that joins with the spinal cord. It consists of three parts: the pons, medulla, and midbrain.

The midbrain regulates vision, hearing, motor control, alertness, and temperature regulation.

The pons contains neural pathways that carry signals from and to the brain.

The medulla is associated with breathing, heart rate, and blood pressure functions.

12. D is correct.

Cerebrospinal fluid is a clear fluid in the brain and spinal cord.

The cerebrospinal fluid acts as a buffer for the brain and provides mechanical and immunological protection.

Red blood cells are usually not present in the cerebrospinal fluid.

13. D is correct.

The dorsal root ganglia of the spinal cord contain cell bodies of sensory neurons known as first-order neurons, which bring information from the periphery to the spinal cord.

14. C is correct.

The prefrontal cortex lies at the front of the brain and is responsible for cognitive behavior, personality, decision making, and social behavior.

The limbic association area helps form memories and guides emotional responses.

The primary somatosensory cortex processes sensations such as touch, pain, and temperature.

The posterior association area is where visual, auditory, and somatosensory association areas meet, giving the body spatial awareness.

15. B is correct.

The sympathetic nervous system is involved in the *fight or flight* response.

Stimulation of the sympathetic branch of the autonomic nervous system increases in the amount of adrenaline secretion and is characterized by dilation of the pupils, an increase in heart rate, an increase in respiratory rate, dilation of the bronchi, increased blood flow to the skeletal muscles, and less blood flow to the digestive organs.

The parasympathetic nervous system produces *rest and digest* responses that are consistent with the other choices.

16. B is correct.

Dendrites are an extension of a nerve cell that receives electrochemical impulses from other cells and carry them inwards toward the cell body.

Axons are nerve fibers distinguished from dendrites in that they usually transmit signals rather than receive them. The axon terminus is the inflated portion of the axon that releases neurotransmitters.

T-tubules are extensions of the cell membrane that pass through muscle cells.

Nodes of Ranvier are gaps in the myelin sheath around an axon or nerve fiber.

17. D is correct.

The myelin sheath covers the axon and increases conduction velocity.

Saltatory conduction occurs by permitting membrane depolarization only at nodes of Ranvier.

The myelin sheath is composed of lipids and is deposited by Schwann cells for peripheral nerve cells and oligodendrocytes for central nerve cells.

18. D is correct.

The synaptic cleft (i.e., synapse) is a small space between the axon terminus (end of axon) and the abutting dendrite between two neurons.

After stimulation, the presynaptic axon releases a neurotransmitter across this cleft, diffuses, and binds receptors on the postsynaptic dendrite of the next neuron.

The propagation of signals is unidirectional; the neurotransmitter is released by the presynaptic axon and received by the postsynaptic dendrite.

A: the dendrite is where input is received and is (often) near the cell body.

B: the axon process of the neuron projects away from the cell body and extends towards the axon terminus (where neurotransmitters are released).

C: myelin sheath covers the axon and increases conduction velocity (i.e., permits saltatory conduction) by preventing (via insulation) the passage of ions during depolarization except at the nodes of Ranvier). The myelin sheath, composed of lipids, is deposited by Schwann cells for peripheral nerve cells and oligodendrocytes for central nerve cells.

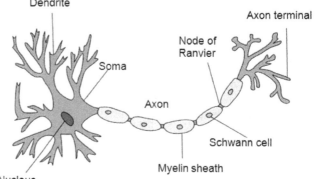

19. D is correct.

The myelin sheath is not produced by the neuron but is synthesized by Schwann cells for peripheral nerve cells and oligodendrocytes for central nerve cells.

Schwann cells and oligodendrocytes wrap around axons to create layers of insulating myelin (composed of lipids), preventing the passage of ions along the axon process and increases the rate of depolarization along the axon.

A: axon hillock is a region in the cell body (i.e., soma) where membrane potentials propagated from synaptic inputs (temporal and spatial summation) are aggregated before being transmitted to the axon.

In its resting state, a neuron is polarized, with its inside at about –70 mV relative to the outside.

The axon hillock "sums" the individual depolarization events to determine if a sufficient magnitude of depolarization has been achieved.

Once the depolarization threshold is reached (between –50 and –40 mV), the *all or none* action potential is propagated along the axon.

C: nodes of Ranvier are openings along the axons that permit depolarization of the membrane for saltatory conduction to increase the rate of transmission along the nerve fiber.

20. A is correct.

The axon hillock is a specialized part of the cell body (or soma) of a neuron that connects to the axon and where membrane potentials propagated from synaptic inputs are summated before being transmitted to the axon.

The axon hillock is like the *accounting center*, where the graded potential is summed (either spatial or temporal summation) to be enough to reach the threshold.

Inhibitory postsynaptic potentials (IPSPs) and excitatory postsynaptic potentials (EPSPs) are summed in the axon hillock.

Once a triggering threshold is exceeded, an action potential propagates – all or none – through the rest of the axon.

21. D is correct.

Myelin is an insulator, preventing ions from passing through the axon membrane and allowing axons to conduct impulses faster.

Ions can only permeate through nodes of Ranvier that are small gaps in the myelin sheath.

The action potential *skips* (i.e., saltatory conduction) from node to node are much faster than conduction through a non-myelinated neuron.

The area requiring depolarization to permit Na^+ in / K^+ out is smaller.

A: action potentials are initiated by graded stimuli that cause depolarization of the axon hillock.

B: the Na+/K+ pump achieves the pumping of Na+ out of the cell.

C: the Na+/K+ pump achieves resting potential.

22. C is correct.

Nodes of Ranvier are unmyelinated regions along the axon process between Schwann cells, which deposit myelin.

The myelin sheath is a lipid that functions to increase the propagation speed for the action potential to travel from the cell body to the axon terminal.

Electrical impulses move by depolarization of the plasma membrane at the unmyelinated (nodes of Ranvier) and "jump" from one node to the next (i.e., *saltatory conduction*).

A: acetylcholine receptors are located on the dendrite of a postsynaptic neuron.

23. B is correct.

Myopia (i.e., nearsightedness) is a condition of the eye where light does not focus directly on the retina but focuses in front.

The image of a distant object is out of focus, while the image of a closer object is in focus.

This condition is generally due to the shape of the eye being too long.

24. A is correct.

The fovea is in the center of the macula region of the retina. The fovea is responsible for the sharp central vision necessary for reading, driving, and visual detail.

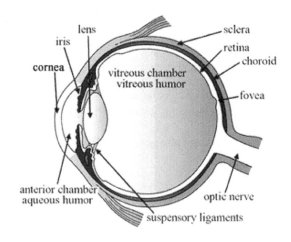

Cone cells are one of two types of photoreceptor cells in the retina and responsible for color vision and sensitivity.

Cone cells function best in relatively bright light.

Rod cells function better in dim light.

Cone cells are densely packed in the fovea (0.3 mm in diameter, rod-free area) but quickly reduce in number towards the periphery of the retina.

The six to seven million cones in a human eye are concentrated towards the macula.

C: rod cells are photoreceptor cells in the retina of the eye that function in less intense light than cone cells.

Rods are concentrated at the outer edges of the retina and are used in peripheral vision.

There are approximately 125 million rod cells in the human retina. Rod cells are more sensitive than cone cells and are almost entirely responsible for night vision.

25. D is correct.

The eye takes approximately 20–30 minutes to fully adapt from bright sunlight to complete darkness, becoming ten thousand to one million times more sensitive than in full daylight.

In this process, the eye's perception of color changes as well.

However, it takes approximately five minutes for the eye to adapt to bright sunlight from the darkness.

This is due to cones obtaining more sensitivity during the first five minutes when entering the light, but the rods take over after five or more minutes.

Rhodopsin is a pigment in the photoreceptors of the retina that immediately photobleaches in response to light.

Rods are more sensitive to light and take longer to adapt to the change in light. Rods' photopigments regenerate more slowly and need about 30 min to reach their maximum sensitivity.

However, their sensitivity improves considerably within 5–10 minutes in the dark.

Cones take approximately 9–10 minutes to adapt to the dark.

Sensitivity to light is modulated by changes in intracellular calcium ions and cyclic guanosine monophosphate.

26. C is correct.

Parasympathetic stimulation elicits *rest and digest* responses (i.e., not stress or immediate survival).

The parasympathetic nervous system stimulates the production of saliva, containing enzymes that help digest food.

A: piloerection is mediated by small arrector pili muscles at the base of each hair; contracting and pulling the hair erect.

This reflex originates from the sympathetic nervous system responsible for most fight-or-flight responses.

B: contraction of abdominal muscles during exercise is the result of somatic nervous system stimulation.

D: increased rate of heart contractions is a sympathetic response.

27. D is correct.

The cornea is the transparent front part of the eye covering the iris, pupil, and anterior chamber.

The cornea, with the anterior chamber and lens, refracts light, with the cornea accounting for approximately two-thirds of the eye's total optical power (43 diopters).

While the cornea contributes most of the eye's focusing power, its focus is fixed.

The curvature of the lens, by comparison, can be adjusted to "tune" the focus depending upon the object's distance

The lens is a transparent, biconvex eye structure that (along with the cornea) helps refract light focused on the retina.

In humans, the refractive power of the lens is about 18 diopters (1/3 of the total refractive power).

The lens, by changing shape, functions to adjust the focal distance of the eye to focus on objects at various distances.

This allows a sharp real image of the object to be formed on the retina.

This adjustment of the lens is known as accommodation.

The lens is flatter on its anterior side than on its posterior side.

A diopter is a unit of measurement of the optical power of a lens or curved mirror.

It is equal to the reciprocal of the focal length measured in meters (i.e., 1/meters) and, therefore, a unit of reciprocal length. For example, a 3-dioptre lens brings parallel rays of light to focus at 0.33 meters.

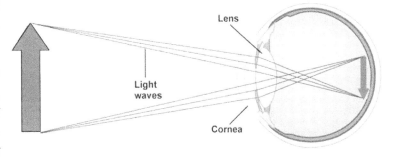

28. C is correct.

A photoreceptor cell is a specialized type of neuron in the retina capable of phototransduction (i.e., light is converted into electrical signals).

Photoreceptors convert light (visible electromagnetic radiation) into signals that can stimulate biological processes by triggering a change in the cell's membrane potential.

Activation of rods and cones involves hyperpolarization.

Rods and cones, when not stimulated, depolarize and release glutamate (neurotransmitter).

In the dark, cells have a relatively high concentration of cGMP (cyclic guanosine monophosphate), which opens ion channels (Na^+ and Ca^{2+}).

The positively charged ions that enter the cell change the cell's membrane potential cause depolarization and leads to glutamate release.

Glutamate depolarizes some neurons and hyperpolarizes others.

29. B is correct.

Otitis is a general term for inflammation or infection of the ear.

A: glaucoma is an increase of pressure in the aqueous humor from blockage of aqueous humor outflow.

C: myopia (nearsightedness) causes the image to form in front of the retina.

D: hyperopia (i.e., hypermetropia or farsightedness) causes the image to form behind the retina.

30. C is correct.

The organ of Corti and the semicircular canals contain hair cells with microcilia (i.e., small hair) projecting from the apical surface of the cell into the surrounding fluid.

Movement of the fluid around the hair cells in the organ of Corti detects sound.

Movement of the fluid around the hair cells in the semicircular canals detects changes in body orientation.

I: hair on the skin is different and is not formed by "hair cells" but by dead epithelial cells.

Notes for active learning

With each topic, reinforce learning by reading review chapters in your *ATI TEAS Science Review* book.

Visit our Amazon store

Notes for active learning

Skeletal System – Explanations

Answer Key

1: C	11: C	21: A
2: C	12: A	22: C
3: B	13: D	23: B
4: D	14: C	24: D
5: D	15: B	25: B
6: A	16: B	26: C
7: A	17: D	27: D
8: A	18: C	
9: A	19: A	
10: B	20: B	

1. C is correct.

The vertebral column consists of 31 bones known as vertebrae.

The curves in the spine help it withstand stress by providing an even distribution of body weight and provide the flexibility of movement.

2. C is correct.

Synovial fluid lubricates and decreases friction between the ends of bones as they move relative to each other.

A: bone cells (i.e., osteocytes) receive blood circulation for adequate nutrition and hydration, but the synovial fluid is not involved in these functions.

3. B is correct.

The lumbar region is in the lower back and bears most of the weight of the body.

The cervical region supports the head.

The thoracic region supports the ribs.

The remaining two regions are the sacral and coccyx, which connect the spine to the hip bones and muscles of the pelvic floor.

4. D is correct.

Osteocytes are derived from osteoprogenitors, some of which differentiate into active osteoblasts that do not divide and have an average half-life of 25 years.

In mature bone, osteocytes reside in lacunae spaces, while their processes reside inside canaliculi spaces.

When osteoblasts become trapped in the matrix that they secrete, they become osteocytes.

Osteocytes are networked via long cytoplasmic extensions occupying tiny canals (i.e., canaliculi) and exchanging nutrients and waste through gap junctions.

Osteocytes occupy the lacuna space.

Although osteocytes have reduced synthetic activity and (like osteoblasts) are not capable of mitotic division, they are actively involved in the dynamic turnover of the bone matrix.

5. D is correct.

There are five types of bones: long, short, flat, irregular, and sesamoid.

Short bones are those bones that are as wide as they are long.

Their primary function of short bones is to provide support and stability with little to no movement (e.g., tarsals in the foot and carpals in the hands).

Cancellous bone (i.e., trabecular or spongy bone) is one of two types of bone tissue.

The other type of bone tissue is cortical bone (i.e., compact bone).

6. A is correct.

The axial skeleton's primary purpose is to support and protect the brain, spinal cord, and internal organs. It consists of the skull, neck bones, vertebral column, and rib cage.

The appendicular skeleton is the part of the skeleton consisting of bones that support limbs.

7. A is correct.

The skeletal system serves the following functions: production of blood cells, storage of minerals, protection of the viscera (internal organs), and toxin removal.

The skeletal system is vital in regulating energy metabolism in the body through the endocrine system.

Vitamin C is an essential nutrient obtained from citrus fruits, leafy greens, and other food sources, and its deficiency leads to scurvy.

8. A is correct.

Compact bone is a dense material used to create the hard outer shell of most bones in the body. Compact bone is the main structure in the body for support, protection, and movement.

Spongy bone is lighter and used for more active functions, filling the inner layer of most bones.

Trabecular bone is another term for spongy bone.

A long bone is a classification of bone by its shape (e.g., femur), as is irregular bone (e.g., vertebra).

9. A is correct.

A deficiency of growth hormone during bone formation can cause decreased epiphyseal plate activity.

The epiphyseal plate is the area of the long bone where new bone growth takes place.

10. B is correct.

Ligaments attach bone to bone.

A: an osteocyte is the most common cell in mature bone and is derived from osteoprogenitors, some of which differentiate into active osteoblasts.

In mature bone, osteocytes and their processes reside inside spaces called lacunae and canaliculi, respectively.

Osteocytes contain a nucleus and a thin ring piece of cytoplasm.

When an osteoblast becomes trapped in the matrix that it secretes, it becomes an osteocyte.

D: periosteum is the membrane covering the surface of bones.

11. C is correct.

Osteon is the functional unit of much compact bone.

Osteons are roughly cylindrical structures that are typically several millimeters long and around 0.2mm in diameter.

Each osteon consists of concentric layers (or *lamellae*) of compact bone tissue surrounding a central canal (the Haversian canal), containing the bone's nerve and blood supplies.

The boundary of an osteon is the cement line.

A: periosteum membrane covers the outer surface of bones, except at the joints of long bones.

B: endosteum lines the inner surface of bones.

D: trabeculae are tissue elements in the form of a small strut or rod (e.g., head of the femur), generally having a mechanical function, and usually composed of dense collagenous tissue (e.g., trabecula of the spleen.)

Trabecula can be composed of other materials.

For example, in the heart, trabeculae consist of muscles that form the trabeculae carneae (meaty ridges) of the ventricles.

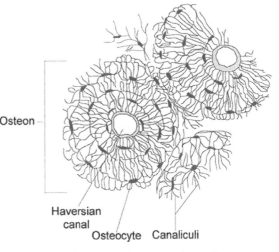

Diagram of compact bone from a transverse section of a long bone's cortex

12. A is correct.

Yellow bone marrow is usually in the medullary cavity of long bones.

Red blood cells, platelets, and most white blood cells arise in red marrow.

Both red and yellow bone marrow contain numerous blood vessels and capillaries.

At birth, bone marrow is red. More is converted to yellow marrow; around half of adult bone marrow is red.

Red marrow is mainly in the flat bones, such as the pelvis, scapulae, sternum, cranium, ribs, vertebrae, and spongy material epiphyseal ends of long bones, such as the femur and humerus.

C: Haversian canals are a series of tubes around narrow channels formed by lamellae, the region of bone called compact bone.

Osteons are arranged in parallel to the long axis of the bone.

The Haversian canals surround blood vessels and nerve cells throughout the bone.

The Haversian canals communicate with osteocytes in lacunae (i.e., spaces within the dense bone matrix that contain the living bone cells) through canaliculi (i.e., canals between the lacunae of ossified bone).

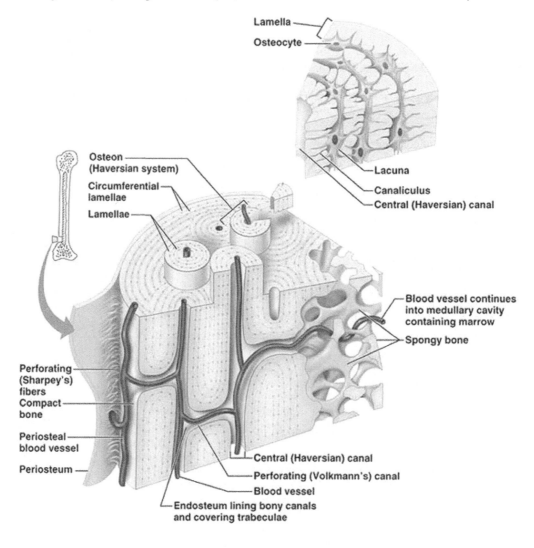

D: Volkmann's canals are microscopic structures in compact bone.

Volkmann's canals run within the osteons perpendicular to the Haversian canals, interconnecting the latter and the periosteum (i.e., a membrane that covers bones).

Volkmann's canals usually run at obtuse angles to the Haversian canals and contain connecting vessels between Haversian capillaries. They carry small arteries throughout the bone.

13. D is correct.

Endochondral ossification, with cartilage, is one of the two essential processes during fetal development of the mammalian skeletal system by which bone tissue is created.

Endochondral ossification is an essential process during the rudimentary formation of long bones, the growth of the length of long bones, and the natural healing of bone fractures.

Appositional growth occurs when the cartilage model grows in thickness due to the addition of more extracellular matrix on the peripheral cartilage surface, accompanied by new chondroblasts that develop from the perichondrium.

B: intramembranous ossification is another essential of rudimentary bone tissue creation during fetal development.

Intramembranous ossification is an essential process during the natural healing of bone fractures and the rudimentary formation of bones of the head.

Unlike endochondral ossification, cartilage is not present during intramembranous ossification.

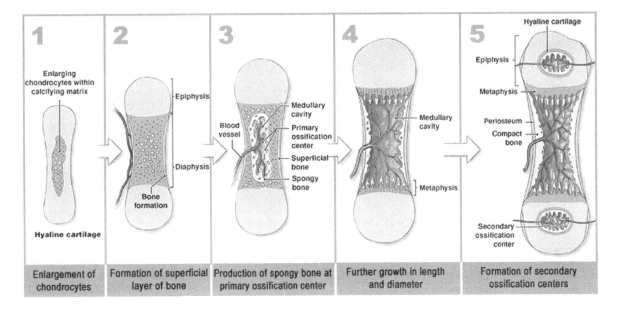

14. C is correct.

Ligaments are the fibrous connective tissue that joins bone to bone.

A: synovium is the smooth lining of synovial joints that produces synovial fluid.

B: osteoprogenitor cells become osteo*blasts* (not osteo*clasts*).

D: sockets are types of joints, such as the ball and socket joint of the hip.

15. B is correct.

The epiphyseal plate is the area of growth in long bones.

When bones increase in diameter, this is referred to as appositional growth.

16. B is correct.

Osseous tissue, or bone tissue, is the primary structural and supportive connective tissue that forms the rigid part of the bones of the skeletal system.

17. D is correct.

The diaphysis is the main shaft of a long bone made of cortical bone and usually contains bone marrow and adipose tissue.

The diaphysis is a middle tubular part composed of compact bone surrounding a central marrow cavity containing red or yellow marrow.

Primary ossification occurs in the diaphysis.

18. C is correct.

Spongy bone (i.e., cancellous bone) is typically at the ends of long bones, proximal to joints, and within the interior of vertebrae.

Cancellous bone is highly vascular and frequently contains red bone marrow where hematopoiesis (i.e., production of blood cells) occurs.

Spongy bone contains blood stem cells for differentiation into mature blood cells.

A: long bones are involved in fat storage.

D: erythrocyte cell storage occurs in the liver and spleen.

19. A is correct.

Trabeculae are thin rods and plates of bone tissue at the ends of long bones.

Despite being porous, the structure provides the strength that allows significant mechanical stresses on the bones.

Osteons are the functional unit of compact bone rather than spongy bone.

Each osteon consists of concentric layers called lamellae.

Haversian canals are microscopic tubes in a bone that allow blood vessels and nerves to travel through them.

20. B is correct.

The epiphyseal plate is a hyaline cartilage plate in the metaphysis at each end of a long bone. The plate is present in children and adolescents. In adults, it is replaced by an epiphyseal line.

21. A is correct.

Hyaline cartilage is a type of cartilage (i.e., flexible connective tissue) found on many joint surfaces.

Hyaline cartilage is pearly bluish with firm consistency, has a considerable amount of collagen, and contains no nerves or blood vessels.

C: areolar connective tissue (or *loose connective tissue*) is a common connective tissue beneath the dermis layer and underneath the epithelial tissue of the body systems with external openings.

Areolar connective tissue holds organs in place and attaches epithelial tissue to other underlying tissues.

Areolar connective tissue serves as a reservoir of H_2O and salts for surrounding tissues.

D: fibrocartilage is a mixture of white fibrous tissue (i.e., toughness) and cartilaginous tissue (i.e., elasticity) in various proportions.

Fibrocartilage is in the pubic symphysis, the annulus fibrosus of intervertebral discs, menisci, and the TMJ (temporomandibular joint of the jaw).

22. C is correct.

Osteoblasts secrete the matrix necessary for bone formation and are formed from osteoprogenitor cells.

Osteoclasts are large cells that dissolve bone.

Osteocytes come from osteoblasts and are cells inside the bone.

Endothelial cells line the interior of blood and lymphatic vessels.

23. B is correct.

Hyaluronic acid is an anionic, non-sulfated glycosaminoglycan distributed widely throughout epithelial, connective, and neural tissues.

24. D is correct.

A tendon connects bone to muscle, while a ligament connects bone to bone.

C: aponeuroses are layers of flat broad tendons.

25. B is correct.

Bones store calcium and phosphate, support and protect the body, produce blood cells and store fat within the yellow bone marrow.

Bones do not regulate the temperature of the blood.

26. C is correct.

A tendon sheath is a layer of membrane around a tendon that permits the tendon to move.

27. D is correct.

Hydroxyapatite composes up to 50% of bone by weight and consists of calcium and phosphate.

Carbonated calcium-deficient hydroxyapatite is the main mineral that dental enamel and dentin are composed of.

Notes for active learning

Notes for active learning

Muscular System – Explanations

Answer Key

1: A	11: A	21: A
2: A	12: A	22: A
3: D	13: C	23: C
4: C	14: D	24: A
5: A	15: C	25: D
6: C	16: B	26: D
7: C	17: D	27: A
8: B	18: B	
9: C	19: C	
10: C	20: B	

1. A is correct.

Cardiac muscle has cross striations formed by alternating segments of myosin thick and actin thin protein filaments.

Like skeletal muscle, the primary structural proteins of cardiac muscle are actin and myosin.

However, in contrast to skeletal and smooth muscle, cardiac muscle cells are often branched rather than linear and longitudinal.

B: histologically, T-tubules in cardiac muscle, compared to skeletal muscle, are larger and broader and run along the Z-discs; there are fewer T-tubules in cardiac muscle than in skeletal muscle.

2. A is correct.

Neither the actin thin filament nor the myosin thick filament change in length during muscle contraction.

Muscle contraction occurs via the *sliding filament model* by increasing the overlap of actin and myosin filaments.

3. D is correct.

Slow-twitch fibers produce 10 to 30 contractions per second, while fast-twitch fibers produce 30 to 70 contractions per second.

4. C is correct.

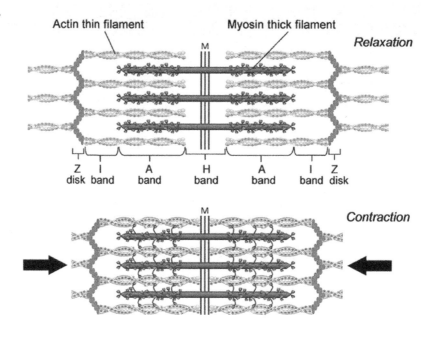

Sliding filament model of skeletal muscle

5. A is correct.

Shivering is a protective mechanism of increases in muscle contractions, which raises core body temperature.

6. C is correct.

Muscle cells share the following properties: extensibility (ability to be stretched), contractility (ability to shorten forcefully), excitability (ability to respond to a stimulus), and elasticity (ability to contract to the original length after being stretched).

Communication is not a property of muscle tissue.

7. C is correct.

Involuntary muscles contract without conscious control.

I: cardiac muscle is another type of involuntary muscle found only in the heart.

II: smooth muscle is in the walls of organs such as the intestines and stomach.

III: skeletal muscle is made up of voluntary muscles attached to the skeleton.

8. B is correct.

Myoglobin is a small protein that carries and stores oxygen in muscle cells. Myoglobin traps oxygen, allowing the cells to produce the energy required for muscular contraction.

9. C is correct.

The ventricles of the heart require long contraction periods to pump the viscous blood.

B: gap junctions permit rapid communication that results in adjacent cardiac muscle cells contracting simultaneously.

D: Na^+ is outside the resting neuron and flows into the cell during the action potential.

K^+ is inside the resting neuron and flows out of the cell during the action potential.

10. C is correct.

Intercalated discs are microscopic identifying features of cardiac muscle.

Cardiac muscle consists of individual heart muscle cells (or *cardiomyocytes*) connected by intercalated discs working as a single functional organ (or *syncytium*).

Intercalated discs support synchronized contraction of cardiac tissue and occur at the Z line of the sarcomere.

11. A is correct.

Muscles move by contracting, which brings the origin and insertion closer.

This contraction often moves the insertion while the origin remains fixed in position.

12. A is correct.

Peristalsis is a contractile process of smooth muscle that propels a ball of food through the intestines. It takes place along the entire length of the digestive system.

13. C is correct.

Myofilaments are microscopic, thread-like structures in myofibrils, which help give muscle its striped appearance.

Muscles contract by sliding the thick and thin myofilaments along each other.

14. D is correct.

Antagonistic muscles move bones in opposite directions relative to a joint and require one muscle to relax while the other muscle contracts.

15. C is correct.

Tendons connect muscle to bone, while ligaments connect bone-to-bone. Tendons are not cartilage.

16. B is correct.

The enteric nervous system (ENS) is an autonomic nervous system division and controls the gastrointestinal tract.

Peristalsis is a contractile process of smooth muscle that propels a ball of food through the intestines.

A: the contraction of the diaphragm is under the control of the autonomic nervous system.

As the diaphragm contracts, the volume of the thoracic cavity increases, and the air is drawn into the lungs.

C: gap junctions conduct cardiac muscle action potentials.

D: a knee-jerk reflex contracts skeletal muscles innervated by the somatic nervous system.

17. D is correct.

Skeletal muscle has multinucleated fibers with a striated appearance from repeating motifs of actin and myosin.

The actin and myosin filaments slide past each other and shorten during contraction.

The contraction process does not require energy, but ATP is needed to release the cross-bridges between the actin and myosin during the next contraction process.

Each muscle fiber is innervated by neurons from the somatic division of the PNS.

The axon releases an action potential to each muscle fiber, but this action potential cannot pass from one muscle fiber to another.

When an action potential reaches the muscle fiber, it causes the release of Ca^{2+} from the sarcoplasmic reticulum to permit the sliding of the actin and myosin filaments.

18. B is correct.

Smooth muscle contains thin actin filaments and thick myosin filaments (albeit not striated) and requires calcium for contraction.

19. C is correct.

The diaphragm is a skeletal muscle innervated by the phrenic nerve of the somatic nervous system.

Smooth muscle and cardiac muscle are involuntary because the autonomic nervous system innervates them.

20. B is correct.

Characteristics of smooth muscle: involuntary, without T-tubules, lacking troponin and tropomyosin, without repeating striations (Z disks) of sarcomeres, single unit with the whole muscle contracting/relaxing.

Smooth muscle cells undergo involuntary contractions and are located 1) in blood vessels for regulating blood pressure, 2) in the gastrointestinal tract to propel food during digestion, and 3) in the bladder to discharge urine.

21. A is correct.

Striated muscle cells (i.e., skeletal muscle) are responsible for the mobility of the body and limbs.

Striated muscle cells are long and cylindrical with many nuclei.

Cardiac muscle cells are in the heart and are single nucleated.

T tubules are in striated and cardiac muscle cells.

Smooth muscle cells are involuntary and primarily in the reproductive, digestive, and endocrine systems.

22. A is correct.

The *somatic nervous system* innervates skeletal muscles.

It consists of myelinated axons without synapses.

The activity of these neurons leads to excitation (contraction) of skeletal muscles; therefore, they are motor neurons.

Motor neurons are never inhibitory.

The somatic fibers are responsible for voluntary movement.

23. C is correct.

Myoglobin is an iron- and oxygen-binding protein in the muscle tissue of vertebrates and most mammals.

Myoglobin has a similar function to hemoglobin, which is the iron- and oxygen-binding protein in red blood cells.

Myoglobin is the primary oxygen-carrying pigment of muscle tissues.

High concentrations of myoglobin allow organisms to hold their breath for extended periods (e.g., diving animals).

24. A is correct.

A muscle is a bundle of parallel fibers. Each fiber is a multinucleated cell created by the fusion of several mononucleated embryonic cells.

I: skeletal muscle is responsible for voluntary movement and is innervated by the somatic nervous system.

Skeletal muscle is made up of individual components known as myocytes (i.e., muscle cells).

These long cylindrical multinucleated cells are called myofibers and are composed of myofibrils.

The myofibrils are composed of actin and myosin filaments repeated in units called a sarcomere – the basic functional unit of the muscle fiber.

The sarcomere is responsible for skeletal muscle's striated appearance and forms the basic machinery necessary for muscle contraction.

II: smooth muscle in the digestive tract, bladder, uterus, and blood vessel walls are responsible for involuntary action and are innervated by the autonomic nervous system.

Smooth muscle does not appear as striated and has one centrally located nucleus.

III: cardiac muscle composes the muscle tissue of the heart.

Cardiac muscle fibers possess characteristics of skeletal and smooth muscle fibers.

As in skeletal muscle, the cardiac muscle has a striated appearance, but cardiac muscle cells generally have one or two centrally located nuclei.

Cardiac muscle is innervated by the autonomic nervous system that modulates the rate of heartbeats.

25. D is correct.

Cardiac muscle contains actin/myosin filaments as in a striated skeletal muscle.

A syncytium is a multinucleated cell that results from the fusion of several individual cells.

Cardiac muscle is not a true syncytium, but adjoining cells are linked by gap junctions that communicate action potentials directly from the cytoplasm of one myocardial cell to another.

The sympathetic nervous system increases heart rate, while parasympathetic stimulation (via the vagus nerve) decreases heart rate.

26. D is correct.

A neuromuscular junction is a synapse between the motor neuron and the muscle fiber.

27. A is correct.

A resting muscle is not entirely relaxed but experiences a slight contraction known as tonus.

B: tonus is the partial sustained contraction in relaxed muscles.

C: isometric contractions involve a constant length and an increase in muscle tension.

D: isotonic contractions involve the shortening of the muscle while the tension remains constant.

Notes for active learning

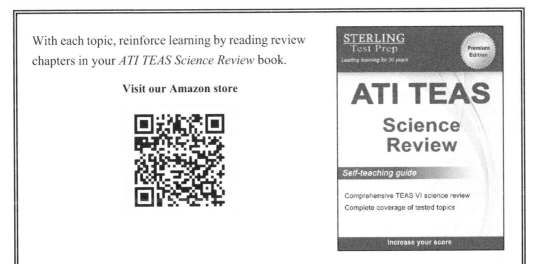

With each topic, reinforce learning by reading review chapters in your *ATI TEAS Science Review* book.

Visit our Amazon store

Notes for active learning

Reproductive System – Explanations

Answer Key

1: D	11: C
2: A	12: C
3: D	13: B
4: A	14: B
5: D	15: B
6: B	16: D
7: C	
8: B	
9: C	
10: A	

1. D is correct.

The menstrual cycle is regulated by several glands: the hypothalamus, anterior pituitary, and ovaries.

FSH is released by the anterior pituitary, which stimulates the maturation of the ova.

Progesterone, synthesized by the ovary and the corpus luteum, regulates the development and shedding of the endometrial lining of the uterus.

The adrenal medulla synthesizes epinephrine (or *adrenaline*) and norepinephrine, which helps the sympathetic nervous system stimulate the *fight or flight* response but are not involved in the menstrual cycle.

2. A is correct.

Oogenesis produces one viable egg and (up to) three polar bodies that result from an unequal distribution of the cytoplasm during meiosis.

Gametes (e.g., egg and sperm) become haploid (1N) through reductive division (i.e., meiosis), in which a diploid cell (2N) gives rise to four haploid sperm or one haploid egg and (up to) three polar bodies.

B: LH stimulates interstitial cells to produce testosterone, which, along with FSH, then stimulates the development of sperm within the seminiferous tubules.

C: FSH stimulates the eggs to develop in follicles within the ovaries.

D: FSH is involved in gamete production for males and females.

3. D is correct.

FSH and LH are secreted by the anterior pituitary and influence the maturation of the follicle.

FSH stimulates the maturation of the gametes (e.g., ova and spermatids).

FSH stimulates the production of estrogen that aids in the maturation of the primary follicle.

LH stimulates ovulation and development of the corpus luteum; the mature corpus luteum secretes progesterone that causes the uterine lining to thicken and becomes more vascular in preparation for implantation of the fertilized egg (i.e., zygote).

4. A is correct.

Sperm synthesis begins within the seminiferous tubules of the testes.

Sperm undergo maturation and storage in the epididymis and, during ejaculation, are released from the vas deferens.

Seminal vesicles are a pair of male accessory glands that produce about 50-60% of the liquid of the semen.

Mnemonic: SEVEN UP—the path of sperm during ejaculation:

Seminiferous tubules > **E**pididymis > **V**as deferens > **E**jaculatory duct > **N**othing > **U**rethra > **P**enis

5. D is correct.

About day 14, LH surges, causing the mature follicle to burst and release the ovum from the ovary (i.e., ovulation).

After ovulation, LH induces the ruptured follicle to develop into the corpus luteum, secreting progesterone and estrogen.

Prolactin stimulates milk production after birth.

A: ovary secretes estrogen and progesterone, while the anterior pituitary secretes LH.

B: progesterone and estrogen inhibit GnRH release, which inhibits the release of FSH and LH and prevents other follicles from maturing.

C: progesterone stimulates the development and maintenance of the endometrium in preparation for implantation of the embryo.

6. B is correct.

Luteinizing hormone (LH) stimulates the release of testosterone in males by Leydig cells.

Testosterone is necessary for the proper development of the testes, penis, and seminal vesicles.

Testosterone surges between the first and fourth months of life, and testosterone inadequacy is a primary cause of cryptorchidism.

During puberty, testosterone is necessary for secondary male sex characteristics (e.g., growth of body hair, broadening of the shoulders, enlarging of the larynx, deepening of the voice, and increased secretions of oil and sweat glands)

A: cortisol is a stress hormone that elevates blood glucose levels.

7. C is correct.

Leydig cells are located adjacent to the seminiferous tubules in the testicle.

Leydig cells are androgens (i.e., hormones as_19-carbon steroids) that secrete testosterone, androstenedione, and dehydroepiandrosterone (DHEA) when stimulated by luteinizing hormone (LH) released by the pituitary gland.

LH increases the conversion of cholesterol to pregnenolone leading to testosterone synthesis and secretion by Leydig cells.

Prolactin (PRL) increases the response of Leydig cells to LH by increasing the number of LH receptors expressed on Leydig cells.

8. B is correct.

Spermatozoon development produces motile, mature sperm, which fuses with an ovum to form the zygote.

Eukaryotic cilia are structurally like eukaryotic flagella, but distinctions are made based on function and length.

Microtubules form the sperm's flagella, necessary for movement through the cervix, uterus, and along the fallopian tubes (i.e., oviducts).

A: acrosomal enzymes digest the outer zona pellucida, a glycoprotein membrane surrounding the plasma membrane of an oocyte) to permit fusion of sperm and egg.

C: sperm's midpiece has many mitochondria used for ATP production for the sperm's movement (via the flagellum) through the female cervix, uterus, and Fallopian tubes.

D: testosterone is necessary for spermatogenesis.

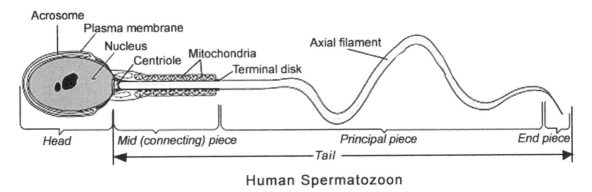

Human Spermatozoon

9. C is correct.

Chlamydia and other infections may scar the reproductive tract, which prevents the ova from reaching the uterus, resulting in infertility.

10. A is correct.

The estrous cycle (i.e., sexual desire) comprises the recurring physiologic changes induced by reproductive hormones in most mammalian females.

Estrous cycles start after sexual maturity in females and are interrupted by anestrous phases or pregnancies.

The menstrual cycle is the cycle of changes that occurs in the uterus and ovary for sexual reproduction. The menstrual cycle is essential to produce eggs and for the preparation of the uterus for pregnancy.

In humans, the length of a menstrual cycle varies significantly among women (ranging from 21 to 35 days), with 28 days designated as the average length.

Each cycle is divided into three phases based on the ovary (ovarian cycle) events or uterus (uterine cycle).

The ovarian cycle consists of the *follicular phase*, *ovulation*, and *luteal phase*, whereas the uterine cycle is divided into menstruation, proliferative phase, and secretory phase.

The endocrine system controls both cycles, and the regular hormonal changes that occur can be interfered with using hormonal contraception to prevent reproduction.

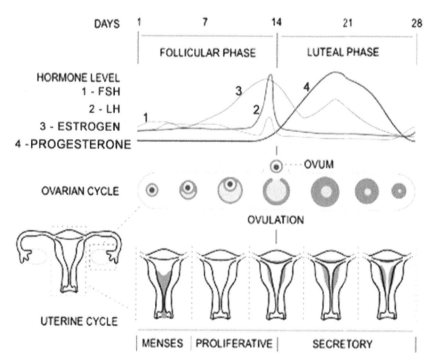

11. C is correct.

Progesterone is a steroid hormone involved in the female menstrual cycle, pregnancy (supports *gestation*), and embryogenesis.

In women, progesterone levels are relatively low during the pre-ovulatory phase of the menstrual cycle, rise after ovulation, and are elevated during the luteal phase.

If pregnancy occurs, human chorionic gonadotropin is released, which maintains the corpus luteum and allows it to maintain levels of progesterone.

At around 12 weeks, the placenta begins to produce progesterone in place of the corpus luteum – this process is called the luteal-placental shift.

After the luteal-placental shift, progesterone levels start to rise further.

After delivery of the placenta and during lactation, progesterone levels are low.

Progesterone levels are relatively low in children and postmenopausal women.

Adult males have levels similar to those in women during the follicular phase of the menstrual cycle.

12. C is correct.

Estrogen is a steroid hormone necessary for normal female maturation.

Estrogen stimulates the development of the female reproductive tract and contributes to developing secondary sexual characteristics and libido.

Estrogen is also secreted by the follicle during the menstrual cycle and is responsible for the thickening of the endometrium in preparation for implantation of the fertilized egg.

A: luteinizing hormone (LH) induces the ruptured follicle to develop into the corpus luteum.

B: LH also stimulates testosterone synthesis in males.

D: FSH is released by the anterior pituitary and promotes the development of the follicle, which matures and then begins secreting estrogen.

13. B is correct.

Sperm mature and are stored until ejaculation in the epididymis.

During ejaculation, sperm flow from the lower portion of the epididymis.

They have not been activated by-products from the prostate gland, and they are unable to swim.

The sperm is transported via the peristaltic action of muscle layers within the vas deferens and form semen.

The sperm mixes with the diluting fluids of the seminal vesicles and other accessory glands before ejaculation.

A: the seminiferous tubules secrete testosterone.

The primary functions of the testes are to produce sperm (i.e., spermatogenesis) and androgens (e.g., testosterone).

Leydig cells are localized between seminiferous tubules and produce and secrete testosterone and other androgens (e.g., DHT, DHEA) necessary for sexual development and puberty, secondary sexual characteristics (e.g., facial hair, sexual behavior, libido), supporting spermatogenesis and erectile function.

C: luteinizing hormone (LH) results in testosterone release.

The presence of testosterone and follicle-stimulating hormone (FSH) is needed to support spermatogenesis.

14. B is correct.

The inner lining of the Fallopian tubes is covered with cilia that help the egg move towards the uterus, where it implants if it is fertilized.

Fertilization usually happens when a sperm fuses with an egg in the Fallopian tube.

C: cilia lining the respiratory tract perform this function.

D: Fallopian tubes are isolated from the external environment, so pH fluctuations are not an issue.

15. B is correct.

If fertilization of the ovum does not occur, the corpus luteum stops secreting progesterone and degenerates.

A: menstruation phase follows decreased progesterone secretion but does not result from increased estrogen levels.

C: increased estrogen secretion (not LH) causes the luteal surge, which occurs earlier in the cycle.

D: thickening of the endometrial lining occurs while estrogen and progesterone levels are high.

16. D is correct.

The anatomy of the male reproductive system from the urethra and into the body is:

urethra → prostate → ejaculatory duct → vas deferens → epididymis → seminiferous tubules

Notes for active learning

Notes for active learning

Integumentary System – Explanations

Answer Key

1: B	11: A	21: A
2: A	12: B	22: C
3: B	13: A	23: C
4: A	14: A	24: C
5: A	15: D	25: B
6: C	16: B	26: C
7: B	17: A	
8: A	18: B	
9: C	19: B	
10: B	20: D	

1. B is correct.

Melanin is a natural pigment in most organisms.

Melanogenesis is produced by melanin in the skin after exposure to UV radiation, causing the skin to appear tan.

Melanin is an effective absorber of light, whereby the pigment dissipates over 99.9% of absorbed UV radiation and protects skin cells from UVB radiation damage, thereby reducing the risk of cancer.

2. A is correct.

The subcutaneous tissue (also known as hypodermis, subcutis, or superficial fascia) is the lowermost layer of the integumentary system.

However, it is not part of the skin, and it lies below the dermis.

The subcutaneous tissue attaches the skin to underlying bone and muscle and supplies it with blood vessels and nerves.

Hypodermis consists of loose connective tissue and elastin.

3. B is correct.

Apocrine glands, which begin functioning at puberty under hormonal influence, are not crucial for thermoregulation.

The odor from sweat is due to bacterial activity on the oily compound, which acts as a pheromone from the apocrine sweat glands (e.g., axillary, parts of the external genitalia).

The armpits are referred to as *axillary*.

4. A is correct.

The reticular dermis is the lower layer of the skin under the papillary dermis, composed of densely packed collagen fibers comprising irregular connective tissue.

The reticular dermis strengthens the skin and provides structure and elasticity.

Additionally, the reticular dermis supports sweat glands and hair follicles.

5. A is correct.

Eccrine glands are the major sweat glands of the human body and are responsible for thermoregulation through the cooling of the body by evaporation of sweat.

6. C is correct.

Arrector pili are small muscles attached to hair follicles that occasionally contract, which causes hairs to stand on end. This can involuntarily occur when a person is cold or experiences strong emotions such as fear.

7. B is correct.

Sebaceous glands are glands in the skin that secrete an oily/waxy matter (sebum) to lubricate and waterproof the skin and hair.

Sebaceous glands are in the highest abundance on the face and scalp, though they are distributed throughout the skin (except for the palms and soles).

In the eyelids, meibomian sebaceous glands secrete a particular type of sebum into tears.

8. A is correct.

Sweat glands (also known as sudoriferous glands) are small tubular structures of the skin that produce sweat.

There are two main types of sweat glands:

Eccrine sweat glands are distributed over the body, though their density varies from region to region.

Humans utilize eccrine sweat glands as a primary form of cooling.

Apocrine sweat glands are larger, have a different secretion mechanism, and are mostly limited to the axilla (armpits) and perianal areas in humans.

Apocrine glands contribute little to cooling in humans but are the effective sweat glands in hoofed animals such as cattle, camels, horses, and donkeys.

The term eccrine is correctly used to designate merocrine secretions from sweat glands (eccrine sweat glands).

Merocrine is used to classify exocrine glands and their secretions for histology.

A cell is classified as merocrine if the secretions are excreted via exocytosis from secretory cells into an epithelial-walled duct or ducts and then onto a bodily surface (or into the lumen).

Merocrine is the most common manner of secretion.

The merocrine gland releases its product, and no part of the gland is lost or damaged (compare holocrine and apocrine).

B: apocrine cells release their secretions via exocytosis of the plasma membrane.

Apocrine secretion is less damaging to the gland than holocrine secretion (which destroys a cell) but more damaging than merocrine secretion (exocytosis).

Mammary glands are apocrine glands responsible for secreting breast milk.

C: ceruminous glands are specialized subcutaneous sudoriferous (i.e., sweat) glands in the external auditory canal.

They produce cerumen (earwax) by mixing their secretion with sebum and dead epidermal cells.

Cerumen waterproofs the canal, kills bacteria, keeps the eardrum pliable, lubricates and cleans the external auditory canal, and traps foreign particles (e.g., dust, fungal spores) by coating the guard hairs of the ear, making them sticky.

D: Sebaceous glands are glands in the skin that secrete an oily/waxy matter (sebum) to lubricate and waterproof the skin and hair.

Sebaceous glands are in the highest abundance on the face and scalp, though they are distributed throughout the skin (except for the palms and soles).

9. C is correct.

The epidermis contains no blood vessels, and cells in the deepest layers are nourished by diffusion from blood capillaries that extend to the upper layers of the dermis.

10. B is correct.

The dermis is a layer of skin between the epidermis (i.e., cutis) and subcutaneous tissues that consists of connective tissue and cushions the body from stress and strain.

The dermis is divided into two layers, the superficial area adjacent to the epidermis (i.e., papillary region) and a deep thicker area is known as the reticular dermis.

The dermis is tightly connected to the epidermis through a basement membrane.

Structural components of the dermis are collagen, elastic fibers, and the extrafibrillar matrix.

The dermis contains mechanoreceptors that provide the sense of touch and heat, sweat glands, hair follicles, sebaceous glands, apocrine glands, blood vessels, and lymphatic vessels.

The blood vessels provide nourishment and waste removal for dermal and epidermal cells.

11. A is correct.

The skin has three layers: the epidermis (outermost layer), the dermis (beneath the epidermis), and the hypodermis, made of fat and connective tissue.

12. B is correct.

The dermis lies beneath the epidermis and contains connective tissue, sweat glands, and hair follicles.

The epidermis is the outermost layer and acts as a physical barrier protecting the body against microbes, UV light, and chemical compounds.

13. A is correct.

The stratum corneum is the outer layer of the epidermis, consisting of dead cells (corneocytes).

The stratum corneum is composed of numerous layers of flattened cells with no nuclei and cell organelles.

These cells contain a dense network of keratin, a protein that helps keep the skin hydrated by preventing water evaporation.

14. A is correct.

Holocrine secretions are produced in the cytoplasm of the cell and released by the rupture of the plasma membrane, which destroys the cell and results in the secretion of the product into the lumen.

The sebaceous gland is an example of a holocrine gland because its secretion product (i.e., sebum) is released with remnants of dead cells.

15. D is correct.

Melanin refers to a group of natural pigments in most organisms.

Melanin is a derivative of the amino acid tyrosine but is not made of amino acids and is not a protein.

The pigment is produced in a specialized group of cells known as melanocytes.

16. B is correct.

The integumentary system refers to the skin and its appendages (hair, nails, glands, nerves).

Adipose tissue accumulates in the deepest, subcutaneous layer of the skin.

17. A is correct.

The order in which a needle would pierce the epidermal layers of the skin is first the corneum, then the lucidum, the granulosum, the spinosum, finally reaching the basale.

The epidermis consists of five layers of cells, whereby each layer has a distinct role in the health, well-being, and functioning of the skin.

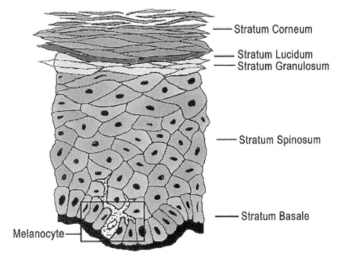

The *stratum corneum* is the outermost layer of the epidermis, consisting of dead cells (corneocytes). Its purpose is to form a barrier to protect underlying tissue from infection, dehydration, chemicals, and mechanical stress.

The *stratum lucidum* is a thin layer of dead skin cells in the epidermis named for its translucent appearance. It is composed of three to five layers of dead, flattened keratinocytes, which do not feature distinct boundaries and are filled with an intermediate form of keratin (eleidin).

The *stratum granulosum* is a thin layer of cells where Keratinocytes that migrated from the underlying stratum spinosum become granular cells containing keratohyalin granules. These granules are filled with proteins and promote hydration and crosslinking of keratin.

At the transition between this layer and the stratum corneum, cells secrete lamellar bodies (containing lipids and proteins) into the extracellular space.

This results in the formation of the hydrophobic lipid envelope responsible for the skin's barrier properties.

Cells lose their nuclei and organelles, causing the granular cells to become non-viable corneocytes in the stratum corneum.

The *stratum spinosum* is where keratinization begins.

This layer comprises polyhedral keratinocytes active in synthesizing fibrillar proteins (cytokeratin), built up within the cells by aggregating to form tonofibrils.

The tonofibrils form the desmosomes allowing strong connections to form between adjacent keratinocytes.

The *stratum basale* is the deepest layer of the five layers of the epidermis and is a continuous layer of cells.

The stratum basale is described as one cell thick (though it may be two to three cells thick in hairless skin and hyperproliferative epidermis).

Other types of cells within the stratum basale are melanocytes (pigment-producing cells), Langerhans cells (immune cells), and Merkel cells (touch receptors).

18. B is correct.

The layer of skin responsible for fingerprints is the papillary dermis, the uppermost layer of the dermis.

19. B is correct.

Adipose tissue serves as an effective shock absorber.

C: basement membrane anchors the epithelium to its loose connective tissue (i.e., dermis) underneath by using cell-matrix adhesions via substrate adhesion SAMs).

20. D is correct.

Keratinocytes accumulate melanin on their surface to form a UV-blocking pigment layer.

21. A is correct.

Stratum basale is primarily basal keratinocytes that divide to form the keratinocytes of the stratum spinosum, which migrate superficially.

22. C is correct.

Perspiration is the secretion of water, salts, and urea from the sweat (i.e., sudoriferous) pores of the skin.

As the sweat comes into contact with air, it evaporates and cools the skin. T

Thus, perspiration is a thermoregulatory mechanism involved in heat dissipation, *not* heat conservation.

Eccrine sweat glands are distributed over the body, though their density varies from region to region. Humans utilize eccrine sweat glands as a primary form of cooling.

Apocrine sweat glands are larger, have a different secretion mechanism, and are mostly limited to the axilla (i.e., armpits) in humans.

A: constriction of selective blood vessels at the skin's surface reroutes blood flow from the skin to deeper tissues, which minimizes the loss of body heat.

B: shivering is a thermoregulatory mechanism that conserves body heat by intensive, rhythmic involuntary contraction of muscle tissue that increases internal heat production.

D: piloerection (i.e., *goosebumps*) is a reflex contraction of the small muscles at the base of skin hairs, which causes the hairs to stand erect, forming an insulating layer that minimizes the loss of body heat.

23. C is correct.

Tactile cells (i.e., Merkel cells) are epithelial mechanoreceptor cells for the sensation of light touch.

A: nociceptors (i.e., pain receptors) detect mechanical, thermal, or chemical changes above a set threshold. Nociception is the neural process mechanism of perceiving stimuli.

24. C is correct.

Burn Type	Layers affected	Sensation	Healing time	Prognosis
Superficial (1°)	Epidermis	Painful	5–10 days	Heals well; Repeated sunburns increase the risk of skin cancer later
Superficial partial thickness (2°)	Extends into the superficial (papillary) dermis	Very painful	2–3 weeks	Local infection/cellulitis but no scarring typically
Deep partial thickness (2°)	Extends into the deep (reticular) dermis	Pressure and discomfort	3–8 weeks	Scarring, contractures (may require excision and skin grafting)
Full thickness (3°)	Extends through the entire dermis	Painless	Months and incomplete	Scarring, contractures, amputation (early excision recommended)
Fourth degree (4°)	Extends - entire skin and into underlying fat, muscle, and bone	Painless	Requires excision	Amputation, significant functional impairment, or death

25. B is correct.

The integumentary (or *skin*) system functions in thermoregulation, UV protection, and infection resistance.

It is the site of vitamin D synthesis, but it does not function in the synthesis of vitamin E; plants synthesize vitamin E.

26. C is correct.

A mechanoreceptor is a sensory receptor that responds to mechanical pressure (or distortion).

The four main types are Pacinian corpuscles, Meissner's corpuscles, Merkel's discs, and Ruffini endings.

Meissner's (i.e., tactile) corpuscles are mechanoreceptors and a type of nerve endings in the skin responsible for sensitivity to light touch.

Merkel discs are mechanoreceptors in the skin and mucosa (i.e., linings of endodermal organs).

Merkel discs detect pressure and texture and transmit the information to the brain.

A: Ruffinian endings are in the deep layers of the skin and register mechanical deformation within joints.

B: bulboid corpuscles (end-bulbs of Krause) are thermoreceptors that sense cold.

D: Pacinian corpuscles are nerve endings in the skin that sense vibrations and pressure.

With each topic, reinforce learning by reading review chapters in your *ATI TEAS Science Review* book.

Visit our Amazon store

STERLING
Test Prep
Leading learning for 30 years

Premium Edition

ATI TEAS

Science Review

Self-teaching guide

Comprehensive TEAS VI science review
Complete coverage of tested topics

Increase your score

Notes for active learning

Notes for active learning

Endocrine System – Explanations

Answer Key

1: D	11: D	21: D
2: A	12: C	22: A
3: A	13: B	23: D
4: D	14: D	24: C
5: D	15: D	25: A
6: C	16: C	26: B
7: C	17: A	27: C
8: C	18: C	28: B
9: B	19: A	
10: B	20: C	

1. D is correct.

Hormones are steroid or peptide molecules released from glands that travel through the blood to affect distant targets.

A: paracrine signals are hormones released by a cell to induce a nearby cell's behavior or differentiation.

C: autocrine signals (i.e., hormones or growth factors) released from a cell and then affect the same cell that synthesized the molecule.

Autocrine signals are common during development, releasing growth factors.

2. A is correct.

Steroid hormones can pass through the plasma membrane of the cell and enter the nucleus.

Once in the cytoplasm of the cell, the steroid hormone binds to its cytosolic receptor.

Once bound, the complex migrates into the nucleus of the cell and binds to the DNA.

The hormone/receptor complex functions as a transcription factor to activate or inactivate gene transcription.

B: eicosanoids are signaling molecules made by the oxidation of 20-carbon fatty acids.

They exert sophisticated control over many bodily systems, mainly in inflammation and immunity, and as messengers in the central nervous system. Examples include prostaglandins and arachidonic acid.

C: peptide (similar to an amino acid) hormones cannot enter through the cell's plasma membrane but bind (as a ligand) to receptors on the cell's surface via second messengers.

D: amino acid (similar to peptide) hormones cannot enter through the cell's plasma membrane but bind (as a ligand) to receptors on the cell's surface via second messengers.

3. A is correct.

The primary exception to negative feedback control of hormones is the female reproduction cycle.

D: ducts are present in the exocrine (not endocrine) system, whereby hormones are released from a gland and distributed throughout the body via the bloodstream.

4. D is correct.

Parathyroid hormone (PTH) controls blood Ca^{2+} levels via two mechanisms by stimulating osteoclasts activity (i.e., bone resorption) and decreasing the Ca^{2+} loss in urine by the kidney.

PTH is secreted by the parathyroid gland to increase blood calcium by removing calcium from bones and other calcium-containing tissues.

The removal of calcium from bones is primarily done via osteoclasts (i.e., bone-releasing = breakdown bone).

Humans usually have four parathyroid glands, which are on the posterior surface of the thyroid gland.

5. D is correct.

Most second messenger systems are initiated by peptide hormones (i.e., ligands), which cannot pass through the plasma membrane and instead bind to receptors on the cell surface.

Peptide hormones are hydrophilic and cannot cross the hydrophobic phospholipid bilayer.

Peptide hormones bind to a receptor on the surface of the target cell's membranes.

The ligand-receptor complex may trigger the release of a second messenger (e.g., G-protein or cAMP), or the ligand-receptor complex may be carried into the cytoplasm by receptor-mediated endocytosis.

In the event of a second messenger, a series of events within the cell are responsible for the hormone's activity.

Thus, peptide hormones do not directly influence mRNA transcription because peptide hormones do not enter the nucleus of their target cells and activate transcription.

Cholesterol-derived steroid hormones enter the cell and bind to a cytosolic receptor.

With the receptor, the hormone-receptor complex passes through the nuclear envelope and enters the nucleus to function as a transcription factor and increase/decrease gene expression.

6. C is correct.

The posterior pituitary releases two hormones: oxytocin and antidiuretic hormone (ADH - also known as vasopressin).

A: TSH (thyroid-stimulating hormone) is released by the anterior pituitary.

B: prolactin is produced in the pituitary and decidua (uterine lining – endometrium), myometrium (the middle layer of the uterine wall), breasts, lymphocytes, leukocytes, and the prostate.

D: progesterone is produced in the ovaries (corpus luteum), the adrenal glands, and during pregnancy in the placenta. It is synthesized from the precursor – pregnenolone.

7. C is correct.

The anterior pituitary secretes three gonadotropic hormones (e.g., FSH, LH, placental chorionic gonadotropins hCG). FSH causes the ova to mature and enlarge.

A: oxytocin is synthesized by the hypothalamus and stimulates uterine contractions during birth and milk letdown during lactation. Prolactin stimulates the production of milk for lactation.

D: LH stimulates ovulation.

8. C is correct.

Adrenocorticotropic hormone (ACTH) is produced and released by the anterior pituitary gland to increase the production and release of glucocorticoid steroid hormones (corticosteroids) by adrenal cortex cells.

9. B is correct.

The thyroid hormones T_3 and T_4 (triiodothyronine and thyroxine) are derived from the amino acid tyrosine and accelerate oxidative metabolism throughout the body.

The anterior pituitary secretes thyroid-stimulating hormone (TSH) to stimulate the thyroid gland to produce T_4 and then T_3, stimulating the metabolism of most tissues in the body.

10. B is correct.

The pancreas is an exocrine (*via* ducts) and endocrine (*via* the bloodstream) gland.

The exocrine function (via a series of ducts) is performed by the cells that secrete digestive enzymes (e.g., amylase, lipase, and maltase) and bicarbonate into the small intestine.

Small glandular structures perform the endocrine function of the pancreas called the islets of Langerhans (i.e., alpha, beta, and delta cells).

Alpha cells produce and secrete glucagon.

Beta cells produce and secrete insulin. Delta cells produce and secrete somatostatin.

11. D is correct.

Cortisol (also known as hydrocortisone) is a steroid hormone.

Cortisol is a glucocorticoid named for its role in the regulation of metabolism (glucose levels).

Cortisol is produced by the adrenal cortex and is released in response to stress and a low blood glucocorticoid level.

Its primary functions are to increase blood sugar through gluconeogenesis, suppress the immune system, and aid in carbohydrate, protein, and fat metabolism.

It decreases bone formation.

Cortisol, the most important human glucocorticoid, is essential for life and regulates/supports important metabolic, cardiovascular, immunologic, and homeostatic functions.

A: adrenaline is also known as epinephrine.

B: norepinephrine (aka noradrenaline) is a catecholamine (i.e., derived from the amino acid tyrosine) with multiple roles, including being a hormone and a neurotransmitter.

Norepinephrine is the hormone and neurotransmitter most responsible for vigilant concentration.

This contrasts with its most chemically similar hormone, dopamine, responsible for cognitive alertness.

The primary function of norepinephrine is its role as the neurotransmitter released from the sympathetic neurons to affect the heart, increasing the heart contraction rate.

Norepinephrine (as a stress hormone) affects parts of the brain (e.g., amygdala), where attention and responses are controlled.

Norepinephrine underlies the fight-or-flight response (in conjunction with epinephrine), directly increases the heart rate, triggers the release of glucose from energy stores, increases the blood flow to skeletal muscle, and increases oxygen supply to the brain.

12. C is correct.

A releasing hormone (or releasing factor) is a hormone whose purpose is to control the release of another hormone.

The hypothalamus is just below the thalamus; a critical function is to link the nervous system to the endocrine system via the pituitary gland (hypophysis).

It is responsible for specific metabolic processes and other activities of the autonomic nervous system.

The hypothalamus synthesizes and secretes releasing hormones, which, in turn, stimulate or inhibit the secretion of pituitary hormones.

The hypothalamus controls body temperature, hunger, thirst, fatigue, sleep, circadian rhythms, and essential aspects of parenting and attachment behaviors.

Examples of releasing factors synthesized by the hypothalamus are thyrotropin-releasing hormone (TRH), Corticotropin-releasing hormone (CRH), Gonadotropin-releasing hormone (GnRH), Growth hormone-releasing hormone (GHRH).

Two other factors are classified as releasing hormones, although they inhibit pituitary hormone release: somatostatin and dopamine.

13. B is correct.

Parathyroid hormone is secreted by the parathyroid gland and increases blood calcium by releasing calcium from bones and other calcium-containing tissues.

The removal of calcium from bones is primarily done via osteoclasts (i.e., bone-releasing = breakdown bone).

A: calcitonin is secreted by the thyroid gland as the antagonist to the parathyroid hormone (PTH).

Calcitonin reduces blood $[Ca^{2+}]$ by depositing it onto bone via osteoblasts (i.e., build bone).

C: aldosterone, secreted by the adrenal cortex, increases Na^+ reabsorption in the kidneys.

D: glucagon (α cells of the islets of Langerhans) from the pancreas raises blood glucose.

14. D is correct.

Antagonistic refers to an action that is opposite, while *agonist* means to mimic the effect.

An antagonistic relationship exists between insulin and glucagon.

The pancreas synthesizes both hormones, but insulin lowers glucose blood levels, while glucagon raises glucose blood levels.

A: ACTH and TSH are unrelated to their actions.

ACTH (adrenocorticotropic hormone) is secreted by the anterior pituitary gland and stimulates the adrenal gland.

TSH (thyroid-stimulating hormone) activates the thyroid to produce thyroxine.

B: oxytocin and prolactin are *agonists* (i.e., same effect) of the same process, specifically milk production by the mammary gland.

Oxytocin is secreted by the *posterior* pituitary gland and stimulates the *release* of milk during lactation.

Prolactin is secreted by the *anterior* pituitary gland and stimulates the *production* of milk during lactation.

C: vitamin D and parathyroid hormone (PTH) are *agonists* of the same process because both increase blood calcium levels.

15. D is correct.

In a positive feedback system, the output enhances the original stimulus, while with negative feedback, the output reduces the effect of the stimulus.

An example of a positive feedback system is childbirth, wherein the hormone oxytocin is released, intensifying the contractions.

16. C is correct.

Glucagon is a peptide hormone secreted by the pancreas that raises blood glucose levels.

Its effect is opposite that of insulin, which lowers blood glucose levels. The pancreas releases glucagon when blood glucose levels are too low.

Glucagon causes the liver to convert stored glycogen into glucose, which is released into the bloodstream.

Conversely, high blood glucose levels stimulate the release of insulin, which allows glucose to be taken up and used by insulin-dependent tissues.

Thus, glucagon and insulin are part of a feedback system that keeps blood glucose levels within a narrow range.

Glucagon generally elevates the amount of glucose in the blood by promoting gluconeogenesis and glycogenolysis.

Glucose is stored in the liver as glycogen, a polymer of glucose molecules.

Liver cells (hepatocytes) have glucagon receptors.

When glucagon binds to the glucagon receptors, the liver cells convert the glycogen polymer into individual glucose molecules and release them into the bloodstream.

This process is known as glycogenolysis. As these stores become depleted, glucagon then signals the liver and kidney to synthesize additional glucose by gluconeogenesis.

Glucagon turns off glycolysis in the liver, causing glycolytic intermediates to be shuttled to gluconeogenesis.

A: calcitonin is secreted by the thyroid gland and lowers blood Ca^{2+} levels.

B: estrogen is secreted by the ovaries and maintains secondary sex characteristics (i.e., menstrual cycles in females) and is responsible for maintaining the endometrium.

D: oxytocin is produced by the hypothalamus and is secreted by the posterior pituitary to stimulate uterine contractions during labor and milk secretion during lactation.

17. A is correct.

Melatonin is an essential and multifunctional hormone secreted by the pineal gland with numerous biological effects triggered by the activation of melatonin receptors.

Also, it is a pervasive and powerful antioxidant with a role in the protection of nuclear and mitochondrial DNA.

Melatonin affects circadian rhythms, mood, the timing of puberty, aging, and other biological processes.

18. C is correct.

Somatostatin, also known as growth hormone-inhibiting hormone (GHIH), is a peptide hormone that regulates the endocrine system and affects neurotransmission and cell proliferation.

Within the GI tract, somatostatin is produced by the delta cells, and it inhibits insulin and glucagon secretion.

19. A is correct.

Epinephrine (also known as adrenaline) is a peptide hormone released by the adrenal medulla and is a physiological stimulant (i.e., *EpiPen* for anaphylaxis) that aids in *fight or flight* responses.

Epinephrine causes bronchial dilation for deeper respiration and increased O_2 intake.

B: the sympathetic nervous system stimulates epinephrine release.

C: epinephrine is a peptide hormone synthesized by the adrenal medulla, while the adrenal cortex synthesizes steroid hormones (e.g., aldosterone and cortisol).

20. C is correct.

Growth-hormone-releasing hormone (GHRH), also known as a growth-hormone-releasing factor, is a 44-amino acid peptide hormone produced in the hypothalamus and carried to the anterior pituitary gland, where it stimulated the secretion of the growth hormone (GH).

The hypothalamus controls secretions from the pituitary. Hypothalamic hormones are referred to as *releasing* and *inhibiting* hormones because of their influence on the anterior pituitary.

The eight hormones of the anterior pituitary:

Adrenocorticotropic hormone (ACTH) targets the adrenal gland and results in secretions of glucocorticoid, mineralocorticoid, and androgens.

Beta-endorphin targets the opioid receptor and inhibits the perception of pain.

Thyroid-stimulating hormone (TSH) targets the thyroid gland and results in secretions of thyroid hormones.

Follicle-stimulating hormone (FSH) targets the gonads and results in the growth of the reproductive system.

Luteinizing hormone (LH) targets gonads to trigger ovulation, maintain corpus luteum and secrete progesterone (in females), or stimulate testosterone secretion (for males).

Growth hormone (aka somatotropin; GH) targets the liver and adipose tissue and promotes growth, lipid, and carbohydrate metabolism

Prolactin (PRL) targets the ovaries and mammary glands and results in secretions of estrogens/progesterone; it also stimulates milk production.

Leptin targets corticotropic and thyrotrophic cells (cell types in the anterior pituitary) and results in secretions of TSH and ACTH.

21. D is correct.

Hormones are classified as steroids (i.e., cholesterol derived) and amino acid hormones.

Amino acid hormones include amines (derived from a single amino acid, either tryptophan or tyrosine), peptide hormones (short chains of amino acids), and protein hormones (longer chains of amino acids).

Steroid hormones are grouped as corticosteroids (i.e., mineralocorticoids and glucocorticoids) or sex steroids (i.e., androgens, estrogens, and progestogens).

22. A is correct.

Insulin is produced by beta cells of the pancreas and decreases blood glucose by stimulating muscle cells to uptake glucose from the blood.

Aldosterone is synthesized by the adrenal gland and increases the reabsorption of Na^+ and H_2O by the distal convoluted tubules of the nephron.

23. D is correct.

Hormones exert their action on target cells by binding to appropriate receptors in or on the tissue of the target.

A cell is a target if it has functional receptors for that specific hormone.

24. C is correct.

The parathyroid gland (via PTH) and the thyroid (via calcitonin) are antagonist hormones that regulate blood calcium concentration.

The thyroid gland is in the middle of the lower neck, below the larynx (i.e., voice box), and just above the clavicles (i.e., collarbone).

Humans typically have four parathyroid glands, which are usually on the posterior surface of the thyroid gland.

Parathyroid hormone (PTH) is a polypeptide hormone-containing 84 amino acids secreted by the chief cells of the parathyroid glands.

PTH acts to increase blood $[Ca^{2+}]$, whereas calcitonin (by the C cells of the thyroid gland) decreases $[Ca^{2+}]$.

PTH increases $[Ca^{2+}]$ in the blood by acting upon the parathyroid hormone 1 receptor (high levels in bone and kidney) and the parathyroid hormone 2 receptor (high levels in the central nervous system, pancreas, testis, and placenta).

25. A is correct.

The posterior pituitary hormones are oxytocin (uterine contraction and lactation) and vasopressin – antidiuretic hormone or ADH – stimulates water retention, raises blood pressure by contracting arterioles and induces male aggression.

26. B is correct.

The hypothalamus is responsible for specific metabolic processes and other activities of the autonomic nervous system.

It synthesizes and secretes certain neurohormones (i.e., releasing hormones), and these, in turn, stimulate or inhibit the secretion of anterior/posterior pituitary hormones.

The hypothalamus regulates many essential human functions, including temperature regulation, sleep/wake cycles, water and salt balance, hunger.

It produces hormones such as vasopressin (aka ADH) and oxytocin (stored in the posterior pituitary).

The hypothalamus also produces releasing factors that control secretions of the anterior pituitary.

A: cerebrum regulates such functions as memory, conscious thought, voluntary motor activity, and the interpretation of sensation.

The cerebrum refers to the part of the brain comprising the cerebral cortex (two cerebral hemispheres); it includes several subcortical structures such as the basal ganglia, hippocampus, and olfactory bulb.

In humans, the cerebrum is the superior-most region of the central nervous system (CNS).

C: medulla oblongata (aka medulla) is the lower half of the brainstem.

The medulla contains the respiratory, cardiac, vomiting, and vasomotor centers and regulates autonomic (i.e., involuntary) functions, such as heart rate, breathing, and blood pressure.

D: pons is part of the brainstem that links the medulla oblongata to the thalamus.

The pons relays signals from the forebrain to the cerebellum.

The pons is involved primarily with sleep, respiration, posture, equilibrium, bladder control, hearing, swallowing, taste, eye movement, facial expressions, and facial sensation.

27. C is correct.

Thyroxine is one of the thyroid hormones secreted by the thyroid gland and plays a vital role in regulating metabolism.

In adults, thyroid deficiency (i.e., hypothyroidism) results in a decreased rate of metabolism, which produces symptoms such as weight gain, fatigue, intolerance to cold, and swelling of the thyroid (i.e., goiter).

A decreased metabolic rate means that the body uses less energy per day, and fewer dietary calories are required.

Thus, unless a hypothyroid patient changes her diet, she will gain weight because excess calories are converted and stored in adipose tissue as fat.

In response to low thyroid hormone levels, the pituitary secretes the thyroid-stimulating hormone (TSH), which increases thyroid hormone production.

However, if the thyroid is unable to increase its hormone synthesis, it undergoes hypertrophy (i.e., increase in mass) and results in the formation of goiter (i.e., a swollen pouch in the throat region).

A: estrogen is not the cause of the patient's symptoms.

B: cortisol deficiency is not the cause of the patient's symptoms.

D: aldosterone deficiency is not the cause of the patient's symptoms.

28. B is correct.

Aldosterone is a steroid hormone secreted from the adrenal gland involved in regulating blood pressure by acting on the distal tubules and collecting ducts of the nephron.

Aldosterone increases the reabsorption of ions and water in the kidney to cause sodium conservation, potassium secretion, water retention, and increased blood pressure.

The renin-angiotensin system regulates blood pressure and water (i.e., fluid) balance.

When blood volume is low, juxtaglomerular cells (in kidneys) activate their prorenin and secrete renin into circulation.

Plasma renin then carries out the conversion of angiotensinogen (released by the liver) to angiotensin I.

Angiotensin I is subsequently converted to angiotensin II by the angiotensin-converting enzyme (located in the lungs).

Angiotensin II is a potent vasoactive peptide that causes blood vessels to constrict, resulting in elevated blood pressure. Angiotensin II stimulates the secretion of aldosterone.

Notes for active learning

Notes for active learning

Genitourinary System – Explanations

Answer Key

1: C	11: B
2: A	12: C
3: B	13: B
4: C	14: C
5: C	15: C
6: D	16: A
7: A	17: A
8: C	18: B
9: C	19: A
10: D	

1. C is correct.

The individual collecting ducts in the kidney empty into much larger ducts called the *minor calyces*, joining to form a *major calyx*.

The major calyces join to form the renal pelvis.

Each of the two ureters originates from the renal pelvis of the kidney and connects to the urinary bladder that stores urine.

A single urethra transports urine from the bladder for discharge from the body.

2. A is correct.

Elimination of solid waste products is the function of the digestive system; the respiratory system eliminates CO_2.

3. B is correct.

A: parasympathetic and sympathetic nerves innervate the ureter.

C: the urinary bladder has a transitional epithelium and does not produce mucus.

D: urine exits the bladder when the autonomically controlled internal sphincter and the voluntarily controlled external sphincter open.

Incontinence results from problems with these muscles.

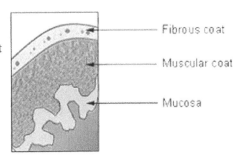

Ureter wall

4. C is correct.

Gout results when uric acid is not adequately eliminated.

The kidneys are the main organs that secrete, eliminate, filter, and reabsorb compounds to maintain homeostasis.

Thus, gout may be caused by a renal (kidney) problem.

A: the spleen is a lymphoid organ that filters blood for pathogens.

B: the large intestine reabsorbs water and is the site of vitamin K synthesis by symbiotic bacteria.

The distal end of the colon is the portion that stores indigestible material as feces.

D: the liver synthesizes blood proteins (e.g., albumins, fibrinogen, some globulins), produces bile, detoxifies metabolites, and stores fat-soluble vitamins (A, D & E).

Vitamin K is fat-soluble but is excreted from the body without being stored.

5. C is correct.

Passive diffusion of Na^+ occurs in the loop of Henle.

The descending limb is permeable to H_2O and less impermeable to salt, and thus indirectly contributes to the concentration of the interstitium.

As the filtrate descends deeper into the medulla, the hypertonic interstitium osmosis causes H_2O to flow out of the descending limb until the osmolarity of the filtrate and interstitium equilibrate.

Longer descending limbs allow more time for H_2O to flow out of the filtrate, so a longer loop of Henle creates a more hypertonic filtrate than shorter loops.

The thin ascending loop of Henle is impermeable to H_2O.

A: the thick segment of the ascending loop of Henle uses active transport for Na^+.

B: the distal convoluted tubule uses active transport for Na^+.

D: the proximal convoluted tubule uses active transport for Na^+.

6. D is correct.

The metabolism of amino acids by the liver involves deamination (i.e., removal of the amino group).

Depending on the organism, nitrogenous wastes are excreted as ammonia, urea, or uric acid.

Organisms where H_2O is abundant (e.g., fish) excrete dilute urine in the form of ammonia.

In contrast, organisms in arid conditions excrete uric acid (e.g., some birds desiccate urine, so it becomes a pellet).

7. A is correct.

The urethra is a tube that connects the urinary bladder to the male or female genitals to remove urine.

During ejaculation, sperm travels from the epididymis through the vas deferens and the urethra that opens to the outside at the tip of the penis.

In males, the urethra functions in the reproductive and excretory systems.

In females, the reproductive and excretory systems do not share a common (i.e., urethral) pathway.

Sperm enter the vagina and travel through the cervix, uterus, and fallopian tubes.

Urine leaves the body through the urethra.

In females, the vagina and urethra never connect because they are separate openings.

B: the ureters serve the same excretory function in males and females. The ureter is the duct connecting the kidney to the bladder. Urine is formed in the kidneys, travels to the bladder via the ureters, and is stored in the bladder until excreted from the body through the urethra.

C: the prostate gland (in males) contributes most of the ejaculated fluid to semen. The prostate secretes prostatic fluid, which is alkaline and neutralizes the acidity of residual urine in the urethra. It protects the sperm from acidic conditions in the female reproductive tract.

D: the vas deferens (also known as ductus deferens) transports sperm from the epididymis to the ejaculatory duct in anticipation of ejaculation.

8. C is correct.

The nephron is the functional renal unit with the proximal convoluted tubule, descending and ascending loops of Henle, distal convoluted tubule, and collecting ducts.

A nephron eliminates wastes, regulates blood volume and pressure, controls levels of electrolytes and metabolites, and regulates blood pH.

The proximal convoluted tubule reabsorbs 2/3 of the H_2O entering the nephron; the descending loop of Henle passively reabsorbs H_2O; the distal convoluted tubule reabsorbs H_2O when stimulated by aldosterone; the collecting duct reabsorbs H_2O when stimulated by the antidiuretic hormone.

Unlike the descending limb, the thin ascending loop of Henle is impermeable to H_2O and is a critical feature of the countercurrent exchange mechanism that concentrates urine.

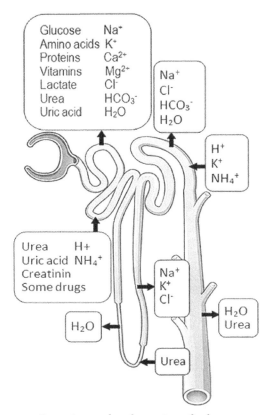

Secretion and reabsorption of solutes

9. C is correct.

For females, the anatomy of the excretory system from the urethra and into the body is:

urethra → bladder → opening to the ureter → ureter → renal pelvis of the kidney

10. D is correct.

Angiotensin II acts at the Na^+/H^+ exchanger in the proximal tubules of the kidney to stimulate Na^+ reabsorption and H^+ excretion, which is coupled with bicarbonate reabsorption.

This increases blood volume, pressure, and pH. ACE (i.e., angiotensin-converting enzyme) inhibitors are major anti-hypertensive drugs.

11. B is correct.

Renin is part of the renin-angiotensin system that influences blood pressure.

Renin is formed by the juxtaglomerular apparatus near the distal convoluted tubule of the nephron and acts indirectly on the adrenal cortex but does not act on the pituitary gland.

When blood pressure falls (e.g., heavy bleeding), renin is released by the kidneys and converts the zymogen of angiotensinogen to angiotensin I by the angiotensin-converting enzyme (ACE).

Angiotensin II causes vasoconstriction (to elevate blood pressure) and aldosterone release from the adrenal cortex that opens ion channels in convoluted tubules (to increase H_2O reabsorption).

12. C is correct.

Water reabsorption in the kidneys is directly proportional to the relative osmolarity of the interstitial tissue compared to the osmolarity of the filtrate.

When the osmolarity of the filtrate is higher than the osmolarity of the kidney tissue, water diffuses *into* the nephron.

When the osmolarity of the filtrate is lower than the osmolarity of the kidney tissue, water diffuses *out* of the nephron.

Infusing the nephron of a healthy person with a concentrated NaCl solution increases the filtrate osmolarity, and water diffuses *into* the nephron.

Since the volume of urine excreted is inversely proportional to the amount of water reabsorption, there is increased urine volume.

13. B is correct.

The glomerulus is the capillary portion of the nephron where glucose, water, amino acids, ions, and urea pass through the capillary bed and enter Bowman's capsule; larger plasma proteins and cells remain within the glomerulus.

Glucose and amino acids pass into the filtrate (i.e., the urine) but are entirely reabsorbed into the blood.

Urea is filtered and excreted in the urine, and Na^+ and other salts are filtered but partially reabsorbed.

14. C is correct.

Vasopressin (also known as anti-diuretic hormone; ADH) is released from the posterior pituitary in response to reductions in plasma volume or increased osmolarity.

Aldosterone is a mineral corticoid released by the adrenal cortex in response to low blood pressure.

It regulates blood pressure mainly by acting on the distal tubules and collecting ducts of the nephron.

15. C is correct.

The primary function of the loop of Henle is in the recovery of water and sodium chloride from the filtrate to produce a small volume of concentrated urine for excretion.

Water is reabsorbed in the descending limb, while electrolytes are actively reabsorbed in the ascending limb.

16. A is correct.

Renal clearance is the amount of liquid filtered out of the blood or the amount of substance cleared per time (i.e., volume/time).

However, the kidney does not entirely remove a substance from the renal plasma flow.

In physiology, clearance is the rate at which waste substances are cleared from the blood (e.g., renal plasma clearance).

Substances have a specific clearance rate that depends on their filtration characteristics (e.g., glomerular filtration, secretion from the peritubular capillaries, and reabsorption from the nephron).

A constant fraction of the substance is eliminated per unit time.

However, the overall clearance is variable because the amount of substance eliminated per unit time changes with the concentration of the substance in the blood.

17. A is correct.

Aldosterone is produced by the adrenal cortex and stimulates the reabsorption of Na^+ from the collecting duct and the secretion of K^+ because aldosterone activates the Na^+/K^+ pumps at the distal convoluted tubule.

Na^+ reabsorption draws H_2O with it, increasing blood volume, elevating blood pressure, and producing concentrated urine.

Aldosterone release is stimulated by angiotensin II (AT), which is influenced by renin (i.e., the renin-angiotensin system).

Vasopressin (ADH; antidiuretic hormone) is secreted by the hypothalamus and stored in the posterior pituitary.

Vasopressin increases H_2O reabsorption by opening water channels in the collecting ducts of the nephron (compared to the indirect action of aldosterone that increases salt reabsorption).

18. B is correct.

Glucose, amino acids, and phosphate are reabsorbed in the proximal convoluted tubule through secondary active transport.

Urea is a waste product that may (or may not) be reabsorbed by the kidney but does not involve active transport.

Reabsorption Site	Reabsorbed nutrient	Comments
Early proximal tubule	Glucose (100%), amino acids (100%), bicarbonate (90%), Na^+, Cl^-, phosphate, H_2O (65%)	PTH inhibits phosphate excretion AT II stimulates Na^+, H_2O, and HCO_3^- reabsorption
Thin descending loop of Henle	H_2O	Reabsorbs via medullary hypertonicity and makes urine hypertonic
Thick ascending loop of Henle	Na^+ (10–20%), K^+, Cl^-; indirectly induces paracellular reabsorption of Mg^{2+}, Ca^{2+}	This region is impermeable to H_2O, and the urine becomes less concentrated as it ascends
Early distal convoluted tubule	Na^+, Cl^-	PTH causes Ca^{2+} reabsorption
Collecting tubules	Na^+ (3–5%), H_2O	Na^+ is reabsorbed in exchange for K^+, and H^+, regulated by aldosterone ADH acts on V2 receptors and inserts aquaporins on the luminal side

19. A is correct.

The proximal tubule of the nephron is divided into an initial convoluted portion and a straight (descending) portion.

The proximal convoluted tubule reabsorbs into the peritubular capillaries approximately two-thirds of the salts (i.e., electrolytes), water, and filtered organic solutes (e.g., glucose and amino acids).

With each topic, reinforce learning by reading review chapters in your *ATI TEAS Science Review* book.

Visit our Amazon store

Notes for active learning

Section II

Life and Physical Sciences

Basic Macromolecules in a Biological System

Chromosomes, Genes, and DNA

Mendel's Laws of Heredity

Basic Atomic Structure

Characteristic Properties of Substances

Changing States of Matter

Chemical Reactions

Basic Macromolecules in a Biological System – Explanations

Answer Key

1: B	11: A	21: B	31: D
2: B	12: B	22: B	32: A
3: B	13: A	23: B	33: C
4: C	14: B	24: C	34: D
5: D	15: A	25: B	35: C
6: A	16: B	26: D	36: C
7: A	17: C	27: A	37: A
8: C	18: B	28: C	38: B
9: C	19: C	29: A	39: D
10: D	20: D	30: C	40: B

1. B is correct.

When plasma glucose levels are low, the body utilizes other energy sources for cellular metabolism.

These sources are used in preferential order: glucose → other carbohydrates → fats → proteins.

These molecules are first converted to glucose or glucose intermediates, which are then degraded in the glycolytic pathway and the Krebs cycle (i.e., citric acid cycle).

Proteins are used last for energy because there is no protein storage in the body.

Catabolism of protein results in muscle wasting and connective tissue breakdown, which is harmful in the long term.

2. B is correct.

The quaternary structure of proteins involves two or more polypeptide chains.

The quaternary structure is maintained between the different polypeptide chains (e.g., 4 chains of 2 α and 2 β in hemoglobin) by hydrophobic interactions and by disulfide bridges between cysteines.

3. B is correct.

The primary structure is the linear sequence of amino acids within the polypeptide or protein.

4. C is correct.

Glycogen is a storage form of a polysaccharide (i.e., carbohydrate) composed of glucose monomers that are highly branched.

The extensive branching provides numerous ends to the molecule to facilitate the rapid hydrolysis (i.e., cleavage and release) of individual glucose monomers when needed *via* a release by epinephrine (i.e., adrenaline).

Glycogen is synthesized in the liver because of high plasma glucose concentrations and stored in muscle cells for release during exercise.

A: glycogenesis involves the synthesis of glycogen.

B: glycogenolysis involves the degradation of glycogen.

D: plants produce starch (i.e., analogous to glycogen) as their storage carbohydrates.

5. D is correct.

DNA and ribozymes of RNA are capable of self-replication.

Some functions of proteins include:

      1) peptide hormones as chemical messengers transported within the blood,

      2) enzymes that catalyze chemical reactions by lowering the energy of activation,

      3) structural proteins for physical support within the cells, tissues, and organs,

      4) transport proteins as carriers of essential materials, and

      5) antibodies of the immune system that bind foreign particles (antigens).

6. A is correct.

Phospholipids are a class of lipids that are a significant cell membrane component, as they can form lipid bilayers.

Phospholipids contain a glycerol backbone, a phosphate group, and a simple organic molecule (e.g., choline).

The 'head' is hydrophilic (attracted to water), while the 'tails' are hydrophobic (repelled by water), and the tails are forced to aggregate (via hydrophobic forces).

The hydrophilic head contains the negatively charged phosphate group and glycerol.

B and C: the hydrophobic tail usually consists of 2 long fatty acid (saturated or unsaturated) hydrocarbon chains.

D: cholesterol is embedded within the lipid bilayer in animals but is absent in plant cell membranes.

7. A is correct.

Osmosis is a particular type of diffusion involving water and is a form of passive transport.

Hypertonic means high solute and low solvent concentrations.

Hypotonic means high solvent and low solute concentrations.

Solvents flow spontaneously from an area of high solvent to an area of low solvent concentration.

During osmosis, water flows from a hypotonic to a hypertonic environment.

8. C is correct.

Like carbohydrates and lipids, proteins contain carbon, hydrogen, oxygen.

Proteins also contain nitrogen and often have sulfur or phosphorus.

Amino acids are the building blocks of proteins, and nitrogen is an essential component of amino acids and urea. Organic nitrogen describes a nitrogen compound originating from a living organism.

9. C is correct.

Lipids are the primary means of food storage in animals, and lipids release more energy per gram (9 kcal/gram) than carbohydrates (4 kcal/gram) or proteins (4 kcal/gram).

Lipids provide insulation and protection against injury as the primary component of adipose (fat) tissue.

A: proteins are mainly composed of amino acids with the elements C, H, O, and N but may also contain S (i.e., sulfur in cysteine).

B: α helices and β pleated sheets are secondary structures of proteins.

D: the C:H:O ratio of carbohydrates is 1:2:1 ($C_nH_{2n}O_n$).

10. D is correct.

Sulfur is found in the amino acid cysteine but is absent in nucleic acids.

The Hershey-Chase (i.e., blender) experiment used radiolabeled molecules of phosphorus (^{32}P for nucleic acids) and sulfur (^{35}S for proteins) to determine whether nucleic acids (phosphorus) or protein (sulfur) carried the genetic information.

Nucleic acids contain the elements C, H, O, N, and P.

Nucleic acids are polymers of nucleotide subunits and encode the information needed by the cell of the organism to synthesize proteins and replicate via cell division.

11. A is correct.

Phospholipids are a class of lipids that are a significant cell membrane component, as they can form lipid bilayers.

Phospholipids contain a glycerol backbone, a phosphate group, and a simple organic molecule (e.g., choline).

The 'head' is *hydrophilic* (attracted to water), while the 'tails' are *hydrophobic* (repelled by water), and the tails are forced to aggregate (via hydrophobic forces).

The hydrophilic head contains the negatively charged phosphate group and glycerol.

B and C: the hydrophobic tail usually has 2 long fatty acids (i.e., saturated or unsaturated) hydrocarbon chains.

D: cholesterol is embedded within the lipid bilayer in animals but is absent in plant cell membranes.

12. B is correct.

Albumins are globular proteins in the circulatory system.

A: carotenoids are organic pigments in the chloroplasts of plants and some other photosynthetic organisms, such as some bacteria and fungi.

Carotenoids are fatty acid-like carbon chains containing conjugated double bonds and sometimes have six-membered carbon rings at each end.

As pigments, carotenoids produce red, yellow, orange, and brown colors in plants and animals.

C: waxes (esters of fatty acids and alcohols) are protective coatings on the skin, fur, leaves of higher plants, and on the exoskeleton cuticle of many insects.

D: steroids (e.g., cholesterol, estrogen) have three fused cyclohexane rings and one fused cyclopentane ring.

13. A is correct.

The primary structure of a protein is the linear sequence of amino acids.

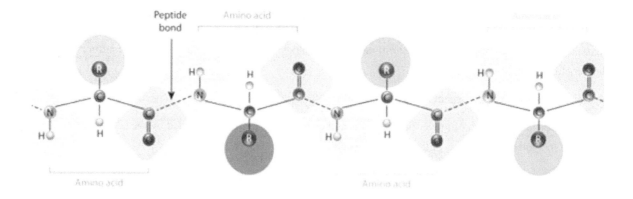

14. B is correct.

All the molecules in the body are divided into four categories.

These biomolecular categories are carbohydrates, lipids, nucleic acids, and proteins.

15. A is correct.

Hormones are substances secreted by a gland and released into the blood to affect a target tissue/organ.

Insulin is a hormone composed of amino acids (i.e., peptide hormones) and a protein molecule.

Insulin is composed of two peptide chains (A chain and B chain).

Two disulfide bonds link the chains, and an additional disulfide is formed within the A chain.

In most species, the A chain consists of 21 amino acids and the B chain – of 30 amino acids.

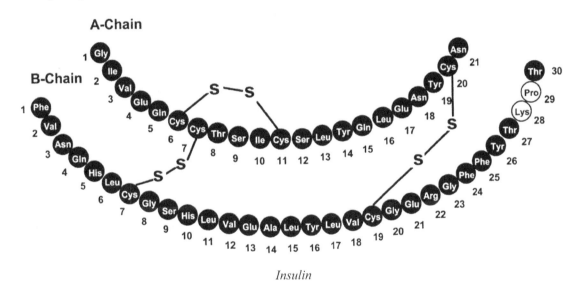

Insulin

Hormones can be lipids, such as steroid derivatives (e.g., testosterone, progesterone, estrogen).

16. B is correct.

The primary structure of a protein is the amino acid sequence formed by covalent peptide linkages.

Hydrogen bonds hold the alpha-helix between every N–H (amino group) and the oxygen of the C=O (carbonyl) in the next turn of the helix; four amino acids along the chain.

The typical alpha helix (shown below) is about 11 amino acids long.

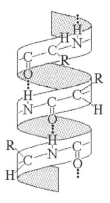

The other type of secondary structure is the beta-pleated sheet.

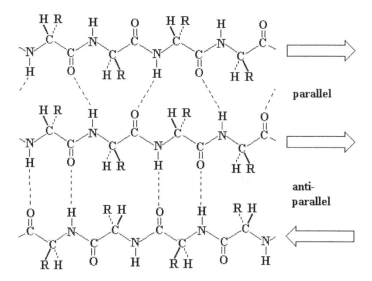

Beta pleated sheets are either parallel or *anti*parallel (i.e., reference to the amino terminus).

17. C is correct.

The primary structure of a protein is the amino acid sequence formed by covalent peptide linkages.

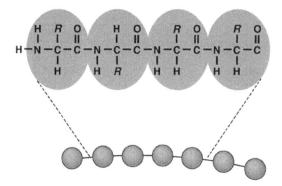

The amino acids (circles) are joined by covalent peptide bonds (lines)

A: only proteins containing more than one peptide subunit have a quaternary structure.

B: proteins are denatured by heating, and they lose their 3D conformation above 35-40 °C.

D: many proteins contain more than one peptide chain (i.e., have quaternary structure).

18. B is correct.

Amino acids are the building blocks of proteins.

Humans need 20 amino acids (see diagram below), some are made by the body (i.e., nonessential), and others must be obtained from the diet (i.e., essential nutrients).

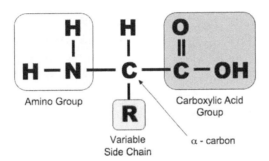

Amino acids contain an amine group, a carboxylic acid, an α-carbon, and an R group

The following table is shown *not* for memorization but for identifying characteristics (e.g., polar, nonpolar) of the side chains. Note: the following amino acids illustrate similarities and differences; they are not to be memorized.

Nonpolar side chains

Glycine (G)
Gly

Alanine (A)
Ala

Valine (V)
Val

Leucine (L)
Leu

Isoleucine (I)
Ile

Methionine (M)
Met

Phenylalanine (F)
Phe

Tryptophan (W)
Trp

Proline (P)
Pro

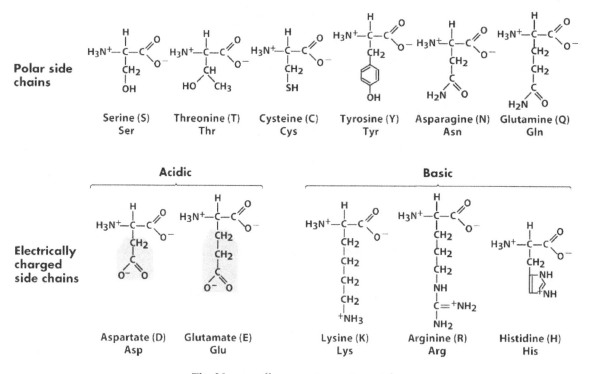

The 20 naturally occurring amino acids

19. C is correct.

Amino acids are the basic building blocks for proteins.

Two amino acids (dimer) with peptide bonds indicated by arrows

The peptide bond is rigid due to the resonance hybrids involving the lone pair of electrons on nitrogen, forming a double bond to the carbonyl carbon (and oxygen develops a negative formal charge).

20. D is correct.

Collagen is a protein that supports hair, nails, and skin. It is composed of a triple helix, and the most abundant amino acids in collagen include glycine, proline, alanine, and glutamic acid.

Much of the excess protein that is consumed in an animal's diet is used to synthesize collagen.

21. B is correct.

The secondary structure for proteins involves localized bonding.

The most critical intermolecular interaction is hydrogen bonding, responsible for maintaining both the alpha-helix and beta-pleated (parallel and antiparallel) sheet structures.

Alpha helix structure with hydrogen bonding shown as dotted lines

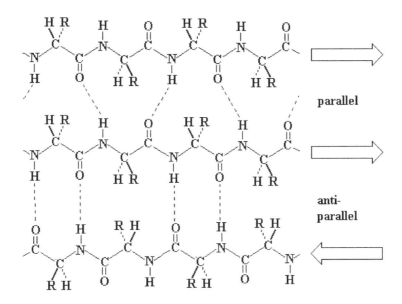

Beta-pleated sheets (parallel and antiparallel) with hydrogen bonding shown

22. B is correct.

Essential amino acids are obtained from the diet.

Nonessential amino acids can be synthesized by the body and do not need to be consumed.

Semi-essential (conditionally essential) amino acids can be synthesized within the body under special physiological conditions (e.g., in premature infants, under severe catabolic distress).

The nine essential amino acids for humans are histidine, isoleucine, leucine, lysine, methionine, phenylalanine, threonine, tryptophan, and valine.

The six conditionally essential amino acids are arginine, cysteine, glycine, glutamine, proline, and tyrosine.

The five nonessential amino acids are alanine, aspartic acid, asparagine, glutamic acid, and serine.

23. B is correct.

Proteins are biological macromolecules composed of amino acids bonded to each other with peptide (amide) bonds.

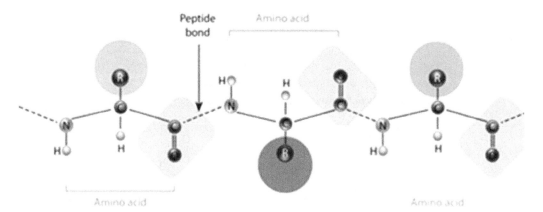

Three amino acids residues of nascent (i.e., growing) polypeptide

24. C is correct.

Cholesterol is a lipid molecule known as a steroid compound.

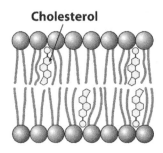

The fused ring structure of steroid molecules makes them rigid and has fewer degrees of motion due to the few conformations available for cyclic molecules *vs.* acyclic molecules.

Molecules, such as phospholipids, lack fused-ring structures, and they exist as straight-chained molecules.

Therefore, cholesterol in the cell membrane acts as a bidirectional regulator of membrane fluidity: at high temperatures, it stabilizes the membrane and raises its melting point, whereas, at low temperatures, it intercalates between the phospholipids and prevents them from clustering and stiffening.

25. B is correct.

Triglycerides (or triacylglycerides) are used for storage and exist in the adipose tissue of animals.

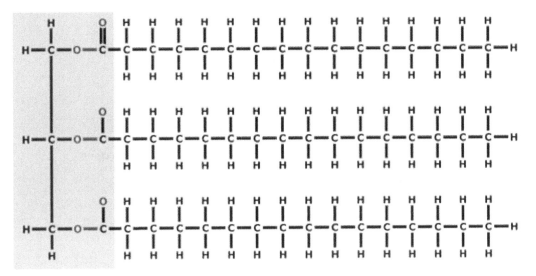

Triglyceride (glycerol and three saturated fatty acid chains)

Phospholipids are the largest component of semi-permeable cell membranes.

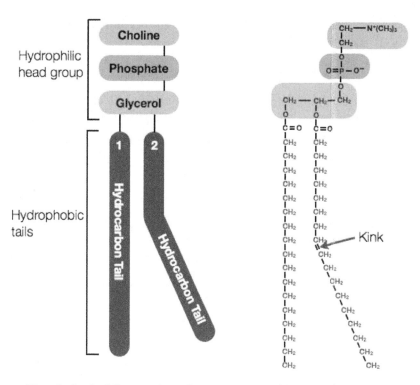

Phospholipids differ mainly in the composition of the polar head region

Steroids (see below) are lipids used for cell-signaling.

Cholesterol is the precursor molecule for several steroid hormones (e.g., progesterone, aldosterone)

26. D is correct.

Estradiol (shown below) is a steroid hormone derived from cholesterol.

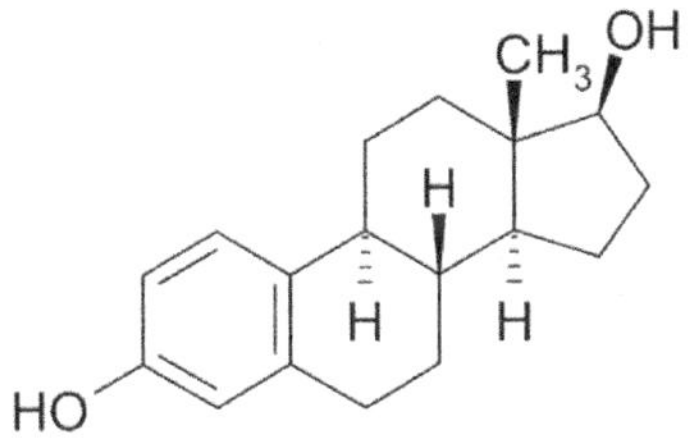

Cholesterol is a lipid made up of four fused rings. Three of the fused rings are six-membered rings, and the fourth ring is five-membered.

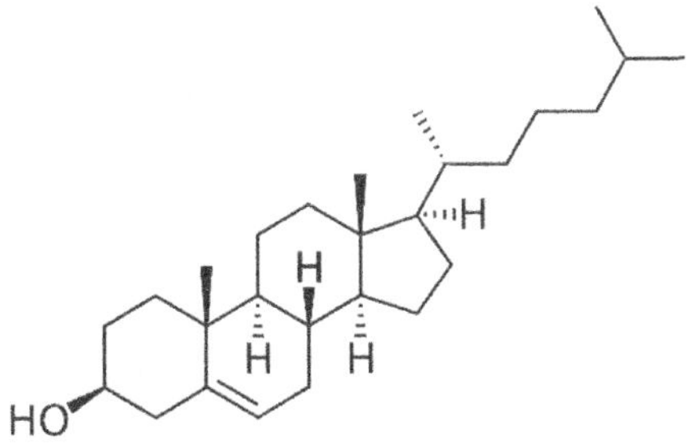

Cholesterol is a steroid, which makes up one of two types of lipid molecules.

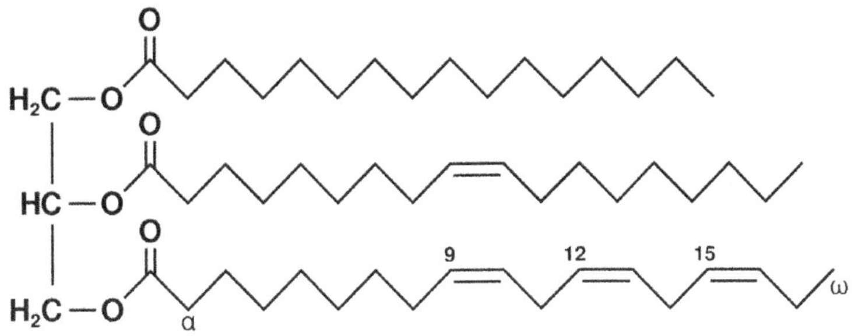

A triglyceride (i.e., glycerol backbone with three fatty acid chains) is the other type of lipid.

27. A is correct.

For unsaturated fats, the molecules are more likely to exist as oils (i.e., liquids) at room temperature.

Saturated fats tend to be solid at room temperature because the reduced forms of these molecules have better stacking properties, which allow them to form solid states.

28. C is correct.

Triacylglycerols are molecules composed of a glycerol substructure and three fatty acids condensed to form a triester.

29. A is correct.

Dietary triglycerides are composed of glycerol and three fatty acids.

The hydrolysis of triglycerides yields glycerol and three fatty acid chains.

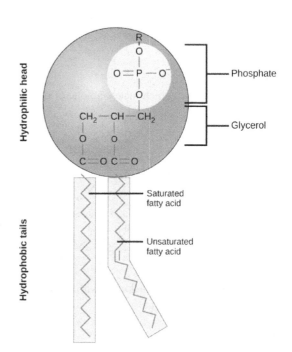

Hydrolysis of a triglyceride

30. C is correct.

Phospholipids are important lipids that make up the bilayer structure of the membranes of cells, organelles, and other enclosed cellular structures.

Phospholipids are composed of two (same or different) fatty acid molecules, a phosphate group, and a glycerol backbone.

The phospholipid contains a hydrophobic (i.e., fatty acid tail) region and a hydrophilic (polar head) region.

The hydrophobic regions point toward each other in the membrane bilayer while the polar heads point towards the inside (i.e., cytosolic) or outside (i.e., extracellular) sides of the bilayer.

31. D is correct.

Fat can be produced from glucose, but glucose is not produced from animal fat.

The excess glucose consumption in the body can lead to increased levels of fat in the body.

32. A is correct.

Lactose is a disaccharide composed of glucose and galactose.

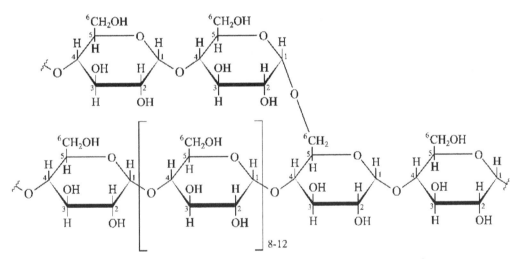

The glycosidic linkage in lactose is a $\beta(1\rightarrow4)$ linkage.

33. C is correct.

Glycogen is a glucose polymer that functions as the energy store of carbohydrates in animal cells (plants use starch).

Glycogen is common in the liver, muscle, and red blood cells.

Glycogen is a large biomolecule consisting of repeating glucose subunits

34. D is correct.

Carbohydrates can be described as organic compounds containing carbon, hydrogen, and oxygen.

The general molecular formula varies by carbohydrate, but many examples have the formula of $C_nH_{2n}O_n$.

35. C is correct.

The "di" prefix in the name suggests that there are two smaller subunits. Monosaccharides are linked through glycosidic (i.e., oxygen bonded to two ethers) functional groups.

Lactose is a disaccharide formed by a $\beta(1 \rightarrow 4)$ linkage between galactose and glucose.

36. C is correct.

Lipids are the primary means of food storage in animals, and lipids release more energy per gram (9 kcal/gram) than carbohydrates (4 kcal/gram) or proteins (4 kcal/gram). Lipids provide insulation and protection against injury as the major component of adipose (fat) tissue.

A: proteins are mainly composed of amino acids with the elements C, H, O, and N but may also contain S (i.e., sulfur in cysteine).

B: α helices and β pleated sheets are secondary structures of proteins.

D: the C:H:O ratio of carbohydrates is 1:2:1 ($C_nH_{2n}O_n$).

37. A is correct.

Carbohydrates (e.g., glucose, fructose, lactose, maltose) and proteins provide 4 calories per gram (i.e. 4 kcal/gram). Fats (i.e., lipids) are energy-dense and provide 9 calories per gram.

38. B is correct.

The proper digestion of macromolecules is required for adequate absorption of nutrients out of the small intestine.

Carbohydrates must be broken down into monosaccharides like glucose, fructose, and galactose.

Lactose is a disaccharide of glucose and galactose; sucrose is a disaccharide of glucose and fructose; maltose is a disaccharide of two glucose units. Disaccharide digestion into monomers occurs at the intestinal brush border of the small intestine via enzymes like lactase, sucrase, and maltase.

A: amino acids are the monomers of proteins. Proteins must be hydrolyzed into mono-, di-, or tri-peptides for absorption in the duodenum of the small intestine.

D: lipids are degraded into free fatty acids and glycerol for absorption in the small intestine.

39. D is correct.

Amino acids are the monomers that comprise proteins.

Nucleotides are comprised of a nitrogenous base (i.e., adenosine, cytosine, guanine, and thymine or uracil), a phosphate group, and a five-carbon sugar (i.e., ribose for RNA or deoxyribose for DNA).

40. B is correct.

Four common nucleotides are in DNA molecules: adenine (A), cytosine (C), guanine (G) and thymine (T)

Four common nucleotides are in RNA molecules:

adenine (A), cytosine (C), guanine (G) and uracil (U)

Notes for active learning

Chromosomes, Genes, DNA – Explanations

Answer Key

1: D	11: A	21: D	31: C	41: C
2: C	12: D	22: C	32: D	
3: D	13: B	23: B	33: D	
4: A	14: B	24: D	34: A	
5: B	15: B	25: C	35: D	
6: C	16: B	26: A	36: B	
7: B	17: D	27: C	37: A	
8: B	18: B	28: B	38: B	
9: A	19: B	29: A	39: D	
10: B	20: D	30: A	40: C	

1. D is correct.

Histones are basic (i.e., positively charged) proteins associated with DNA within the nucleus to condense it into chromatin.

Nuclear DNA does not appear in free linear strands; instead, it is highly condensed and wrapped around histones to fit inside the nucleus and form chromosomes.

Three major types of RNA involved in gene expression:

1) messenger RNA (mRNA) molecules carry the coding sequences (i.e., "blueprints") for protein synthesis and are called transcripts;

2) ribosomal RNA (rRNA) forms the core of a cell's ribosomes (i.e., macromolecular cellular particles where protein synthesis takes place);

3) transfer RNA (tRNA) molecules transport amino acids (i.e., protein building blocks) to the ribosomes during protein synthesis.

2. C is correct.

A tumor suppressor gene is a gene that protects a cell from the path to cancer.

When this gene mutates to cause a loss (or reduction) in its function, the cell can progress to cancer, usually in combination with other genetic changes.

The loss of these tumor suppressor genes may be even more critical than proto-oncogene/activation to form many kinds of human cancer cells.

Apoptosis is the process of programmed cell death (PCD) that may occur in multicellular organisms.

Biochemical events lead to characteristic cell changes (morphology), including blebbing, cell shrinkage, nuclear fragmentation, chromatin condensation, chromosomal DNA fragmentation, and death.

In contrast to necrosis (i.e., traumatic cell death that results from acute cellular injury), apoptosis confers advantages during an organism's lifecycle.

For example, the separation of fingers and toes in a developing human embryo occurs because cells between the digits undergo apoptosis.

Unlike necrosis, apoptosis produces cell fragments called apoptotic bodies that phagocytic cells can engulf and quickly remove before the contents of the cell can spill out onto surrounding cells and cause damage.

A: telomerase is an enzyme that adds DNA sequence repeats (i.e., TTAGGG) to the 3' end of DNA strands in the telomere regions at the ends of eukaryotic chromosomes.

This region of repeated nucleotides called telomeres contains noncoding DNA and hinders the loss of essential DNA from chromosome ends.

When the chromosome is replicated during the S phase, 100–200 nucleotides are lost without damage to the coding region of the DNA.

Telomerase is a reverse transcriptase that carries its RNA molecule used as a template when it elongates telomeres shortened after each replication cycle.

Embryonic stem cells express telomerase, which allows them to divide repeatedly.

In adults, telomerase is highly expressed in cells that regularly divide (e.g., male germ cells, lymphocytes, and specific adult stem cells). In contrast, telomerase is not expressed in most adult somatic cells.

3. D is correct.

There are 4 different nucleotides (adenine, cytosine, guanine, and thymine/uracil).

Each codon is composed of 3 nucleotides, and therefore there must be 64 (4^3) possible variations of codons to encode for the 20 amino acids.

The genetic code is degenerate (or *redundant*) because several codons encode for the same amino acid.

Sixty-one codons encode for amino acids, and 3 stop codons terminate translation.

5. B is correct.

Chromosomes replicate during the synthesis (S) phase of interphase.

6. C is correct.

The replication fork opens by disrupting hydrogen bonds between complementary nucleotide base pairs (e.g., A bonded to T; C bonded to G).

Gyrase cuts one of the strands of the DNA backbone and relaxes the positive supercoil that accumulates as helicase separates the two strands of DNA.

Ligase seals the backbone of DNA (i.e., joins the Okazaki fragments) by forming phosphodiester bonds between deoxynucleotides in DNA.

7. B is correct.

The percent of adenine cannot be determined because RNA is a single-stranded molecule.

The base-pairing rules of DNA (i.e., Chargaff's rule) determining the possibility for double-stranded DNA do not apply to single-stranded RNA.

8. B is correct.

Adenosine (A) bonds with thymine (T) with two hydrogen bonds; guanine (G) bonds with cytosine (C) with three hydrogen bonds.

9. A is correct.

The addition of a 3' poly-A tail to mRNA (not proteins) is a *post-transcription* event.

The *post transcription* events include adding a 5' cap and splicing of exons (or removing introns) from the RNA molecule.

10. B is correct.

The *central dogma* of molecular biology refers to the direction of genetic information flow within a living system.

The *central dogma* states that DNA is transcribed into RNA, and then RNA is translated into protein:

DNA → RNA → protein

The central dogma of molecular biology was disrupted by the discovery of retroviruses that have RNA genomes using reverse transcriptase to make a copy of their RNA into DNA within the infected cell.

11. A is correct.

Heterochromatin is a tightly packed form of DNA.

Euchromatin refers to uncoiled regions of DNA actively engaged in gene expression because RNA polymerase binds to the relaxed region of DNA.

Heterochromatin mainly consists of genetically inactive satellite sequences (i.e., tandem repeats of noncoding DNA).

Centromeres and telomeres are heterochromatic (i.e., tightly coiled DNA), as is the Barr body of the second, inactivated X-chromosome in females.

12. D is correct.

The nucleolus is the organelle within the nucleus responsible for the synthesis of ribosomal RNA (rRNA).

A: the Golgi apparatus is the organelle responsible for processing, packaging, and distribution of proteins.

B: lysosomes are organelles with low pH that function to digest intracellular molecules.

C: mitochondrion is the organelle, bound by a double membrane, where the reactions of the Krebs (TCA) cycle, electron transport, and oxidative phosphorylation occur.

13. B is correct.

A polynucleotide (e.g., DNA) is the only macromolecule (i.e., nucleic acids, proteins, lipids, and carbohydrates) repaired rather than degraded. DNA repair is essential for maintaining cell function and is performed by biological repair systems (e.g., p53 tumor repressor protein).

Uncontrolled cell growth via disruption to the cell cycle regulation occurs if somatic cell mutations are not repaired.

14. B is correct.

A codon is a three-nucleotide segment of an mRNA molecule that hybridizes (via complementary base pairing) with the appropriate anticodon on the tRNA to encode for one amino acid in a polypeptide chain during protein synthesis.

The tRNA molecule interacts with the mRNA codon after the ribosomal complex binds to the mRNA.

A: tRNA molecule interacts with the mRNA codon after (not before) the mRNA is bound to the ribosomal complex.

C: translation involves the conversion of mRNA into protein.

D: operon regulates the transcription of genes into mRNA and is not involved in translating mRNA into proteins.

15. A is correct.

Ligase is an enzyme used by the cell during DNA replication (and other biochemical processes) that catalyzes the joining of two large molecules (e.g., DNA nucleotides) by forming a new chemical bond.

The newly formed bond is *via* a condensation reaction (joining) and usually involves dehydration with the loss of H_2O when the molecules (e.g., DNA, amino acids) are linked.

16. B is correct.

Gametes are formed via meiosis and are double-stranded haploids. A single chromosome consists of two hydrogen-bonded complementary DNA strands.

17. D is correct.

Genetic recombination is when two DNA strand molecules exchange genetic information (i.e., the base composition within the nucleotides), which results in new combinations of alleles (i.e., alternative forms of genes).

In eukaryotes, the natural process of genetic recombination during meiosis (i.e., the formation of gametes – eggs and sperm) results in genetic information passed to progeny.

Genetic recombination in eukaryotes involves pairing homologous chromosomes (i.e., a set of maternal and paternal chromosomes), which may involve nucleotide exchange between the chromosomes.

The information exchange may occur without physical exchange (a section of genetic material is copied – duplicated – without a change in the donating chromosome) or by the breaking and rejoining of the DNA strands (i.e., forming new molecules of DNA).

Mitosis may involve recombination, where two sister chromosomes form after DNA replication.

In general, new combinations of alleles are not produced because the sister chromosomes are usually identical.

For meiosis and mitosis, recombination occurs between similar DNA molecules (homologous chromosomes or sister chromatids, respectively).

In meiosis, non-sister (i.e., same parent) homologous chromosomes pair with each other, and recombination often occurs between non-sister homologs.

For both somatic cells (i.e., undergo mitosis) and gametes (i.e., undergo meiosis), recombination between homologous chromosomes or sister chromatids is a common DNA repair mechanism.

18. B is correct.

The pseudoautosomal regions get their name because genes within them are inherited like autosomal genes.

The function of these pseudoautosomal regions is that they allow the X and Y chromosomes to pair and properly segregate during meiosis in males.

Males have two copies of these genes: one in the pseudoautosomal region of their Y chromosome, the other in the corresponding portion of their X chromosome.

Typical females have two copies of pseudoautosomal genes, as each of their two X chromosomes contains a pseudoautosomal region.

Crossing over (during prophase I) between the X and Y chromosomes is usually restricted to the pseudoautosomal regions.

Thus, pseudoautosomal genes exhibit an autosomal, rather than sex-linked, pattern of inheritance.

Females can inherit an allele initially present on their father's Y chromosome, and males can inherit an allele initially present on the X chromosome of their father.

19. B is correct.

A primary spermatocyte has completed the synthesis (S) phase of interphase but has not completed the first meiotic division and is still diploid (2N) with 46 chromosomes (i.e., 23 pairs).

20. D is correct.

Klinefelter syndrome describes the set of symptoms resulting from additional X genetic material in males.

A: Turner syndrome describes the condition in females resulting from a single X (monosomy X) chromosome.

B: XYY syndrome is a genetic condition in which a human male has an extra male (Y) chromosome, giving him a total of 47 chromosomes instead of 46. 47, XYY is not inherited but usually occurs during the formation of sperm cells.

A nondisjunction error during anaphase II (of meiosis II) results in sperm cells with an extra copy of the Y chromosome.

If one of these atypical sperm cells contributes to the genetic makeup, the child will have an extra Y chromosome in each somatic cell.

C: Triple X syndrome is not inherited but usually occurs during the formation of gametes (e.g., ovum and sperm) because of nondisjunction in cell division that results in reproductive cells with additional chromosomes.

An error in cell division (nondisjunction) can result in gametes with additional chromosomes.

An egg or a sperm may gain an extra X chromosome as a result of nondisjunction, and if one of these gametes contributes to the genetic makeup of the zygote, the child will have an extra X chromosome in each cell.

21. D is correct.

DNA replication occurs during the synthesis (S) phase of interphase (i.e., G1, S, G2) to form sister chromatids joined by the centromere.

Replication occurs during the S phase of the cell cycle.

However, transcription (in the nucleus) and translation (in the cytoplasm) still occur during the S phase.

22. C is correct.

X-linked dominance is a mode of inheritance whereby a dominant gene is carried on the X chromosome.

X-linked dominant is less common than X-linked recessive.

For X-linked dominant inheritance, one copy of the allele is sufficient to cause the disorder inherited from a parent who has the disorder.

X-linked dominant traits do not necessarily affect males more than females (unlike X-linked recessive traits).

An affected father will give rise to all affected daughters, but no affected sons will be affected (unless the mother is also affected).

23. B is correct.

Meiosis is a particular process of cell division that occurs in sexually reproducing eukaryotes (animals, plants, and fungi), whereby the chromosome number is reduced by half, resulting in four genetically distinct haploid daughters.

In meiosis, DNA replication is followed by two rounds of cell division to produce four cells.

The two rounds of this meiotic division are Meiosis I and Meiosis II.

Meiosis I is known as *reductive division*, as the cells are reduced diploid to haploid.

Meiosis II (only G phase occurs) is known as *equational division*, as the cells begin and end as haploid cells.

24. D is correct.

Point mutations occur when a single nucleotide base (A, C, G, T) is substituted by another.

A silent mutation is a point mutation that either 1) occurs in a noncoding region or 2) does not change the amino acid sequence due to the degeneracy of the genetic code.

A frameshift mutation is either an insertion or deletion of some nucleotides.

These mutations have severe effects on the coded protein since nucleotides are series of triplets.

The addition or loss of nucleotides (except in multiples of three) changes the reading frame of the mRNA and often gives rise to premature polypeptide termination (i.e., nonsense mutation).

Even without a consequential frameshift mutation, insertions or deletions are often severe.

A missense mutation results from the insertion of a single nucleotide that changes the amino acid sequence of the specified polypeptide.

25. C is correct.

The DNA damage checkpoint is a signal transduction pathway that blocks cell cycle progression in G1, G2, and metaphase and slows down the rate of S phase progression when DNA is damaged.

It leads to a pause in the cell cycle, allowing the cell time to repair the damage before dividing.

Cell cycle progression:

G1 → S → G2 → prophase → metaphase → anaphase → telophase

Interphase   Mitosis (PMAT)

26. A is correct.

G-C base pairs are linked in the double helix by three hydrogen bonds.

Two hydrogen bonds join A-T base pairs.

Therefore, it takes more energy to separate G-C base pairs.

The less G-C rich a piece of double-stranded DNA is, the less energy is required to separate (i.e., denature) the two strands of the double helix.

Because of complementary base pairing, double-stranded DNA has equal quantities of G and C (and of A and T).

This is *Chargaff's rule*.

27. C is correct.

During meiosis I, homologous chromosomes separate. During meiosis II, sister chromatids (identical copies, except for recombination) separate.

In Klinefelter syndrome (XXY karyotype), sperm to cause the defect must contain an X and Y chromosome.

X and Y would be "homologous chromosomes" and would typically separate during meiosis I.

Failure to do so could create a sperm containing both an X and a Y, which causes Klinefelter syndrome.

Anaphase is when the centromere splits, and the homologous chromosomes / sister chromatids are drawn away (via spindle fibers) from each other toward opposite sides of the two cells.

The separation of homologous chromosomes occurs during anaphase I, while the separation of sister chromatids occurs during anaphase II.

Turner's syndrome is observed in females due to the single X karyotype (single X chromosome and no Y).

28. B is correct.

Only human gametes formed during meiosis are cells with a single copy (1N) of the genome.

Cells have a single unreplicated copy (i.e., devoid of a sister chromatid) after the second meiotic division.

29. A is correct.

During transcription, the two nucleic acid strands of DNA dissociate, and mRNA is synthesized (i.e., transcription) using the nitrogen bases of DNA as a template.

Therefore, the mRNA strand is a complementary strand to the DNA strand.

The mRNA then exits the nucleus to be used as a template for producing proteins (i.e., translation).

30. A is correct.

When DNA is replicated in the cell, one of the strands of DNA acts as a template for a new strand synthesized as the replication fork opens.

This continuously synthesized strand is known as the leading strand and, when combined with one of the old strands of DNA, makes up one new DNA molecule.

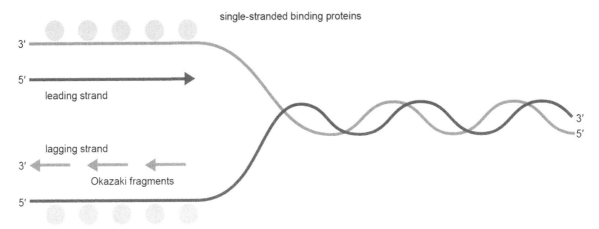

Furthermore, an additional DNA molecule is created in the process, as the other parent strand acts as a template for its complementary strand.

This lagging strand is made up of smaller segments called Okazaki fragments (about 150-200 nucleotides long).

Okazaki fragments are combined with the enzyme DNA ligase.

31. C is correct.

DNA molecules hold the genetic information of organisms.

RNA molecules are synthesized from the DNA strand to make proteins for the cell.

Genes are the sections of DNA responsible for the synthesis of proteins in cells.

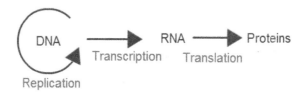

Central dogma of molecular biology (designates information flow)

32. D is correct.

There are five known nucleotides, four of which appear in DNA.

These nucleotides are cytosine, guanine, adenine, and thymine.

In RNA molecules, the thymine is replaced with another pyrimidine nucleotide known as uracil.

Nucleotides consisting of a phosphate group (note the negative charge on oxygens), deoxyribose sugar (lack a 2'hydroxyl) and a nitrogenous base (adenine, cytosine, guanine or thymine).

33. D is correct.

DNA	DNA	mRNA	tRNA
A	T	A	U
C	G	C	G
G	C	G	C
T	A	U	A

Complementary base pairing for nucleotides

DNA → DNA (replication); DNA → RNA (transcription); RNA → protein (translation)

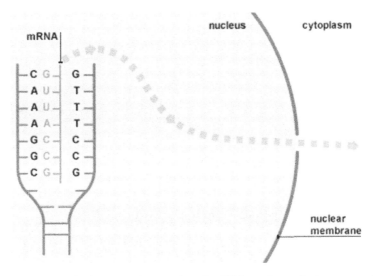

Adenosine (left) and uracil (replaces thymine in RNA)

A single strand of DNA is the template for RNA synthesis during transcription

The mRNA (after processing) is translocated to the cytoplasm for translation to proteins.

34. A is correct.

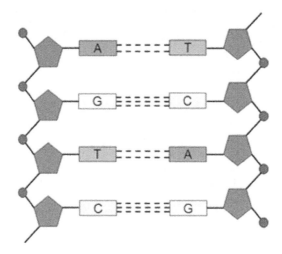

Double-stranded DNA with two hydrogen bonds between A=T and three hydrogen bonds between C≡G.

The backbone is comprised of deoxyribose sugar and phosphates (shown as circles between the pentose sugars).

35. D is correct.

Identical copies of DNA are necessary for cell division; these cells are known as daughter cells.

When the daughter strand is synthesized, a complementary nitrogenous base containing nucleotides (A↔T and C↔G) is incorporated into the growing strand.

Replication (i.e., synthesis of DNA) occurs during the S phase (i.e., within interphase) of the cell cycle.

36. B is correct.

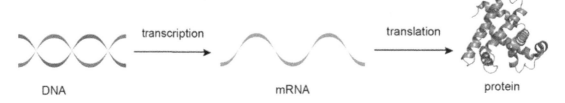

Central dogma of molecule biology: DNA → RNA → protein

tRNA and ribosomes are used to make peptide chains from mRNA.

Nucleotide triplets known as codons are combined with a complementary tRNA (i.e., containing the anticodon that is complementary in base pairing with the codon of the mRNA).

Each tRNA brings an appropriate (i.e., anticodon ↔ amino acid) to the growing polypeptide during translation.

The amino acid residues are combined in the order of the codon sequence.

37. A is correct.

Three nucleotides are combined to make a codon or anticodon required for translation.

A larger segment of DNA is called a gene, and sections of different genes make up nucleic acid strands.

Two single strands of DNA are used to make one DNA double helix.

38. B is correct.

Replication:

DNA → DNA during the S phase of the cell cycle.

A: translation is the process of synthesizing proteins from mRNA.

C: transcription is the process of synthesizing mRNA from DNA.

D: complementation is observed in genetics when two organisms with different homozygous recessive mutations produce the same mutant phenotype (e.g., thorax differences in *Drosophila* flies), when mated or crossed, produce offspring with the wild-type phenotype.

Complementation occurs if the mutations are in different genes.

Each organism's genome supplies the wild-type allele as the *complement* of the mutated allele of the other. Since the mutations are recessive, the offspring display the wild-type phenotype.

Complementation (i.e., *cis/trans*) test determines whether the mutations are in different (*trans*) genes.

39. D is correct.

Central dogma of molecular biology: DNA → RNA → protein

DNA → RNA is known as transcription.

RNA → protein is known as translation.

DNA is the nucleic acid biomolecule that can give rise to other nucleic acids and proteins.

DNA strands are synthesized from parental DNA strands during replication.

40. C is correct.

The peptide chain is assembled depending on the amino acid residue order, dictated by the mRNA sequence.

rRNA is the nucleic acid that comprises the ribosome used during translation (conversion of the codon into a corresponding amino acid in the growing polypeptide chains of the nascent protein).

Each codon of RNA has a corresponding anticodon located on the tRNA.

tRNA molecules have the 3-nucleotide sequence of the anticodon and the appropriate amino acid at its 3' end corresponding to the anticodon.

The genetic code is the language for converting DNA (i.e., nucleotides) to proteins (i.e., amino acids).

DNA → mRNA → protein

> DNA to mRNA is transcription.

> mRNA to protein is translation.

There are 20 naturally occurring amino acids.

There is one start codon (i.e., methionine) and three stop codons (containing releasing factors that dissociate the ribosome).

41. C is correct.

DNA (deoxyribonucleic acid) is a long biological molecule composed of smaller units called nucleotides (i.e., sugar, phosphate, and base).

The sugar is deoxyribose (compared to ribose for RNA), and the bases are either adenine, cytosine, guanine, and thymine (with uracil replacing thymine in RNA).

The strands that these nucleotides make up are called nucleic acids.

Notes for active learning

Notes for active learning

Mendel's Laws of Heredity – Explanations

Answer Key

1: B	11: D	21: D
2: A	12: A	22: D
3: B	13: C	23: A
4: C	14: A	24: A
5: B	15: C	25: D
6: C	16: D	
7: B	17: D	
8: D	18: C	
9: D	19: D	
10: B	20: C	

1. B is correct.

Only human gametes formed during meiosis have a single copy (1N) of the genome.

Cells have a single unreplicated copy (i.e., devoid of a sister chromatid) after the second meiotic division.

2. A is correct.

Centrioles are the organizational sites for microtubules (i.e., spindle fibers) that assemble during cell division (e.g., mitosis and meiosis).

The four phases of mitosis are prophase, metaphase, anaphase, and telophase, followed by cytokinesis.

Cytokinesis physically divides the cell into two identical daughter cells.

The condensed (heterochromatin) chromosomes are aligned along the equatorial plane in mitotic metaphase before the centromere (i.e., heterochromatin region on the DNA) splits.

The two sister chromosomes migrate to the respective poles of the cell.

3. B is correct.

For a recessive trait to appear in a phenotype of an offspring (e.g., long hair), offspring inherit a recessive allele (Mendel called it *traits*) from each parent (i.e., two copies of the recessive gene).

The short-haired parent carries one copy (i.e., heterozygous) of the recessive long-haired allele (or *gene*) passed to some offspring.

Combined with the second copy from the other long-haired parent, it produced the long-haired offspring.

4. C is correct.

Eye color is sex-linked in *Drosophila*.

Determine the phenotype of the parents.

A red-eyed fly with red-eyed and sepia-eyed parents must be heterozygous because a sepia-eyed parent only contributes to the recessive sepia allele.

When the heterozygous (Rr) red-eyed fly is crossed with a homozygous recessive (rr) sepia-eyed fly, ½ the offspring are red-eyed (Rr) because of the dominant (red) allele from the heterozygous fly.

The Punnett square is:

Red eyed parent

	R	r
r	Rr (red)	rr (sepia)
r	Rr (red)	rr (sepia)

Sepia eyed Parent

Since the question does not assign the gender to the sepia and red-eyed parents, the Punnett squares for two possible combinations for sex-linked traits are:

Red-eyed female (♀)

	R	r
r	Rr (red)	rr (sepia)
y	Ry (red)	ry (sepia)

Sepia eyed male (♂)

Red-eyed male (♂)

	R	y
r	Rr (red)	ry (sepia)
r	Rr (red)	ry (sepia)

Sepia eyed female (♀)

5. B is correct.

Hardy-Weinberg law states that the gene ratios (P + Q =1) and the allelic frequencies ($p^2 + 2pq + q^2 = 1$) remain constant between generations in a population that is not evolving.

The Hardy-Weinberg law requires five criteria: 1) a large population, 2) random mating, 3) no gene flow, 4) no mutations, and 5) no selection.

These conditions are required for the gene frequency to remain constant.

If all of the criteria are met, the gene frequencies remain constant.

If one or more of these criteria are not met, the gene frequencies (and allele frequencies) change and evolution occurs.

6. C is correct.

The cross of spherical-seeded and wrinkled-seeded pea plants in Mendel's experiment inherited alleles (or *gene variants*) from both parents.

However, only spherical-seeded plants resulted from the cross.

The wrinkled-seed gene is a recessive allele compared to the spherical-seed (i.e., dominant gene).

A dominant gene is a gene variant, which for many reasons, is expressed more strongly than other variants (or *alleles*) of the gene (i.e., recessive) present.

7. B is correct.

Notation 2N indicates that a given cell line is diploid, two homologous versions of each chromosome.

Human somatic cells are diploid and have 23 different chromosome pairs (N = 23) for 46 chromosomes (2N = 46).

Gamete cells are haploid (i.e., 1N).

Mitosis is the mode of cell division used by somatic cells, which results in two diploid daughter cells genetically identical to the diploid parent cell.

8. D is correct.

The degree of genetic linkage measures the physical distance of two genes that are on the same chromosome.

The probability of a crossover and corresponding exchange between gene loci (location on the chromosome) is generally directly proportional to the distance between the loci.

Pairs of genes that are far apart from each other on a chromosome have a higher probability of being separated during crossover than genes physically close.

Thus, the frequency of genetic recombination between two genes is related to the distance between them.

Recombination frequencies can be used to construct a genetic map.

One map unit (Morgan units) is defined as a 1 percent recombinant frequency.

Recombination frequencies are roughly additive but merely an approximation for small percentages.

The percentage of recombinants cannot exceed 50%, which results when the two genes are at the opposite ends of the same chromosome.

In this situation, a crossover event results in an exchange of genes.

However, only an odd number of crossover events (a 50/50 chance between an even and odd number of crossover events) results in a recombinant product.

9. D is correct.

From Mendel's law of independent assortment, the probability of a cross resulting in a particular genotype is equal to the *product* of the individual probabilities.

This cross involves two heterozygous individuals for the three genes (A, B, and C) to produce an offspring that is homozygous dominant for each trait.

Both parents are heterozygous for A, genotype = Aa.

The ratio of their offspring = 1/4 AA, 1/2 Aa, and 1/4 aa; typical 1:2:1 ratio for heterozygous crosses.

Both parents are heterozygous for genes B and C; the probability of their offspring being BB is 1/4, and CC is 1/4.

Therefore, the probability that a particular offspring will have the genotype AABBCC.

AABBCC = the product of the individual probabilities: $1/4 \times 1/4 \times 1/4 = 1/64$.

10. B is correct.

The basic laws of inheritance explain the patterns of disease transmission.

The inheritance patterns of single-gene diseases are referred to as "Mendelian" after Gregor Mendel, who first observed the different patterns of gene segregation for specific traits of garden peas.

Mendel calculated probabilities of trait recurrence in the next generations.

Most genes have one or more versions (alleles) because of mutations or polymorphisms.

Individuals can carry a normal allele, mutant or rare allele, depending on the impact of the mutation/polymorphism and the frequency of the allele within a population.

Single-gene diseases are usually inherited in one of several patterns depending on the location of the gene and whether one or two normal copies of the gene are needed for the disease to manifest (i.e., affected individual).

The expression of the mutated allele is characterized as dominant, co-dominant, or recessive.

The five basic patterns of inheritance for single-gene diseases:

Autosomal dominant:

every affected person has an affected parent

manifests in every generation

Autosomal recessive:

both parents of an affected person are carriers (i.e., unaffected)

typically, NOT seen in every generation

X-linked dominant:

females affected more frequently

can affect males and females in the same generation

X-linked recessive:

males affected more frequently

often affects males in each generation

Mitochondrial:

both males and females can be affected but passed by females

can appear in every generation

When a family is affected by a disease, accurate family history is essential to determine a pattern of inheritance.

11. D is correct.

Let T = tall and t = short; B = brown eyes and b = blue eyes.

The father is homozygous tall and homozygous blue-eyed with a genotype of TTbb.

The mother is heterozygous tall and heterozygous brown-eyed with a genotype of TtBb.

Determine the probability that these parents could produce a tall child with blue eyes (T_bb).

The genes for height and eye color are unlinked.

The father (TTbb) contributes T and b alleles, so his gametes have both T and b alleles.

The mother (TtBb) contributes T or t and B or b, so her gametes are (in equal amounts): TB, tB, Tb, or tb.

Possible genotypes of the offspring: TTBb, TTbb, TtBb, Ttbb.

Half the offspring are tall and brown-eyed (T_B_), and half are tall and blue-eyed (T_bb).

Therefore, the probability of a tall child with blue eyes is ½.

A faster method is calculating phenotype ratios for height and eye-color separately and then combining them.

The mating of TT × Tt = 100% tall.

The mating of Bb × Bb = ½ blue and ½ brown.

Multiplying 1 tall × ½ blue = ½ tall blue.

12. A is correct.

Recombination is the exchange of genetic information between homologous chromosomes during prophase I.

In meiosis, crossing over occurs between non-sister homologs and results in a new combination of alleles (e.g., AB / ab can yield Ab / aB).

Recombination has been reported in eukaryotes during mitosis, but between sister chromatids, which are copies (replicated during the S phase), do not lead to novel genotypes.

Recombination is a DNA repair mechanism between homologous chromosomes.

B: recombination frequency would be the same for *cis*- and *trans*-heterozygotes.

The distance would be the same between the genes regardless of whether they are on the same chromosome (i.e., *cis*) or homologous chromosomes (*trans*).

Recombination frequency is not a completely random event.

Specific regions within the chromosome have differences in the propensity to undergo recombination; the presence of hotspots and architectural features increase or decrease recombination frequencies.

C: recombination frequency increases (not decreases) with distance.

D: different genes have different distances from each other.

Therefore, with different distances, the recombination frequency changes.

13. C is correct.

There are two possible alleles for each of the three genes.

If the genes assort independently (not linked), then there are $2^3 = 8$ possible combinations.

14. A is correct.

In the *autosomal dominant* inheritance pattern, every affected person has an affected parent.

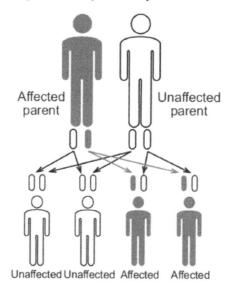

15. C is correct.

Parents are Aa × Aa (carriers but not afflicted with the disease).

The children (i.e., progeny) could be AA, Aa, Aa, or aa.

From the Punnett square, eliminate aa because this is the disease state.

The question asks what the chance is she is heterozygous (Aa) but not homozygous (AA) = 2/3

16. D is correct.

Afflicted children are either AA, Aa or Aa (but not aa), representing 3 of 4 possibilities.

Probability = ¾ or 75%.

	A	a
A	AA	Aa
a	Aa	aa

17. D is correct.

Autosomal dominant is the most common type of inheritance.

For autosomal dominant traits, a person needs a single copy of the mutant gene to exhibit the disease.

Usually, equal numbers of males and females are affected, traits do not skip generations, and father-to-son transmission is observed.

18. C is correct.

In males, spermatogonia are (2N) cells that undergo mitosis to produce (2N) cells called 1° spermatocytes, which undergo the first round of meiosis to yield 2° spermatocytes (1N).

The 2° spermatocytes undergo another round of meiosis to produce four spermatids (1N) that mature into sperm (i.e., male gamete).

In females, the 1° oocyte is (2N), whereby the 2° oocyte undergoes the second meiotic division to produce two (1N) cells – a mature oocyte (i.e., ovum – female gamete) and another polar body.

A: primary oocyte is a diploid cell. During fertilization, a (1N) ovum and a (1N) sperm fuse to produce a (2N) zygote.

B: spermatogonium is a diploid (2N) cell.

D: zygote is a fertilized egg.

19. D is correct.

The probability that a child will be male (or female) is ½.

Each event is independent; the first (or second or third) child is a particular gender that does not affect future events.

Therefore, the probability for 4 children is calculated as ½ × ½ × ½ × ½ = 1/16.

The same would be the probability that the first and third child is female, with the second and fourth as male (or other combinations).

20. C is correct.

Let C designate the wild type and c designate the color bind allele.

Mother is Cc, and father is CY (normal allele with a single copy of X gene).

From mating, the mother's gamete (as a carrier due to her dad) can be either C or c with a 50% probability of the gamete inheriting either the C or c allele.

Assuming the child is a boy (i.e., father transmits Y and not X), so the father's allele of Y (boy) is 100%, and the probability of the mother passing a c (color-blind) is 50%.

The probability of the son being color blind is 50% or ½.

If the question had asked, "what is the probability that they will have a color-blind child?" the analysis changes to determine the probability among all children (not just among boys in the original question).

The same gametes are produced by the mother: C and c with 50% probability each.

The affected child is a boy.

What is the probability that the father passes the X or Y gene to the offspring; the probability is 50%.

The individual probabilities are multiplied to determine the overall probability: ½ × ½ = ¼

21. D is correct.

Color blindness is a sex-linked trait because the gene is on the X chromosome.

The mother is a carrier (not afflicted with the condition) and is heterozygous for the recessive allele (color blindness).

The father has the allele on his X chromosome (the Y chromosome lacks the gene).

The genotype and phenotype of a son depend entirely on the mother (afflicted vs. carrier) since the afflicted father transmits the gene on his X.

Since the mother is heterozygous, a son would have a 50% chance of receiving the color-blindness allele from her.

22. D is correct.

Loss of heterozygosity is a chromosomal event that results in loss of the entire gene and the surrounding chromosomal region.

Most diploid cells (e.g., human somatic cells) contain two copies of the genome, one from each parent.

Each copy contains approximately 3 billion bases, and for most positions in the genome, the base present is consistent between individuals.

However, a small percentage may contain different bases.

These positions are called single nucleotide polymorphisms (or SNP).

When the genomic copies from each parent have different bases for these regions, the region is heterozygous.

Most of the chromosomes within somatic cells of individuals are paired, allowing SNP locations to be potentially heterozygous.

However, one parental copy of a region can sometimes be lost, which results in the region having one copy.

If the copy lost contained the dominant allele, the remaining recessive allele appears as the phenotype.

23. A is correct.

A *gene* is a fundamental physical and functional unit of heredity transferred from a parent to offspring and determines some characteristics of the offspring.

Genes are DNA sequences encoding for proteins.

Alleles are forms of the same gene with slight differences in their sequence of DNA bases.

A *genome* is a complete set of genetic information of an organism.

A genome contains the genetic information needed for an organism and allows it to develop, grow and reproduce.

24. A is correct.

The desired phenotype is green smooth peas, and both green and smooth are dominant phenotypes.

Therefore, the genotypes selected for the cross must avoid the two recessive alleles (g and s).

For GgSs × GGSS, one parent (GGSS) is a double dominant, and therefore all offspring have the dominant phenotype (G and S) regardless of the genotype of the other parent.

B: Gg × gg yields 1/2 yellow (g) phenotype offspring.

C: ss × Ss yields 1/2 wrinkled (s) phenotype offspring.

D: Gg × Gg yields 1/4 yellow (g) phenotype offspring.

25. D is correct.

True breeding means that the organism is homozygous (e.g., AA or aa) for the trait.

All progeny are heterozygous Aa (shown below) and exhibit the dominant phenotype.

	A	A
a	Aa	Aa
a	Aa	Aa

Notes for active learning

Basic Atomic Structure – Explanations

Answer Key

1: D	11: A	21: D	31: A	41: D
2: C	12: B	22: C	32: C	
3: C	13: B	23: C	33: D	
4: B	14: D	24: D	34: A	
5: C	15: D	25: C	35: C	
6: B	16: A	26: D	36: D	
7: B	17: A	27: B	37: A	
8: A	18: A	28: C	38: A	
9: D	19: B	29: D	39: B	
10: B	20: C	30: B	40: D	

1. D is correct.

English chemist John Dalton is known for his Atomic Theory, which states that *elements are made of tiny particles called atoms, which cannot be created or destroyed.*

2. C is correct.

The number of valence electrons for an element can be determined by its group (i.e., vertical column) on the periodic table.

Except for the transition metals (i.e., groups 3-12), the group number identifies how many valence electrons are associated with an element.

Elements of the same group have the same number of valence electrons.

Atoms are most stable when they contain 8 electrons (i.e., complete octet) in the valence shell.

3. C is correct.

Dalton's Atomic Theory, developed in early 1800s, states that atoms of a given element are identical in mass and properties.

The masses of atoms of an element need not be identical; although atoms of an element have the same number of protons; they can have different numbers of neutrons (i.e., isotopes).

4. B is correct.

The atomic number (Z) is the number of protons within the nucleus that characterizes the element's nuclear and chemical properties.

5. C is correct.

The mass number (A) is the total number of nucleons (i.e., protons and neutrons) in an atom.

The atomic number (Z) is the number of protons in an atom.

The number of neutrons in an atom is calculated by subtracting the atomic number (Z) from the mass number (A).

Mass number – atomic number = number of neutrons

6. B is correct.

A nucleon is a particle that makes up the nucleus of an atom.

The two known nucleons are protons and neutrons.

7. B is correct.

The atomic number (Z) is the sum of protons in an atom that determines an element's chemical properties and location on the periodic table.

The mass number (A) is the sum of protons and neutrons in an atom.

The mass number approximates the atomic weight of the element as amu (grams per mole).

Atomic mass – atomic number = number of neutrons

$9 - 4 = 5$ neutrons

8. A is correct.

A molecular formula expresses the actual number of atoms of each element in a molecule.

An empirical formula is the simplest formula for a compound.

For example, if the molecular formula of a compound is C_6H_{16}, the empirical formula is C_3H_8.

Elemental formula and atomic formula are not valid chemistry terms.

9. D is correct.

All atoms of a given element have the same number of protons (i.e., atomic number).

Elements may have different numbers of neutrons, forming isotopes of the same elements.

Elements may have different numbers of electrons, forming charged particles called ions (anions and cations).

10. B is correct.

The nucleus, the dense central core of an atom, contains most of the atom's mass.

The nucleus consists of protons and neutrons, each having a mass of approximately 1 amu.

A cloud of orbiting electrons surrounds the nucleus, and each electron has a mass of approximately 1/1,837 amu. The electrons contribute a tiny fraction of the mass of an atom.

11. A is correct.

The atomic number (Z) depends on the number of protons.

The mass number (A) is the sum of the number of protons and neutrons.

This element has 7 protons, 7 electrons, and (13 – 7) = 6 neutrons.

12. B is correct.

Atoms with an electrical charge are ions.

If an atom gains electrons, it becomes negatively charged as an *anion*.

If an atom loses electrons, it becomes positively charged as a *cation*.

An element is a pure chemical substance that consists of a single type of atom (e.g., O, N, Cl).

A compound is a chemical substance that consists of two or more elements (e.g., O_2, N_2, H_2O, PBr_5, H_2SO_4).

Isotopes of an element have different numbers of neutrons, although they have the same number of protons.

Some isotopes are radioactive, whereby the nucleus of the atom is unstable, causing it to emit ionizing radiation.

13. B is correct.

Isotopes are variants of the same element that have a different number of neutrons.

Since they are the same element, they have the same number of protons.

Ions are elements that have the same number of protons but a different number of electrons.

14. D is correct.

An element is a pure chemical substance that consists of a single type of atom, distinguished by its atomic number (Z) (i.e., the number of protons it contains).

One hundred eighteen elements have been identified, of which the first 94 occur naturally on Earth, with the remaining 24 being synthetic elements.

The properties of the elements on the periodic table repeat at regular intervals, creating "groups" or "families" of elements.

Each column on the periodic table is a group, and elements within each group have similar physical and chemical characteristics due to the orbital location of their outermost electron.

These groups exist because the elements of the periodic table are listed by increasing atomic numbers.

15. D is correct.

Isotopes are variants of an element that differ in the number of neutrons.

Isotopes of the element have the same number of protons and occupy the same position on the periodic table.

The number of protons within the atom's nucleus is the atomic number (Z) and is equal to the number of electrons in the neutral (non-ionized) atom.

Each atomic number identifies a specific element but not the isotope; an atom of a given element may have a wide range in its number of neutrons.

The number of protons and neutrons (i.e., nucleons) in the nucleus is the atom's mass number (A), and each isotope of an element has a different mass number.

16. A is correct.

Neutrons are the neutral particles located inside the nucleus of an atom.

1 amu is 1/12 the mass of ^{12}C atoms.

1 amu is approximately the mass of 1 proton.

Neutrons have approximately the same mass as a proton.

17. A is correct.

Isotopes are variants of an element, which differ in the number of neutrons.

Isotopes of the element have the same number of protons and occupy the same position on the periodic table.

The number of protons within the atom's nucleus is the atomic number (Z) and is equal to the number of electrons in the neutral (non-ionized) atom.

Each atomic number identifies a specific element but not the isotope; an atom of a given element may have a wide range in its number of neutrons.

The number of protons and neutrons (i.e., nucleons) in the nucleus is the atom's mass number (A), and each isotope of an element has a different mass number.

The ^{1}H is the most common hydrogen isotope with an abundance of more than 99.98%.

The ^{1}H is protium, and its nucleus consists of a single proton.

The ^{2}H isotope is deuterium, and ^{3}H is tritium.

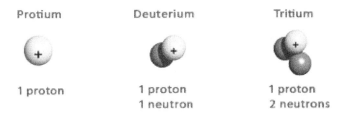

Three isotopes of hydrogen

18. A is correct.

All atoms of an element have the same chemical properties, and the same number of protons denoted as the atomic number (Z) of the element.

Atoms of an element do not necessarily have the same mass (A) because they may have different numbers of neutrons (i.e., they are isotopes of the element).

Atoms of an element may have different numbers of electrons, forming charged ions.

19. B is correct.

Ions do not have the same number of electrons and protons.

Ions have a positive or negative electrical charge.

If an element has more electrons than protons, it is negatively charged (i.e., anion).

If an element has more protons than electrons, it is positively charged (i.e., cation).

20. C is correct.

Neutrons, like protons, are nucleons.

Neutrons are a particle that make up the nucleus of an atom.

Neutrons are closely associated with protons, held by the nuclear force.

Both neutrons and protons have a mass of about 1 amu and are therefore much more massive than electrons.

Neutrons are **neu**tral and thus have a charge of 0.

This makes them more difficult to detect than protons (with a +1 charge) or electrons (with a –1 charge).

21. D is correct.

The mass number (A) is the sum of protons and neutrons (i.e., nucleons) in an atom.

The mass number approximates the atomic weight of the element as amu (grams per mole).

22. C is correct.

Elements are defined by the number of protons (i.e., atomic number).

The isotopes are neutral atoms: # electrons = # protons.

Isotopes are variants of an element that differ in the number of neutrons.

Isotopes of the element have the same number of protons and occupy the same position on the periodic table.

The number of protons within the atom's nucleus is the atomic number (Z) and is equal to the number of electrons in the neutral (non-ionized) atom.

Each atomic number identifies a specific element but not the isotope; an atom of a given element may have a wide range in its number of neutrons.

For example, hydrogen has the fewest number of isotopes (3), while cesium and xenon have the highest known isotopes (36).

The number of protons and neutrons (i.e., nucleons) in the nucleus is the atom's mass number (A), and each isotope of an element has a different mass number.

23. C is correct.

The nucleus of an atom is bound by the strong nuclear force from the nucleons within it.

The strong nuclear force must overcome the Coulomb repulsion of the protons (due to their like charges).

Neutrons help stabilize and bind the nucleus by contributing to the strong nuclear force so that it is greater than the Coulomb repulsion experienced by the protons.

24. D is correct.

The atomic number indicates the number of protons within the nucleus of an atom.

25. C is correct.

The sum of protons and neutrons in the nucleus is the mass number.

26. D is correct.

Atomic mass is specified by the sum of the protons and neutrons within the nucleus of an atom. Isotopes have more or fewer neutrons than the characteristic element; thus, they have different masses.

27. B is correct.

An element is a pure chemical substance that consists of a single type of atom, distinguished by its atomic number (Z) (i.e., the number of protons it contains).

One hundred eighteen elements have been identified, of which the first 94 occur naturally on Earth, with the remaining 24 being synthetic elements.

The properties of the elements on the periodic table repeat at regular intervals, creating "groups" or "families" of elements.

Each column on the periodic table is a group, and elements within each group have similar physical and chemical characteristics due to the orbital location of their outermost electron.

These groups exist because the elements of the periodic table are listed by increasing atomic numbers.

28. C is correct.

Most elements on the periodic table (over 100 elements) are metals.

Currently, there are 84 metal elements on the Periodic Table.

Seventeen elements are generally classified as nonmetals.

Eleven are gases: hydrogen (H), helium (He), nitrogen (N), oxygen (O), fluorine (F), neon (Ne), chlorine (Cl), argon (Ar), krypton (Kr), xenon (Xe) and radon (Rn).

One nonmetal is a liquid – bromine (Br).

Five are solids: carbon (C), phosphorus (P), sulfur (S), selenium (Se), and iodine (I).

Therefore, with the ratio of 84:17, there are about five times more metals than nonmetals.

29. D is correct.

The attraction of the nucleus on the outermost electrons determines the ionization energy, which increases towards the right and increases up on the periodic table.

30. B is correct.

Seventeen elements are generally classified as nonmetals.

Eleven are gases: hydrogen (H), helium (He), nitrogen (N), oxygen (O), fluorine (F), neon (Ne), chlorine (Cl), argon (Ar), krypton (Kr), xenon (Xe) and radon (Rn).

One nonmetal is a liquid – bromine (Br) – and five are solids: carbon (C), phosphorus (P), sulfur (S), selenium (Se), and iodine (I).

Alkali metals (group IA) include lithium (Li), potassium (K), sodium (Na), rubidium (Rb), cesium (Cs) and francium (Fr).

Alkali metals lose one electron to become +1 cations, and the resulting ion has a complete octet of valence electrons.

Alkaline earth metals (group IIA) include beryllium (Be), magnesium (Mg), calcium (Ca), strontium (Sr), barium (Ba), and radium (Ra).

Alkaline earth metals lose two electrons to become +2 cations, and the resulting ion has a complete octet of valence electrons.

31. A is correct.

Congeners are chemical substances related by origin, structure, or function.

Regarding the periodic table, congeners are the elements of the same group that shares similar properties.

For example, copper, silver, and gold are congeners of Group 11.

Stereoisomers, diastereomers, and epimers are terms commonly used in organic chemistry.

Stereoisomers: are chiral molecules (attached to 4 different substituents and are non-superimposable mirror images.

They have the same molecular formula and the same sequence of bonded atoms but are oriented differently in 3-D space (e.g., *R / S* enantiomers).

Diastereomers are chiral molecules that are not mirror images.

The most common form is a chiral molecule with more than 1 chiral center.

Additionally, *cis / trans* (*E / Z*) geometric isomers are diastereomers.

Epimers: diastereomers that differ in absolute configuration at only one chiral center.

32. C is correct.

The atom has 47 protons, 47 electrons, and 60 neutrons.

Because the periodic table is arranged by atomic number (Z), the fastest way to identify an element is to determine its atomic number.

The atomic number is equal to the number of protons or electrons, which means that this atom's atomic number is 47.

Use this information to locate element #47 in the table, which is Ag (silver).

Check the atomic mass (A), which is equal to atomic number + number of neutrons.

For this atom, the mass is $60 + 47 = 107$.

The mass of Ag on the periodic table is listed as 107.87, which is the average mass of the Ag isotopes.

Usually, isotopes of an element have similar masses (e.g., within 1-3 amu).

33. D is correct.

In general, the size of neutral atoms increases down a group (i.e., increasing shell size) and decreases from left to right across the periodic table.

Positive ions (cations) are *much smaller* than the neutral element (due to greater effective nuclear charge), while negative ions (anions) are *much larger* (due to smaller effective nuclear charge).

34. A is correct.

Electronegativity is the ability of an atom to attract electrons when it bonds with another atom.

The most common use of electronegativity pertains to polarity along the *sigma* (or single) bond.

The trend for increasing electronegativity within the periodic table is up and toward the right.

The most electron negative atom is fluorine (F), while the least electronegative atom is francium (Fr).

The greater the difference in electronegativity between two atoms, the more polar of a bond these atoms form.

The atom with the higher electronegativity is the partial (delta) negative end of the dipole.

35. C is correct.

Polonium (Po), element 84 is highly radioactive, with no stable isotopes, and is classified as either a metalloid or a metal.

Alkali metals (group IA) include lithium (Li), potassium (K), sodium (Na), rubidium (Rb), cesium (Cs) and francium (Fr).

Alkaline earth metals (group IIA) include beryllium (Be), magnesium (Mg), calcium (Ca), strontium (Sr), barium (Ba), and radium (Ra).

Halogens (Group VIIA) include fluorine (F), chlorine (Cl), bromine (Br), iodine (I), and astatine (At).

Halogens gain one electron to become –1 anion, and the resulting ion has a complete octet of valence electrons.

Noble gases (group VIIIA) include helium (He), neon (Ne), argon (Ar), krypton (Kr), xenon (Xe), radon (Rn), and oganesson (Og).

Except for helium (which has a complete octet with 2 electrons, $1s^2$), the noble gases have complete octets with ns^2 and np^6 orbitals.

Representative elements on the periodic table are groups IA and IIA (on left) and groups IIIA – VIIIA (on the right).

36. D is correct.

Electronegativity is the ability of an atom to attract electrons when it bonds with another atom.

The most common use of electronegativity pertains to polarity along the sigma (single) bond.

The trend for increasing electronegativity within the periodic table is up and toward the right.

The most electron negative atom is fluorine (F), while the least electronegative atom is francium (Fr).

37. A is correct.

The mass number (A) is the total number of nucleons (i.e., protons and neutrons) in an atom.

The number of protons and neutrons is denoted by the superscript on the left.

The atomic number (Z) is the number of protons in an atom.

The number of neutrons in an atom is calculated by subtracting the atomic number (Z) from mass number (A).

38. A is correct.

The periods are the horizontal rows and correlate with the principal quantum number (n).

The groups are the vertical columns and correlate with the number of valence electrons.

39. B is correct.

Periods are the horizontal rows on the periodic table, while groups are the vertical columns.

From left to right across a period, the atomic number increases, but this does not mean that the elements tend to get more metallic.

The elements across a period get incrementally larger since it is one proton being added to each subsequent element across a period.

The properties of the elements are similar within columns (groups), indicating that they must change across periods on the periodic table.

40. D is correct.

Transition metals (or transition elements) are elements with a partially-filled *d* or *f* subshell in a common oxidative state.

Transition metals occur in groups (vertical columns) 3–12 of the period table. They occur in periods (horizontal rows) 4–7. This group of elements includes silver, iron, and copper.

The *f*-block lanthanides (i.e., rare earth metals) and actinides (i.e., radioactive elements) are transition metals and inner transition metals.

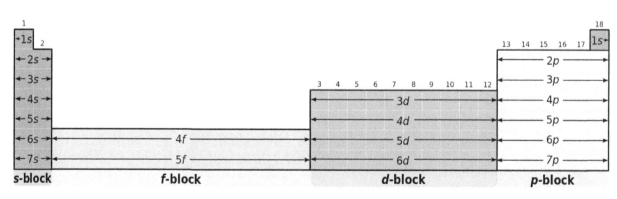

Transition elements have characteristics not found in other elements, which result from the partially filled *d* shell.

These include the formation of compounds whose color is due to *d* electronic transitions, the formation of compounds in many oxidation states due to the relatively low reactivity of unpaired *d* electrons.

The incomplete *d* sub-shell can give rise to cations with an incomplete *d* sub-shell.

Transition elements form many paramagnetic (i.e., attracted to an externally applied magnetic field) compounds due to the presence of unpaired *d* and *f* electrons.

A few compounds of main group elements are paramagnetic (e.g., nitric oxide and oxygen).

41. D is correct.

Elements with atomic numbers of 84 and higher are radioactive because the strong nuclear force binding the nucleus cannot overcome the Coulomb repulsion from the high number of protons within the atom.

Thus, these nuclei are unstable and emit alpha radiation to decrease the number of protons within the nucleus.

Notes for active learning

Characteristic Properties of Substances – Explanations

Answer Key

1: D	11: D	21: B	31: D	41: C	51: D
2: D	12: C	22: B	32: C	42: B	
3: A	13: C	23: C	33: D	43: B	
4: C	14: B	24: D	34: D	44: C	
5: D	15: C	25: D	35: D	45: B	
6: B	16: D	26: D	36: D	46: A	
7: C	17: C	27: B	37: B	47: A	
8: C	18: D	28: D	38: D	48: B	
9: A	19: D	29: B	39: A	49: C	
10: D	20: C	30: D	40: B	50: D	

1. D is correct.

Metals are the elements that form positive ions by losing electrons during chemical reactions. Thus, metals are electropositive elements.

Metals are characterized by bright luster, hardness, resonate sound, and excellent conductors of heat and electricity.

Metals, except mercury, are solids under normal conditions. Potassium has the lowest melting point of the solid metals at 146 °F.

2. D is correct.

The metalloids have some properties of metals and some properties of nonmetals.

Metalloids are semimetallic elements (i.e., between metals and nonmetals).

The metalloids are boron (B), silicon (Si), germanium (Ge), arsenic (As), antimony (Sb), and tellurium (Te).

Some literature reports polonium (Po) and astatine (At) as metalloids.

They have properties between metals and nonmetals.

They typically have a metallic appearance but are fair conductors of electricity (as opposed to metals that are excellent conductors), making them useable in the semiconductor industry.

Metalloids tend to be brittle, and chemically they behave more like nonmetals.

However, the elements in the IIIB group are transition metals, not metalloids.

3. A is correct.

Metals, except mercury, are solids under normal conditions.

Potassium (K) has the lowest melting point of the solid metals at 146 °F.

The relatively low melting temperature for potassium is due to its fourth shell ($n = 4$), which means its valence electrons are further from the nucleus; therefore, there is less attraction between its electrons and protons.

4. C is correct.

Seventeen elements are generally classified as nonmetals. Eleven are gases: hydrogen (H), helium (He), nitrogen (N), oxygen (O), fluorine (F), neon (Ne), chlorine (Cl), argon (Ar), krypton (Kr), xenon (Xe) and radon (Rn). One nonmetal is a liquid – bromine (Br) – and five are solids: carbon (C), phosphorus (P), sulfur (S), selenium (Se), and iodine (I).

Metals, except mercury, are solids under normal conditions. Potassium has the lowest melting point of the solid metals at 146 °F.

5. D is correct.

An element is a pure chemical substance that consists of one type of atom.

Every element has an atomic number based on the number of protons.

Hydrogen has the atomic number 1, and it is the first element on the periodic table of elements.

Hydrogen gas (H_2) is a compound.

The other choices contain more than one type of atom bonded and are chemical compounds.

Glucose and methanol contain carbon, oxygen, and hydrogen atoms bonded.

Sodium chloride, as its name suggests, contains sodium and chlorine bonded.

Brass contains copper and zinc bonded.

6. B is correct.

A compound consists of two or more different types of atoms that associate via chemical bonds.

An element is a pure chemical substance that consists of a single type of atom, defined by its atomic number (Z), the number of protons.

One hundred eighteen elements have been identified, of which the first 94 occur naturally on Earth.

7. C is correct.

An element is a pure chemical substance that consists of a single type of atom, distinguished by its atomic number (Z) (i.e., the number of protons it contains).

One hundred eighteen elements have been identified, of which the first 94 occur naturally on Earth, with the remaining 24 being synthetic elements.

The properties of the elements on the periodic table repeat at regular intervals, creating "groups" or "families" of elements.

Each column on the periodic table is a group, and elements within each group have similar physical and chemical characteristics due to the orbital location of their outermost electron.

These groups exist because the elements of the periodic table are listed by increasing atomic numbers.

8. C is correct.

Cohesion is the property of like molecules sticking (e.g., water to water).

Hydrogen bonds join water molecules.

Water molecules stick to each other due to the collective action of hydrogen bonds between water molecules.

Hydrogen bonds are continually breaking and reforming; these bonds hold many molecules.

Adhesion is the attraction between dissimilar molecules. For example, the meniscus observed from water molecules adhering to a graduated cylinder.

Water sticks to surfaces (i.e., adhesion) because of water's polarity.

On an exceptionally smooth surface (e.g., glass), the water may form a thin film because the molecular forces between glass and water molecules (adhesive forces) are stronger than the water molecules' cohesive forces.

Polarity is the differences in electronegativity between bonded molecules.

Polarity gives rise to the delta plus (on H) and the delta minus (on O), which permits hydrogen bonds to form between water molecules.

9. A is correct.

Hydrogen bonds are the strongest intermolecular forces (i.e., between molecules), followed by dipole–dipole, dipole–induced dipole, and van der Waals forces (i.e., London dispersion).

Hydrogens, bonded directly to F, O, or N, participate in hydrogen bonds.

H–bonding is a polar interaction involving hydrogen forming bonds to the electronegative atoms such as F, O, or N, which accounts for the high boiling points of water.

The hydrogen is partially positive (i.e., delta plus or $\partial+$) due to the bond to these electronegative atoms.

The lone pair of electrons on the F, O, or N interacts with the $\partial+$ hydrogen to form a hydrogen bond.

Molecular geometry of H₂S

Polar molecules have high boiling points because of polar interaction. H_2S is a polar molecule but does not form hydrogen bonds; it forms dipole–dipole interactions.

10. D is correct.

Colligative properties are for solutions that depend on the ratio of the number of solute particles to the number of solvent molecules in a solution and not on the type of chemical species present.

Colligative properties include: lowering of vapor pressure, the elevation of boiling point, depression of freezing point, and increased osmotic pressure

Dissolving a solute into a solvent alters the solvent's freezing point, melting point, boiling point, and vapor pressure.

11. D is correct.

Gases form homogeneous mixtures, regardless of the identities or relative proportions of the component gases. There is a relatively large distance between gas molecules; compare to solids or liquids where the molecules are much closer.

When pressure is applied to gas, its volume readily decreases, and thus gases are highly compressible.

There are no attractive forces between gas molecules, which is why gas molecules move freely.

12. C is correct.

Solids have a definite shape and volume.

A solid granite does not change its shape or volume regardless of the container.

Molecules in a solid are tightly packed due to the strong intermolecular attractions, which prevent the molecules from freely moving.

13. C is correct.

Molecules in solids have the most attraction to their neighbors, followed by liquids (significant motion between the individual molecules) and then gas (randomized motion of particles).

A molecule in an ideal gas has no attraction to other gas molecules.

The particles are far apart for a low-pressure gas, with no attractive forces between the individual gas molecules.

14. B is correct.

Volatility is the tendency of a substance to vaporize (phase change from liquid to vapor).

Volatility is directly related to a substance's vapor pressure.

At a given temperature, a substance with higher vapor pressure vaporizes more readily than a substance with lower vapor pressure.

Molecules with weak intermolecular attraction increase their kinetic energy by transferring less heat due to a smaller molecular mass.

The increase in kinetic energy is required for individual molecules to move from the liquid to the gaseous phase.

15. C is correct.

Gas molecules have a large amount of space between them; therefore, they can be pushed together, and gases are compressible.

Molecules in solids and liquids are close; therefore, they cannot get significantly closer and are thus nearly incompressible.

16. D is correct.

Boiling occurs when the vapor pressure of a liquid equals atmospheric pressure.

Vapor pressure is the pressure exerted by a vapor in equilibrium with its condensed phases (i.e., solid or liquid) in a closed system at a given temperature.

Atmospheric pressure is the pressure exerted by the weight of air in the atmosphere.

Vapor pressure is inversely correlated with the strength of the intermolecular force.

With stronger intermolecular forces, the molecules are more likely to stick in liquid form.

Fewer of them participate in the liquid-vapor equilibrium; therefore, the molecules boil at a higher temperature.

17. C is correct.

Atmospheric pressure is the pressure exerted by the weight of air in the atmosphere.

Boiling occurs when the vapor pressure of the liquid is higher than the atmospheric pressure.

At standard atmospheric pressure and 22 °C, the vapor pressure of water is less than the atmospheric pressure, and it does not boil.

However, when a vacuum pump is used, the atmospheric pressure is reduced until it has a lower vapor pressure than water, allowing water to boil at a much lower temperature.

18. D is correct.

Liquids take the shape of the container they are in (i.e., they have an indefinite shape).

For example, a liter of water poured into a cylindrical bucket or a square box; water takes the shape of the container.

Liquids have a definite volume. The volume of water in the example is 1 L, regardless of the container.

19. D is correct.

Liquids have a definite volume but take the shape of their container.

They have moderate intermolecular attractions, compared to the strong intermolecular attractions of solids (that consist of tightly-packed molecules) and weak, almost non-existent, intermolecular attractions of gas molecules (that move freely).

20. C is correct.

Gases do *not* have definite volumes and shapes; instead, they take the volume and shape of their container.

This is different from liquids (which have a definite volume but take the shape of the container they are in) and solids (which have a definite volume and a definite shape).

Ideal gases are modeled as having perfectly elastic collisions, meaning that they have no intermolecular interactions. Essentially, the molecules in a gas (ideal or low pressure) are separate from one another.

21. B is correct.

Heat is energy, and the energy from the heat is transferred to the gas molecules, which increases their movement (i.e., kinetic energy).

Temperature is a measure of the average kinetic energy of the molecules.

22. B is correct.

The temperature (i.e., average kinetic energy) of a substance remains constant during a phase change (e.g., solid to liquid or liquid to gas).

For example, heat (i.e., energy) breaks bonds between the ice molecules as they change phases into the liquid phase.

Since the molecules' average kinetic energy does not change at the moment of the phase change (i.e., melting), the temperature of the molecules does not change.

23. C is correct.

Solubility is the property of a solid, liquid, or gaseous substance (i.e., solute); it dissolves in a solid, liquid, or gaseous solvent to form a solution (i.e., solute in the solvent).

The solubility of a substance depends on the physical and chemical properties of the solute and solvent and the temperature, pressure, and pH of the solution.

Gaseous solutes (e.g., oxygen) exhibit complex behavior with temperature. As the temperature rises, gases usually become less soluble in water but more soluble in organic solvents.

24. D is correct.

Immiscible refers to the property (of solutions) when two or more substances (e.g., oil and water) are mixed and eventually separate into two layers.

Miscible is when two liquids are mixed but do not necessarily interact chemically.

In contrast to miscibility, *soluble* means the substance (solid, liquid, or gas) *dissolves* in another solid, liquid, or gas.

A substance *dissolves* when it becomes incorporated into another substance.

In contrast to miscibility, solubility involves a *saturation point*, where a substance cannot dissolve further and a mass, the *precipitate*, begins to form.

25. D is correct.

Solutes dissolve in the solvent to form a solution.

A *solute* can be a *gas*, *liquid*, or *solid*.

26. D is correct.

When most people hear the term solvent, they associate it with a liquid medium.

However, in the chemical sense, solvents, like solutes, can be gases, liquids, or solids.

The definition of a solvent is incorporated into a solution whereby the substance present in the larger quantity is the solvent. The substance present in the smaller quantity is the solute.

Based on this definition, a solvent can be liquid, solid, or gas.

For example, a solid phase solvent is copper in a brass mixture consisting of approximately 2/3 copper and 1/3 zinc.

27. B is correct.

An acid is a chemical substance with a pH of less than 7, which produces H^+ ions in water.

An acid can be neutralized by a base (i.e., a substance with a pH above 7) to form a salt.

Acids are known to have a sour taste (e.g., lemon juice) because the sour taste receptors on the tongue detect the dissolved hydrogen (H^+) ions.

However, acids are not known to have a slippery feel; this is characteristic of bases.

Bases feel slippery because they dissolve the fatty acids and oils from the skin and reduce friction between skin cells.

28. D is correct.

The properties of turning litmus paper blue, bitter taste, slippery feel are true of basic solutions.

A base is a chemical substance with a pH greater than 7 and feels slippery because it dissolves the fatty acids and oils from the skin and reduces friction between skin cells.

Many bitter foods are alkaline because bitter compounds often contain amine groups, which are weak bases.

An acidic solution has opposite qualities.

It has a pH lower than 7 and therefore turns litmus paper red.

It tastes sour and does not feel slippery. Acids are known to have a sour taste (e.g., lemon juice) because the sour taste receptors on the tongue detect the dissolved hydrogen (H^+) ions.

29. B is correct.

Percent composition is a breakdown of each component's percentage in a compound.

30. D is correct.

Temperature is the measure of the average kinetic energy of the molecules.

The greater the kinetic energy of the gas, the higher is the temperature.

An increase in kinetic energy results in a more rapid motion of the molecules, and this rapid motion results in the breaking of intermolecular bonds.

The breaking of bonds allows molecules to escape from the solution, thus affecting the solubility of gas molecules.

31. D is correct.

Solutions can be gases, liquids, or solids. The three statements are possible types of solutions.

An example of a gas-in-liquid solution (statement III) is a hydrochloride/HCl.

In its pure form, HCl is a gas and is passed through water to create an aqueous HCl solution.

32. C is correct.

Density = mass / volume

Gas molecules have a large amount of space between them.

Gas molecules can be pushed together, and thus gases are compressible.

Because there is much space between gas molecules, the extent to which the gas molecules can be pushed together is greater than for liquid molecules.

Therefore, gases have greater compressibility than liquids.

Gas molecules are further apart than liquid molecules, which is why gases have a smaller density.

33. D is correct.

Neither bond energy nor vapor pressure change with a change in atmospheric pressure.

Boiling occurs when the vapor pressure of a liquid equals the atmospheric pressure.

At high altitudes, water boils at a lower temperature because the atmospheric pressure decreases as altitude increases.

34. D is correct.

Metals are excellent conductors of heat and electricity because the molecules in metal are closely packed (i.e., have a high density).

Metals are generally in a solid phase at room temperature.

Metals are malleable; they can be pressed or hammered into various shapes without breaking.

35. D is correct.

Metals are good heat and electrical conductors because of their bonding structure.

In metallic bonding, the outer electrons are held loosely and can travel freely.

Electricity and heat require high electron mobility.

Thus, the looseness of the outer electrons in the materials allows them to be excellent conductors.

36. D is correct.

A nonmetal tends to be highly volatile (i.e., easily vaporized), have low density, and are good insulators of heat and electricity.

Nonmetals tend to have high ionization energy and electronegativity and share (or gain) an electron when bonding with other elements.

Seventeen elements are generally classified as nonmetals.

Most are gases (e.g., hydrogen, helium, nitrogen, oxygen, fluorine, neon, chlorine, argon, krypton, xenon, radon).

One nonmetal is a liquid (bromine), and a few are solids (e.g., carbon, phosphorus, sulfur, selenium, iodine).

37. B is correct.

Electrolytes dissociate into ions in an aqueous solution and conduct electricity when current is applied to the solution.

Sucrose is a disaccharide with the molecular formula of $C_{12}H_{22}O_{11}$.

Sucrose does not dissociate into ions; only individual sucrose molecules separate.

38. D is correct.

The object sinks when the buoyant force is less than the weight of the object.

Since the buoyant force is equal to the weight of the displaced fluid, an object sinks precisely when the weight of the fluid it displaces is less than the weight of the object itself.

39. A is correct.

Surface tension increases as temperature decreases. Generally, the cohesive forces maintaining surface tension decrease as molecular thermal activity increases.

40. B is correct.

The *density* of an object is its mass per unit volume:

density = mass / volume

Density is expressed in SI units of kg/m^3; it may be given in g/cm^3.

The least dense known element is hydrogen at $8.99 \times 10^{-5} \, g/cm^3$, which is about 250,000 times less dense than osmium.

41. C is correct.

For most substances, the solid form is denser than the liquid phase.

Therefore, a block of most solids sinks in the liquid.

With regards to pure water, though, a block of ice (solid phase) floats in liquid water because ice is less dense.

Like other substances, when liquid water is cooled from room temperature, it becomes increasingly dense.

However, at approximately 4 °C (39 °F), water reaches its maximum density, and as it is cooled further, it expands and becomes less dense.

This phenomenon is negative thermal expansion and attributed to strong intermolecular interactions that are orientation-dependent.

The density of water is about 1 g/cm^3 and depends on the temperature.

When frozen, the density of water is decreased by about 9%.

This is due to the decrease in intermolecular vibrations, allowing water molecules to form stable hydrogen bonds with other water molecules.

As these hydrogen bonds form, molecules are locking into positions similar to form hexagonal structures.

Even though hydrogen bonds are shorter in the crystal than in the liquid, this position locking decreases the average coordination number of water molecules as the liquid reaches the solid phase.

42. B is correct.

Specific heat is the amount of heat (i.e., energy) needed to raise the temperature of the unit mass of a substance by a given amount (usually one degree).

43. B is correct.

Body heat gives energy to the water molecules in the sweat.

This energy is transferred via collisions until some molecules have enough energy to break the hydrogen bonds and escape the liquid (evaporation).

However, if a body stayed dry, the heat would not be given to the water, and the person stays hot because heat is not lost due to the evaporation of water.

44. C is correct.

Conduction is a form of heat transfer in which the collisions of the molecules transfer energy through the material.

Higher temperature of the material causes the molecules to collide with more energy which eventually is transferred throughout the material through subsequent collisions.

Radiation is a form of heat transfer in which electromagnetic waves carry energy from the emitting object and deposit the energy to the object that absorbs the radiation.

Convection is a form of heat transfer in which the mass motion of a fluid (i.e., liquids and gases) transfers energy from the source of heat.

45. B is correct.

Convection is a form of heat transfer in which the mass motion of a fluid (i.e., liquids and gases) transfers energy from the source of heat.

46. A is correct.

Radiation is the transmission of energy as particles or waves through space or a material medium. Examples include electromagnetic radiations such as X-rays, alpha particles, beta particles, radio waves, and visible light.

47. A is correct.

Conduction is a form of heat transfer in which the collisions of the molecules transfer energy through the material.

Higher temperature of the material causes the molecules to collide with more energy which eventually is transferred throughout the material through subsequent collisions.

48. B is correct.

Steel is a conductive material that can transfer thermal energy.

The steel feels colder than the plastic because its higher thermal conductivity allows it to remove more heat and makes touching it feel colder.

49. C is correct.

Conduction is a form of heat transfer in which the collisions of the molecules transfer energy through the material.

Higher temperature of the material causes the molecules to collide with more energy which eventually is transferred throughout the material through subsequent collisions.

50. D is correct.

Warm air is less dense than cold air.

It follows that a mass of warm air is subject to buoyancy force, which is due to the density gradient in the cold air.

The direction of the buoyancy force is toward lower density. Air with lower density has lower pressure.

51. D is correct.

Convection is a form of heat transfer in which the mass motion of a fluid (i.e., liquids and gases) transfers energy from the source of heat.

Notes for active learning

Changing States of Matter – Explanations

Answer Key

1: A	11: C	21: B	31: B
2: C	12: D	22: C	32: A
3: C	13: A	23: B	33: B
4: B	14: D	24: C	34: C
5: B	15: B	25: C	35: A
6: A	16: A	26: D	36: D
7: D	17: D	27: C	37: D
8: A	18: B	28: C	38: A
9: B	19: C	29: D	
10: A	20: C	30: C	

1. A is correct.

Vaporization refers to the change of state from a liquid to a gas.

The two types of vaporization are boiling and evaporation, which is differentiated based on the temperature at which they occur.

Evaporation occurs at a temperature below the boiling point.

Boiling occurs at a temperature at or above the boiling point.

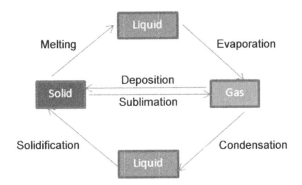

Interconversion of states of matter

2. C is correct.

When more than two H_2O molecules are present (e.g., liquid water), more bonds (between 2 and 4) are possible because the oxygen of one water molecule has two lone pairs of electrons that can form a hydrogen bond with a hydrogen on another water molecule.

This bonding can repeat, so every water molecule is H–bonded with up to four other molecules (two through its two lone pairs of O, and two through its two hydrogen atoms).

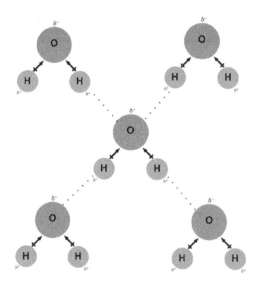

Ice with four hydrogen bonds between the water molecules

Hydrogen bonding affects the crystal structure of ice (hexagonal lattice).

The density of ice is less than the density of water at the same temperature.

Thus, the solid phase of water (ice) floats on the liquid.

The creation of the additional H–bonds (up to 4 for ice) forces the individual molecules further from each other, giving it less density, unlike most other substances in the solid phase.

For most substances, the solid form is denser than the liquid phase.

Therefore, a block of most solids sinks in the liquid. With regards to pure water, though, a block of ice (solid phase) floats in liquid water because ice is less dense.

Like other substances, when liquid water is cooled from room temperature, it becomes increasingly dense. However, at approximately 4 °C (39 °F), water reaches its maximum density, and as it is cooled further, it expands and becomes less dense.

This phenomenon is known as *negative thermal expansion* and is attributed to strong intermolecular interactions that are orientation-dependent.

The density of water is about 1 g/cm^3 and depends on the temperature.

When frozen, the density of water is decreased by about 9%.

This decreased density is due to decreased intermolecular vibrations, allowing water molecules to form stable hydrogen bonds with other water molecules.

As these hydrogen bonds form, molecules are locking into positions similar to the hexagonal structure.

Even though hydrogen bonds are shorter in the crystal than in the liquid, this position locking decreases the average coordination number of water molecules as the liquid reaches the solid phase.

3. C is correct.

The substantial difference between the two forms of carbon (i.e., graphite and diamonds) is mainly due to their crystal structure, hexagonal for graphite and cubic for diamond.

The conditions to convert graphite into diamond are high pressure and high temperature.

Creating synthetic diamonds is time-consuming, energy-intensive, and expensive since carbon is forced to change its bonding structure.

4. B is correct.

Ideal gas law:

$$PV = nRT$$

where P is pressure, V is volume, n is the number of molecules, R is the ideal gas constant, and T is the temperature of the gas.

R and n are constant.

From this equation, if pressure and temperature are halved, there is no effect on the volume.

5. B is correct.

Sublimation is the direct change of state from a solid to a gas, skipping the intermediate liquid phase.

An example of a compound that undergoes sublimation is solid carbon dioxide (i.e., dry ice).

CO_2 changes phases from solid to gas (i.e., bypasses the liquid phase) and is often used as a cooling agent.

6. A is correct.

An ideal gas has no intermolecular forces, indicating that its molecules have no attraction to each other.

However, the molecules of a real gas do have intermolecular forces, although these forces are extremely weak.

Therefore, the molecules of a real gas are slightly attracted to one another, although the attraction is nowhere near as strong as the attraction in liquids and solids.

7. D is correct.

Evaporation describes the phase change from liquid to gas.

The mass of the molecules and the attraction of the molecules with their neighbors (to form intermolecular attractions) determine their kinetic energy.

The increase in kinetic energy is required for individual molecules to move from the liquid to the gaseous phase.

8. A is correct.

Kinetic theory explains the macroscopic properties of gases (e.g., temperature, volume, pressure) by their molecular composition and motion.

The gas pressure is due to the collisions on the walls of a container from molecules moving at different velocities.

Temperature = $\frac{1}{2}mv^2$

9. B is correct.

The kinetic theory of gases describes a gas as many small particles in constant rapid motion. These particles collide with each other and with the walls of the container.

Their average kinetic energy depends only on the absolute temperature of the system.

$$temperature = \frac{1}{2}mv^2$$

At high temperatures, the particles are moving greater velocity, and at a temperature of absolute zero (i.e., 0 K), there is no movement of gas particles.

As temperature decreases, kinetic energy decreases, and so does the velocity of the gas molecules.

10. A is correct.

Sublimation is the direct change of state from a solid to a gas, skipping the intermediate liquid phase.

An example of a compound that undergoes sublimation is solid carbon dioxide (i.e., dry ice).

CO_2 changes phases from solid to gas (i.e., bypasses the liquid phase) and is often used as a cooling agent.

11. C is correct.

Scientists found that the relationships between pressure, temperature, and volume of a sample of gas holds for gases, and the gas laws were developed.

Boyle's law (i.e., pressure-volume law) states that pressure and volume are inversely proportional:

$$(P_1V_1) = (P_2V_2)$$

or

$$P \times V = constant$$

If the volume of a gas increases, its pressure decreases proportionally.

Charles' law (i.e., law of volumes) explains how, at constant pressure, gases behave when temperature changes:

$$(V_1 / T_1) = (V_2 / T_2)$$

Gay-Lussac's law (i.e., pressure-temperature law) states that pressure is proportional to temperature:

$P \alpha T$

or

$(P_1 / T_1) = (P_2 / T_2)$ or $(P_1T_2) = (P_2T_1)$

or

$P / T = $ constant

If the pressure of a gas increases, the temperature increases.

12. D is correct.

Ideal gas law:

$PV = nRT$

where P is pressure, V is volume, n is the number of molecules, R is the ideal gas constant, and T is the temperature of the gas. R and n are constants.

Therefore, decreasing the volume, increasing temperature, or increasing the number of molecules increases the pressure of a gas.

13. A is correct.

ΔH refers to enthalpy (or heat).

Endothermic reactions have heat as a reactant.

Exothermic reactions have heat as a product.

Exothermic reactions release heat and cause the temperature of the immediate surroundings to rise (i.e., a net loss of energy).

An endothermic process absorbs heat and cools the surroundings (i.e., a net gain of energy).

Endothermic reactions absorb energy to break strong bonds to form a less stable state (i.e., positive enthalpy).

Exothermic reactions release energy during the formation of stronger bonds to produce a more stable state (i.e., negative enthalpy).

14. D is correct.

During phase changes, only the mass and heat of specific phase change is required to calculate the energy released or absorbed.

Because water is turning into ice, the specific heat required is the heat of solidification.

15. B is correct.

A change is exothermic when energy is released to the surroundings.

Energy loss occurs when a substance changes to a more rigid phase (e.g., gas → liquid or liquid → solid).

16. A is correct.

For the same magnitude, phase changes must be the reverse of each other (between the same phases).

Here, both phase changes of the heat of sublimation and deposition are between gas and solid phases.

Therefore, heats of sublimation and deposition are equal in magnitude.

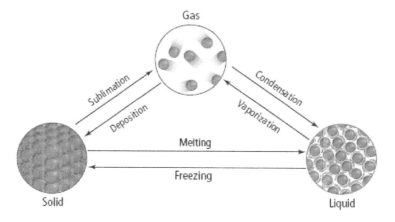

17. D is correct.

Evaporation is the phase change from a liquid to a gas.

This occurs in Earth's water cycle when solar energy heats water and causes it to evaporate and become vapor.

Evaporation is an endothermic process (i.e., heat is absorbed).

Sublimation is when a solid becomes a gas without becoming a liquid during the phase change.

18. B is correct.

Vapor pressure is inversely proportional to the strength of the intermolecular force.

With stronger intermolecular forces, the molecules are more likely to stick in the liquid form, and less of them participate in the liquid-vapor equilibrium.

19. C is correct.

Vaporization refers to the change of state from a liquid to a gas. There are two types of vaporization: boiling and evaporation, which are differentiated based on the temperature at which they occur.

Evaporation occurs at a temperature below the boiling point.

Boiling occurs at a temperature at or above the boiling point.

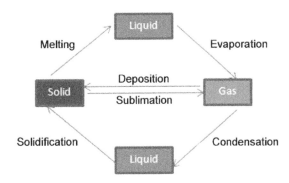

Interconversion of states of matter

20. C is correct.

The kinetic theory assumes random motion of molecules, elastic collisions, no significant volume occupied by molecules, and little attraction between molecules.

For the same temperature, the average kinetic energy of molecules of different gases is the same, regardless of differences in mass.

21. B is correct.

Boiling is the rapid vaporization of a liquid where its phase changes from a liquid to a gas. It occurs when the liquid's vapor pressure is equal to or greater than the external pressure.

The lower the pressure of a gas above a liquid, the lower the temperature at which the liquid boils.

22. C is correct.

For most substances, the solid form is denser than the liquid phase.

Therefore, a block of most solids sinks in the liquid.

Regarding pure water, though, a block of ice (solid phase) floats in liquid water because ice is less dense.

Like other substances, when liquid water is cooled from room temperature, it becomes increasingly dense.

However, at approximately 4 °C (39 °F), water reaches its maximum density, and as it is cooled further, it expands and becomes less dense.

This phenomenon is negative thermal expansion and is attributed to strong intermolecular interactions that are orientation-dependent.

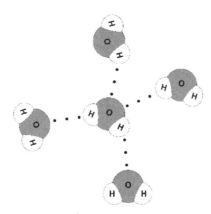

Ice with four hydrogen bonds between the water molecules

The density of water is about 1 g/cm^3 and depends on the temperature.

When frozen, the density of water is decreased by about 9%.

This is due to the decrease in intermolecular vibrations, allowing water molecules to form stable hydrogen bonds with other water molecules.

As these hydrogen bonds form, molecules are locking into positions similar to the hexagonal structure.

Even though hydrogen bonds are shorter in the crystal than in the liquid, this position locking decreases the average coordination number of water molecules as the liquid reaches the solid phase.

23. B is correct.

Vapor pressure is proportional to temperature.

Vapor pressure is the pressure exerted by a vapor in thermodynamic equilibrium with its condensed phases (i.e., solid or liquid) at a given temperature in a closed system.

The equilibrium vapor pressure is an indicator of a liquid's evaporation rate.

24. C is correct.

The ideal gas law:

$$PV = nRT$$

where P is pressure, V is volume, n is the number of molecules, R is the ideal gas constant, and T is the temperature of the gas.

The volume and temperature are directly proportional; if one increases, the other increases.

25. C is correct.

The kinetic theory of gases describes a gas as a large number of small molecules in constant, random motion.

However, it does not state that the molecules have the same kinetic energy, same velocity, or individual temperature. It does not state that the molecular collisions must have the same energy.

26. D is correct.

Decreasing external pressure increases the distance between gas molecules.

Therefore, the phase change is likely from liquid → gas.

27. C is correct.

Phase changes occur at a constant temperature. Once the phase change is complete, the temperature of the substance then either increases or decreases.

For example, water remains at 0 °C until it has completely changed phase to ice before the temperature decreases further.

28. C is correct.

Fusion is the process whereby a substance changes from a solid to a liquid (i.e., melting).

Condensation is the process whereby a substance changes from a vapor to a liquid.

Sublimation is the process whereby a substance changes directly from a solid to the gas phase without passing through the liquid phase.

29. D is correct.

Condensation refers to a change of state from a gas to a liquid.

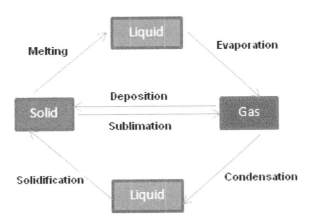

Interconversion of states of matter

For example, condensation occurs when atmospheric water vapor in clouds condenses to form droplets of liquid water that become heavy enough to fall due to gravity.

This results in rain, an essential part of the Earth's water cycle.

30. C is correct.

Vaporization is the process whereby a substance changes from a liquid to a gas.

The process can be either boiling or evaporation.

Sublimation is the process whereby a substance changes from a solid to a gas.

31. B is correct.

During a change of state, the addition of heat does not change the temperature (i.e., a measure of the kinetic energy).

The heat energy added adds to the potential energy of the substance until the substance completely changes state.

32. A is correct.

When a liquid freezes, it undergoes a phase change from liquid to solid.

For this phase change to occur, heat energy must be dissipated (removed).

During a phase change, the temperature remains constant.

33. B is correct.

During a change of state, the addition of heat does not change the temperature (i.e., a measure of the kinetic energy).

The heat energy added only adds to the potential energy of the substance until the substance completely changes state.

34. C is correct.

Standing in a breeze while wet feels colder than when dry because of the evaporation of water off the skin.

Water requires heat to evaporate, so this is taken from the body, making a person feel colder than if they were dry, and the evaporation did not occur.

35. A is correct.

After 5 minutes, the sample is at a constant temperature indicating a phase change from solid to liquid (a mixture of solid and liquid).

B: heat capacity of the liquid phase is much greater than that of the solid.

C: the sample begins to boil at the second plateau, representing the liquid to gas phase change.

D: the heat of fusion is less than the heat of vaporization.

36. D is correct.

Ionic bonds hold salt crystals. Salts are composed of cations and anions and are electrically neutral.

When salts dissolve in solution, they separate into their constituent ions by breaking of noncovalent interactions.

Water: the hydrogen atoms in the molecule are covalently bonded to the oxygen atom.

Hydrogen peroxide: the molecule has one more oxygen atom than the water molecule and is held by covalent bonds.

Ester (RCOOR'): undergo hydrolysis and breaks covalent bonds to separate into its constituent carboxylic acid (RCOOH) and alcohol (ROH).

37. D is correct.

Condensation is the transition from the gaseous to the liquid phase. It is an essential part of the Earth's water cycle. Condensation occurs when atmospheric water vapor in clouds condenses to form droplets of liquid water that become heavy enough to fall due to gravity, which results in rain.

38. A is correct.

Deposition is the thermodynamic process where gas transitions directly into a solid without first becoming a liquid.

An example of deposition occurs in sub-freezing air when water vapor changes directly into ice without becoming a liquid.

Notes for active learning

Chemical Reactions – Explanations

Answer Key

1: C	11: B	21: C
2: C	12: A	22: B
3: A	13: C	23: D
4: A	14: C	24: C
5: C	15: D	25: A
6: D	16: B	26: A
7: A	17: A	27: A
8: A	18: C	28: C
9: B	19: B	29: B
10: A	20: D	30: D

1. C is correct.

A chemical reaction is a rearrangement of a substance's molecular or ionic structure when one or more substances (i.e., reactants) are converted to different substances (i.e., products).

During a *chemical reaction,* constituent atoms of the reactants rearrange to create different substances as products.

2. C is correct.

ΔH refers to enthalpy (or heat).

Endothermic reactions have heat as a reactant.

Exothermic reactions have heat as a product.

Exothermic reactions release heat and cause the temperature of the immediate surroundings to rise (i.e., a net loss of energy).

An endothermic process absorbs heat and cools the surroundings (i.e., a net gain of energy).

Endothermic reactions absorb energy to break strong bonds to form a less stable state (i.e., positive enthalpy).

Exothermic reactions release energy by forming stronger bonds to produce a more stable state (i.e., negative enthalpy).

The reaction is nonspontaneous (i.e., endergonic) if the products are less stable than the reactants and ΔG is positive.

The reaction is spontaneous (i.e., exergonic) if the products are more stable than the reactants and ΔG is negative.

3. A is correct.

ΔH refers to enthalpy (or heat).

Endothermic reactions have heat as a reactant.

Exothermic reactions have heat as a product.

The reaction is nonspontaneous (i.e., endergonic) if the products are less stable than the reactants and ΔG is positive.

The reaction is spontaneous (i.e., exergonic) if the products are more stable than the reactants and ΔG is negative.

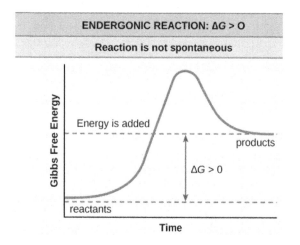
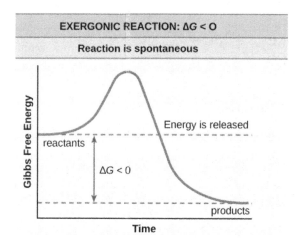

Exothermic reactions release heat and cause the temperature of the immediate surroundings to rise (i.e., a net loss of energy).

An endothermic process absorbs heat and cools the surroundings (i.e., a net gain of energy).

Endothermic reactions absorb energy to break strong bonds to form a less stable state (i.e., positive enthalpy).

Exothermic reactions release energy by forming stronger bonds to produce a more stable state (i.e., negative enthalpy).

4. A is correct.

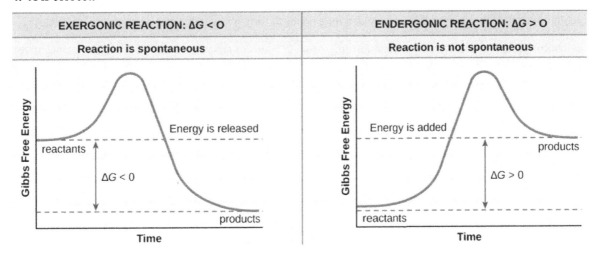

$\Delta G = \Delta H - T\Delta S$ refers to exergonic when ΔG is negative and endergonic when ΔG is positive.

If ΔS is 0 then $\Delta G = \Delta H$ because the $T\Delta S$ term cancels because it equals zero).

ΔH refers to exothermic when ΔH is negative and endothermic when ΔH is positive.

5. C is correct.

ΔH refers to enthalpy (or heat).

Endothermic reactions have heat as a reactant.

Exothermic reactions have heat as a product.

Exothermic reactions release heat and cause the temperature of the immediate surroundings to rise (i.e., a net loss of energy).

An endothermic process absorbs heat and cools the surroundings (i.e., a net gain of energy).

Endothermic reactions absorb energy to break strong bonds to form a less stable state (i.e., positive enthalpy).

Exothermic reactions release energy by forming stronger bonds to produce a more stable state (i.e., negative enthalpy).

The reaction is nonspontaneous (i.e., endergonic) if the products are less stable than the reactants and ΔG is positive.

The reaction is spontaneous (i.e., exergonic) if the products are more stable than the reactants and ΔG is negative.

6. D is correct.

Endothermic reactions absorb energy to break strong bonds to form a less stable state (i.e., positive enthalpy).

Exothermic reactions release energy when forming stronger bonds to produce a more stable state (i.e., negative enthalpy).

To predict spontaneity of reaction, use the Gibbs free energy equation:

$$\Delta G = \Delta H° - T\Delta S$$

The reaction is nonspontaneous (i.e., endergonic) if the products are less stable than the reactants and ΔG is positive.

The reaction is spontaneous (i.e., exergonic) if the products are more stable than the reactants and ΔG is negative.

It is the total amount of energy that is determinative. Some bonds are stronger than others, so there is a net gain or net loss of energy when formed.

7. A is correct.

The higher the energy of activation, the slower the reaction is.

The height of this barrier is independent of the determination of spontaneous (ΔG is negative with products more stable than reactants) or nonspontaneous reactions (ΔG is positive with products less stable than reactants).

8. A is correct.

The primary function of catalysts is lowering the reaction's activation energy (i.e., energy barrier), thus increasing its rate (k).

Although catalysts decrease the energy required to reach the rate-limiting transition state, they do *not* decrease the relative energy of the products and reactants. Therefore, a catalyst does not affect ΔG.

A catalyst provides an alternative pathway for the reaction to proceed to product formation. It lowers the energy of activation (i.e., relative energy between reactants and transition state) and speeds the reaction rate.

Catalysts do not affect the Gibbs free energy (ΔG: stability of products vs. reactants) or the enthalpy (ΔH: bond breaking in reactants or bond making in products).

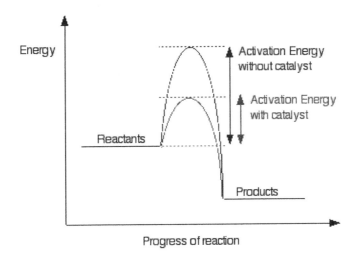

9. B is correct.

A catalyst lowers the energy of activation, which increases the rate of the reaction.

The primary function of catalysts is lowering the reaction's activation energy (energy barrier), thus increasing its rate (k).

Although catalysts decrease the amount of energy required to reach the rate-limiting transition state, they do *not* decrease the relative energy of the products and reactants.

Therefore, a catalyst does not affect ΔG.

10. A is correct.

All the choices are possible events of chemical reactions, but they do not need to happen for a reaction to occur, except that reactant particles must collide (i.e., make contact) with each other.

11. B is correct.

The activation energy is the energy barrier for a reaction to proceed. For the forward reaction, it is measured from the energy of the reactants to the highest energy level in the reaction.

12. A is correct.

Lowering the temperature decreases the reaction rate because the molecules involved in the reaction move and collide more slowly, so the reaction occurs at a slower speed.

Increasing the concentration of reactants due to the increased probability that the reactants collide with sufficient energy and orientation to overcome the energy of activation barrier and proceed toward products.

The primary function of catalysts is lowering the reaction's activation energy (energy barrier), thus increasing its rate (k).

13. C is correct.

Increased pressure or increased concentration of reactants increases the probability that the reactants collide with sufficient energy and orientation to overcome the energy of activation barrier and proceed toward products.

14. C is correct.

The reaction rate is the speed at which reactants are consumed or a product forms.

The rate of a chemical reaction at a constant temperature depends only on the concentrations of the substances that influence the rate.

The reactants influence the rate of reaction, but occasionally products can influence the rate of the reaction.

15. D is correct.

A redox reaction, or oxidation-reduction reaction, involves the transfer of electrons between two reacting substances.

An oxidation reaction refers explicitly to a substance that is losing electrons, and a reduction reaction refers explicitly to a substance that is gaining reactions.

The oxidation and reduction reactions are half-reactions because they always occur together during a reaction.

This question is about *transferring* electrons between *two* species, referring to the whole redox reaction, not one half-reaction.

An electrochemical reaction takes place during the passage of electric current and does involve redox reactions.

However, it is not the correct answer to the question.

16. B is correct.

Use the mnemonic OIL RIG: Oxidation Is Loss, Reduction Is Gain (of electrons).

Oxidation is the loss of electrons, while reduction is the gain of electrons.

An oxidizing agent undergoes reduction, while a reducing agent undergoes oxidation.

If the substance loses electrons (being oxidized), another substance must be gaining electrons (being reduced).

The original substance is a reducing agent, even though it is being oxidized.

17. A is correct.

$PbO + C \rightarrow Pb + CO$ is a single replacement reaction because only one element is being transferred from one reactant to another.

It is a redox reaction because the lead (Pb^{2+}), which dissociates, is reduced (gains electrons), the oxygen (O^{2-}) is oxidized (loses electrons)

One of the products is a single element (Pb), which is a clue that it is a redox reaction.

C: the reaction is double-replacement and not combustion because the combustion reactions must have hydrocarbons and O_2 as reactants.

Double-replacement reactions often result in the formation of a solid, water, and gas.

18. C is correct.

A double-replacement reaction occurs when parts of two ionic compounds (e.g., HBr and KOH) are exchanged to make two new compounds (H_2O and KBr).

$2\ HI \rightarrow H_2 + I_2$ is a decomposition reaction where a compound is degraded into its constituent elements.

$SO_2 + H_2O \rightarrow H_2SO_4$ is a synthesis (or composition) reaction when two species combine to form a more complex chemical product.

$CuO + H_2 \rightarrow Cu + H_2O$ is a single-replacement reaction, which occurs when one element is transferred from one reactant to another element (i.e., the oxygen atom leaves the Cu and joins H_2).

19. B is correct.

$2\ H_2O_2\ (s) \rightarrow 2\ H_2O\ (l) + O_2\ (g)$ is incorrectly classified.

The decomposition part of the classification is correct because one complex compound (H_2O_2) is degraded into two or more parts (H_2O and O_2).

However, it is a redox reaction because oxygen is being lost from H_2O_2, which is one of the three indicators of a redox reaction (i.e., electron loss/gain, hydrogen loss/gain, oxygen loss/gain).

One of the products is a single element (O_2), a clue for a redox reaction.

$AgNO_3\ (aq) + KOH\ (aq) \rightarrow KNO_3\ (aq) + AgOH\ (s)$ is correctly classified as a non-redox reaction because the reactants and products are compounds (i.e., no single elements), and there is no change in oxidation state (i.e., no gain or loss of electrons).

It is a precipitation reaction because the chemical reaction occurs in an aqueous solution, and one of the products formed (AgOH) is insoluble, which makes it a precipitate.

$Pb(NO_3)_2\ (aq) + 2\ Na\ (s) \rightarrow Pb\ (s) + 2\ NaNO_3\ (aq)$ is correctly classified as a redox reaction because the nitrate (NO_3^-), which dissociates, is oxidized (loses electrons), the Na^+ is reduced (gains electrons).

The two combine to form the ionic compound $NaNO_3$.

It is a single-replacement reaction because one element is substituted for another element in a compound, making a new compound (2 $NaNO_3$) and an element (Pb).

HNO_3 (*aq*) + LiOH (*aq*) → $LiNO_3$ (*aq*) + H_2O (*l*) is correctly classified as a non-redox reaction because the reactants and products are compounds (i.e., no single elements), and there is no change in oxidation state (i.e., no gain or loss of electrons).

It is a double-replacement reaction because parts of two ionic compounds are exchanged to make two new compounds.

20. D is correct.

A redox reaction, or oxidation-reduction reaction, involves the transfer of electrons between two reacting substances.

An oxidation reaction refers explicitly to the substance losing electrons, and a reduction reaction refers explicitly to the substance gaining electrons.

The oxidation and reduction reactions are half-reactions because they always occur together to form a whole reaction.

Therefore, half-reaction can represent either a separate oxidation process or a separate reduction process.

21. C is correct.

Increased pressure or increased concentration of reactants increases the probability that the reactants collide with sufficient energy and orientation to overcome the energy of activation barrier and proceed toward products.

22. B is correct.

CH_4 + 2 O_2 → CO_2 + 2 H_2O is a combustion reaction.

A single-replacement reaction results in the production of a compound and an element, but this reaction results in the production of two compounds.

This reaction is a combustion reaction where methane (CH_4) reacts with oxygen.

A: $AgNO_3$ + KCl → KNO_3 + AgCl is correctly classified as a double-replacement reaction, where parts of two ionic compounds ($AgNO_3$ and KCl) are exchanged to make two new compounds (KNO_3 and AgCl).

C: Zn + H_2SO_4 → $ZnSO_4$ + H_2 is correctly classified as a single-replacement reaction, where one element is substituted for another element in a compound, making a new compound ($ZnSO_4$) and an element (H_2).

D: 2 $KClO_3$ → 2 KCl + 3 O_2 is correctly classified as a decomposition reaction, where one chemical compound (2 $KClO_3$) is split into two or more products (2 KCl and 3 O_2).

23. D is correct.

2 KClO$_3$ (*s*) → 2 KCl (*s*) + 3 O$_2$ (*g*) is a decomposition reaction, which occurs when one chemical compound splits into two or more compounds.

The compound KClO$_3$ splits into KCl and O$_2$.

2 Cr (*s*) + 3 Cl$_2$ (*g*) → 2 CrCl$_3$ (*s*) is a synthesis reaction (composition reactions) because it forms a more complex chemical compound from individual elements.

6 Li (*s*) + N$_2$ (*g*) → 2 Li$_3$N (*s*) is a synthesis reaction (composition reactions) because it forms a more complex chemical compound from individual elements.

C$_7$H$_8$O$_2$ (*l*) + 8 O$_2$ (*g*) → 7 CO$_2$ (*g*) + 4 H$_2$O (*l*) is a combustion reaction because the hydrocarbon is reacting with oxygen.

It is not a decomposition reaction because it involves two reactants rather than a single substance.

24. C is correct.

Heat is a product of a spontaneous (exothermic) reaction whereby the products are more stable than the reactants.

Endothermic reactions have a net absorption of energy from a reaction, and the products have more energy than the reactants. Heat is required as a reactant for non-spontaneous (endothermic) reactions.

25. A is correct.

A single-replacement reaction is a chemical reaction in which one element is substituted for another element in a compound, making a new compound and an element.

A double-replacement reaction occurs when parts of two ionic compounds are exchanged to make two new compounds.

BaCl$_2$ + H$_2$SO$_4$ → BaSO$_4$ + 2 HCl is a double-replacement reaction with two products (BaSO$_4$ and 2 HCl).

26. A is correct.

Increasing the concentration of reactants increases the collision rate, resulting in a reaction that proceeds faster.

Vessel a shows the least concentrated reaction conditions and, therefore, the slowest reaction.

27. C is correct.

For a reaction to occur, the molecules must have enough energy during a collision and strike each other with the proper spatial orientation to overcome the energy barrier (activation energy).

28. A is correct.

Increasing the concentration of reactants increases the frequency of collision and, therefore, the relative rate of the reaction.

29. B is correct.

Since atoms cannot be created or destroyed in chemical reactions, there must be equal numbers of atoms on each side of the reaction arrow.

The number of atoms present in a reaction can never vary, even if conditions change.

However, the number of products and reactants does not have to be the same.

For example, two reactants (on the left side of a reaction arrow) combine to form one product (on the right side of a reaction arrow).

Similarly, the number of molecules on each side of the reaction arrow does not have to be equal.

30. D is correct.

Enzymes are proteins that increase the rate of chemical reactions converting substrate into product.

They act as catalysts to increase the rate of a chemical reaction; they do not get consumed in the reactions and remain unchanged.

Catalysts are simple inorganic molecules, while enzymes are complex proteins.

The activation energy is the minimum energy needed for a reaction to take place.

It is thought of as an "energy barrier" because at least this amount of energy must be put into the system.

Enzymes act by decreasing the activation energy and lowering the energy barrier, which allows the reaction to take place more easily.

This increases the rate at which the reaction takes place.

Notes for active learning

Notes for active learning

Section III

Scientific Reasoning

Scientific Measurements and Laboratory Tools

Scientific Explanations Using Logic and Evidence

Relationships Among Events, Objects, and Processes

Analysis and Design of a Scientific Investigation

Scientific Measurements and Laboratory Tools – Explanations

Answer Key

1: B	11: A	21: A
2: B	12: D	22: B
3: C	13: C	
4: A	14: C	
5: D	15: D	
6: C	16: B	
7: D	17: B	
8: A	18: D	
9: D	19: B	
10: D	20: B	

1. B is correct.

Western blotting separates proteins by electrophoresis and is commonly used to identify the presence of HIV antibodies (proteins).

All blotting techniques rely on gel electrophoresis to separate DNA, RNA, or proteins based on size.

After resolution by electrophoresis, the gel (containing the resolved products) is placed next to the blotting paper (e.g., nitrocellulose).

After the transfer of the macromolecules (i.e., DNA, RNA, or proteins) onto the gel by capillary action, the blotting paper is probed by specific markers that hybridize to regions with complementary sequences on the blotting paper.

A: Eastern blotting does not exist.

C: Northern blotting uses RNA in gel electrophoresis.

D: Southern blotting uses DNA in gel electrophoresis.

2. B is correct.

PCR requires knowledge of the sequence at the ends of the fragment being amplified.

From the ends, complementary base pairing is used to design the primers that anneal to the target fragment and permit amplification.

No knowledge of the region between the ends is required because the parent strands are the templates used by the DNA polymerase.

3. C is correct.

Microscopy is the laboratory technique of magnifying objects that cannot be seen with the unaided eye.

Gregor Mendel performed crossbreeding experiments with pea plants to study inheritance patterns and introduced the terms *dominant* and *recessive* for phenotypic traits (or *alleles*).

4. A is correct.

O_2 binding to hemoglobin exhibits positive cooperativity with a Hill coefficient greater than 1.

Positive cooperativity is due to the first (of four) O_2 binding weakly to hemoglobin.

The binding of the first O_2 increases the affinity of the hemoglobin for additional O_2 binding.

The binding curve has a sigmoid shape.

Negative cooperativity is when the ligand binding to the first site decreases the affinity for additional ligands to bind.

5. D is correct.

pH is represented as a log scale:

A pH change of 1 unit (e.g. pH 4 *vs.* 5) = 10× difference.

A pH difference of 2 units (e.g., pH 3 *vs.* 5): $10 \times 10 = 100×$ difference.

A pH difference of 3 units (e.g., pH 2 *vs.* 5): $10 \times 10 \times 10 = 1,000×$ difference.

6. C is correct.

The pH scale has a range from 1 to 14, with 7 being a neutral pH.

A pH change of 1 unit changes the ratio by 10×.

7. D is correct.

Barometers and manometers are used to measure pressure.

Barometers are designed to measure atmospheric pressure.

A manometer can measure lower pressure than atmospheric pressure.

A manometer has both ends of the tube open to the outside (while some may have one end closed), whereas a barometer is a type of closed-end manometer with one end of the glass tube closed and sealed with a vacuum.

The atmospheric pressure is 760 mmHg, so the barometer should be able to accommodate that.

8. A is correct.

Standard temperature and pressure (STP) have a temperature of 273.15 K (0 °C, 32 °F) and a pressure of 10^5 Pa (100 kPa, 750.06 mmHg, 1 bar, 14.504 psi, 0.98692 atm).

The mm of Hg is the pressure generated by a column of mercury one millimeter high.

The pressure of mercury depends on temperature and gravity.

This variation in mmHg and torr is a difference in units of about 0.000015%.

In general,

> 1 torr = 1 mm of Hg
>
> 1 mm of Hg = 0.0013158 atm
>
> 750.06 mmHg = 0.98692 atm

9. D is correct.

Assume a is the equivalent temperature (i.e., has the same value in °C and °F).

Set the equivalent temperature on one side and a conversion factor to the other unit on the other side.

For example, the left side is °C, while the right side is the conversion to °F:

> $a = [(9/5) \times a] + 32$
>
> $a - (9/5)a = 32$
>
> $(-4/5)a = 32$
>
> $-4a = 160$
>
> $a = -40$

At –40, the temperature is the same in °C and °F.

10. D is correct.

At low elevations (i.e., sea level), the boiling point of water is 100 °C.

Atmospheric pressure is the pressure exerted by the weight of air in the atmosphere.

The boiling point decreases with increasing altitude due to the reduced atmospheric pressure above the water at high altitudes.

11. A is correct.

When comparing fuels in various forms (e.g., solid, liquid, gas), it is easiest to compare energy released in terms of the mass because the matter has mass regardless of its state (as opposed to volume, which is convenient for a liquid or gas, but not for a solid).

Moles are more complicated because they must be converted to mass before a direct comparison can be made between fuels.

12. D is correct.

Concentration:

> solute / volume

For example:

> 10 g / 1 liter = 10 g/liter
>
> 2 g / 1 liter = 2 g/liter

13. C is correct.

The pH scale has a range from 1 to 14, with 7 being a neutral pH.

Acidic solutions have a pH below 7, while basic solutions have a pH above 7.

The pH scale is a log scale where 7 has a 50% deprotonated and 50% protonated (neutral) species (1:1 ratio).

At a pH of 6, there are 1 deprotonated : 10 protonated species. The ratio is 1:10.

At a pH of 5, there are 1 deprotonated : 100 protonated species. The ratio is 1:100.

A pH change of 1 unit changes the ratio by 10×.

Decreasing the pH (< 7) results in more protonated species (i.e., cation).

Increasing the pH (> 7) results in more deprotonated species (e.g., anion).

14. C is correct.

The pH scale has a range from 1 to 14, with 7 being a neutral pH.

> pH change of 1 unit changes the ratio by 10×
>
> pH change of 2 units changes the ratio by 100×
>
> pH change of 3 units changes the ratio by 1000×

15. D is correct.

Standard temperature and pressure (STP) have a temperature of 273.15 K (0 °C, 32 °F) and a pressure of 10^5 Pa (100 kPa, 750.06 mmHg, 1 bar, 14.504 psi, 0.98692 atm).

16. B is correct.

Methyl red has a pK_a of 5.1 and is a pH indicator dye that changes color in acidic solutions: it turns red in pH under 4.4, orange in pH 4.4-6.2, and yellow in pH over 6.2.

I: phenolphthalein is used as an indicator for acid-base titrations. It is a weak acid, which can dissociate protons (H^+ ions) in solution.

The phenolphthalein molecule is colorless, and the phenolphthalein ion is pink.

It turns colorless in acidic solutions and pink in basic solutions.

With basic conditions, the phenolphthalein (neutral) $\rightleftharpoons$ ions (pink) equilibrium shifts to the right, leading to more ionization as H^+ ions are removed.

III: bromothymol blue is a pH indicator that is often used for solutions with neutral pH near 7 (e.g., managing the pH of pools and fish tanks).

Bromothymol blue acts as a weak acid in a solution that can be protonated or deprotonated.

Bromothymol blue appears yellow when protonated (lower pH), blue when deprotonated (higher pH), and bluish-green in neutral solution.

17. B is correct.

Phenolphthalein is used as an indicator for acid-base titrations.

Phenolphthalein is a weak acid, which can dissociate protons (H^+ ions) in solution.

The phenolphthalein molecule is colorless, and the phenolphthalein ion is pink.

It turns colorless in acidic solutions and pink in basic solutions.

With basic conditions, the phenolphthalein (neutral) $\rightleftharpoons$ ions (pink) equilibrium shifts to the right, leading to more ionization as H^+ ions are removed.

18. D is correct.

Molarity is the number of moles of solute per liter of solution.

Molarity is based on a specified volume of solution.

Molality (molal concentration) is a measure of the concentration of a solute in a solution in terms of the amount of substance in a specified amount of mass of the solvent.

19. B is correct.

Temperature is a measure of the average kinetic energy ($KE = \frac{1}{2}mv^2$) of the molecules, not the potential energy ($PE = mgh$) of the molecules.

The *temperature of matter* refers to the macroscopic (i.e., aggregate) properties of the matter and not the microscopic (i.e., individual) properties of the matter (i.e., each particle may have different kinetic energy).

There is a temperature difference among the molecules at the microscopic level (due to differences in KE).

Heat is the transfer of thermal energy from high to low temperature regions.

It spontaneously passes between individual molecules within the system (e.g., from one molecule to another) and the system and its surroundings.

20. B is correct.

Heat is energy that is transferred to the molecules and increases their kinetic energy.

Temperature is a measure of the average kinetic energy of the molecules.

21. A is correct.

Vapor pressure increases as the temperature increases.

100 °C is the boiling point of water.

At boiling point, the vapor pressure of a substance is equal to the atmospheric pressure.

Therefore, the vapor pressure of water at 100 °C is 760 mmHg.

22. B is correct.

Litmus (i.e., dyes extracted from lichens) is used to test whether a solution is acidic or basic.

Neutral litmus paper is purple, with color changes occurring outside of the pH range 4.5–8.3 at 25 °C (77 °F).

Under acidic conditions, litmus paper is red, and under basic conditions, it is blue.

Litmus paper can be used to test for water-soluble gases that affect acidity or alkalinity; the gas dissolves in the water, and the resulting solution colors the litmus paper.

For example, alkaline ammonia gas causes the litmus paper to change from red to blue.

Litmus can be prepared as an aqueous solution that functions similarly.

Under acidic conditions, the solution is red, and under basic conditions, the solution is blue.

Notes for active learning

With each topic, reinforce learning by reading review chapters in your *ATI TEAS Science Review* book.

Visit our Amazon store

Notes for active learning

Scientific Explanations Using Logic and Evidence – Explanations

Answer Key

1: D	11: D
2: C	12: B
3: A	13: C
4: A	14: B
5: A	
6: B	
7: A	
8: C	
9: A	
10: D	

1. D is correct.

The decimating fire was a random event unrelated to the apparent fitness of the fly in its typical environment.

Genetic drift is the random change over time in the allele frequency within a population, such as the one caused by the decimating fire in the loss of allele(s) for the altered structure.

A: reproduction is not involved in the loss of the advantageous modification.

B: natural selection is not the cause since the death of the flies was unrelated to their fitness, and a decimating fire would likely have killed all flies, regardless of their advantageous modification.

C: Hardy-Weinberg describes ideal circumstances which do not apply to this situation.

2. C is correct.

Thyroxine is one of the thyroid hormones secreted by the thyroid gland and plays an essential role in regulating metabolism. In adults, thyroid deficiency (i.e., hypothyroidism) results in a decreased rate of metabolism, which produces symptoms such as weight gain, fatigue, intolerance to cold, and swelling of the thyroid (i.e., goiter).

A decreased metabolic rate means that the body uses less energy per day, and fewer dietary calories are required. Thus, unless a hypothyroid patient changes her diet, she will gain weight because excess calories are converted and stored in adipose tissue as fat.

In response to low thyroid hormone levels, the pituitary secretes the thyroid-stimulating hormone, which increases thyroid hormone production. However, if the thyroid cannot increase its hormone synthesis, it will hypertrophy (i.e., increase in mass), resulting in goiter (i.e., a swollen pouch in the throat region).

A: estrogen is not the cause of the patient's symptoms.

B: cortisol deficiency is not the cause of the patient's symptoms.

D: aldosterone deficiency is not the cause of the patient's symptoms.

3. A is correct.

The radio-labeled hormone enters the nucleus of the liver cells, which means the hormone is soluble in the plasma membrane.

Steroid hormones are hydrophobic and therefore pass through the plasma membrane and enter the target cells where the hormone binds to an intracellular (i.e., cytoplasmic) receptor and then, bound to the receptor, the hormone/receptor complex enters the nucleus and directly binds to the DNA (i.e., transcription factor) and therefore influences the transcription of mRNA.

Peptide hormones (i.e., ligand) bind to a receptor on the target cell's membranes' surface.

The ligand-receptor complex may trigger the release of a second messenger (e.g., G-protein or cAMP), or the ligand-receptor complex may be carried into the cytoplasm by receptor-mediated endocytosis.

For a second messenger, events within the cell are responsible for the hormone's activity (i.e., phosphorylation or dephosphorylation to change the shape/activity of enzymes within the cell).

Thus, peptide hormones do not directly influence mRNA transcription because peptide hormones do not enter the nucleus of their target cells and activate transcription.

B: steroid hormones are often derivatives of cholesterol (i.e., hydrophobic).

D: amino acids contain hydrophilic residues and cannot cross the hydrophobic lipid bilayer of the plasma membrane or the nuclear membrane.

4. A is correct.

Autosomal recessive inheritance is the product of mating two carriers (i.e., heterozygous parents).

In the mating of two heterozygotes for an autosomal recessive gene, there is a:

       1) 25% (1/4) probability of a homozygous unaffected child

       2) 25% (1/4) probability of a homozygous affected child

       3) 50% (1/2) probability of a heterozygous (carrier) child

Overall, 75% of children are phenotypically normal (25% AA and 50% Aa).

Out of all children, 50% are phenotypically normal but carry the mutant gene (Aa).

5. A is correct.

Maternal inheritance involves all the progeny exhibiting the phenotype of the female parent.

B: not maternal inheritance because the progeny exhibit the phenotype of only the male parent.

C and D: normal Mendelian 1:1 segregation and not maternal inheritance.

Maternal inheritance is a type of uniparental inheritance by which all progeny have the genotype and phenotype of the female parent.

6. B is correct.

A recessive trait is expressed only when present in both copies or is the only copy of the gene present.

A recessive X-linked allele would only be expressed in unaffected women with two (homozygous) copies of the allele. If one X is present, then all recessive (single copy) alleles on the X are expressed (e.g., hemophilia).

The presence of a Y chromosome (in humans) confers maleness on the organism.

7. A is correct

Surfactants are compounds that lower the surface tension and form micelles.

Micelle formation requires numerous hydrophobic interactions and minimizes exposure to hydrophilic surfaces.

Surfactants are lipid-based compounds.

Micelle formation is necessary during the absorption of lipids (i.e., dietary fats) by the small intestine.

A lack of micelle formation results in lipid-soluble vitamins (A, D, E, K) deficiency.

8. C is correct.

From the diagram, lymph flow increases (to a point) in proportion to the increase in the interstitial fluid pressure. To decide whether an increase in interstitial fluid protein increases lymph flow, determine whether an increase in interstitial fluid protein increases interstitial fluid pressure.

When proteins move from the capillary into the interstitial space, the solute concentration in the interstitial space increases.

Fluid then flows out of the capillaries and into the interstitial space, which increases the interstitial fluid volume and fluid pressure.

A: fluid movement from the interstitial spaces into the capillaries would decrease interstitial fluid pressure, but an increase of proteins in the interstitial causes fluid movement out of the capillaries.

D: an increase in interstitial fluid pressure increases lymph flow (until point 0 – see graph).

9. A is correct.

Bile is formed in the liver and released by the gallbladder to emulsify fats by increasing their surface area to help lipase degrade them.

Bile salt anions are hydrophilic on one side and hydrophobic on the other.

They aggregate around droplets of fat (triglycerides and phospholipids) to form micelles, with the hydrophobic sides towards the fat and hydrophilic sides facing outwards.

The hydrophilic sides are negatively charged, and this charge prevents fat droplets coated with bile from re-aggregating into larger fat particles.

10. D is correct.

Cartilage does not contain nerves.

Unlike other connective tissues, cartilage does not contain blood vessels.

Cells of the cartilage (i.e., chondrocytes) produce a large amount of extracellular matrix composed of collagen fibers, elastin fibers, and abundant ground substance rich in proteoglycan.

Cartilage is classified as *elastic cartilage, hyaline cartilage,* and *fibrocartilage*, which differ in the relative amounts of the three main components.

11. D is correct.

Acromegaly is a condition that results from an oversecretion by the anterior pituitary of growth hormone (GH) that decreases the sensitivity of insulin receptors.

The pancreas secretes insulin in response to high blood glucose.

Acromegaly patients do not bind insulin and do normal cells, and the effects of insulin are diminished.

If insulin cannot exert its effects on the cells, excess glucose is not converted into glycogen.

Hence, the patient has high blood glucose concentrations.

A: high blood glucose concentrations lead to the excretion of glucose, along with the loss of water in the urine, meaning that patients have increased (*not decreased*) urine volume.

B: cardiac output is the volume of blood pumped by the heart/unit time, which is unrelated to the sensitivity of insulin receptors.

C: low blood glucose concentration is the opposite effect.

12. B is correct.

Glucose usually is completely reabsorbed from the filtrate and is not excreted in the urine.

The presence of glucose in the urine signifies that glucose transporters in the proximal convoluted tubule (not the loop of Henle) cannot reabsorb glucose from the filtrate.

13. C is correct.

Most integral proteins span the plasma membrane. The plasma membrane is a phospholipid bilayer with an inner span consisting of hydrophobic (or *water-fearing*) regions. The diameter of a plasma membrane is 20 to 25 amino acids thick. Therefore, spans of 20-25 hydrophobic residues prefer to be embedded in the plasma membrane and isolated from water.

Hydropathy analysis determines the degree of hydrophobicity (i.e., nonpolar or *water-fearing*) or hydrophilicity (i.e., polar or *water-loving*) of amino acids in a protein. It characterizes the possible structure or domains of a protein. Each residue (i.e., individual amino acid) has a hydrophobicity value assigned to it (analogous to electronegativity). The hydropathy plot has the amino acid sequence of a protein on the *x*-axis and the degree of hydrophobicity (or hydrophilicity) on the *y*-axis. The graph shows amino acids *vs.* hydrophobicity.

Amino acids have lower energy when polar amino acids occupy a polar environment (e.g., cytoplasm) and nonpolar amino acids occupy a nonpolar environment (e.g., interior of plasma membrane).

14. B is correct.

Mitochondria have DNA genetic material and machinery to manufacture RNA and proteins.

In the example above, the trait must be recessive (not observed in the limited number of offspring) and encoded by a nuclear gene.

A: mice, like organisms that reproduce sexually, inherit the mitochondrial organelle from their mother and display maternal inheritance of mitochondrial genes.

C: if X-linked, then selectively male (not female) progeny would display the trait.

D: mitochondrial genes cannot be recessive because all mitochondria are inherited from the mother.

Notes for active learning

Relationships Among Events, Objects, and Processes – Explanations

Answer Key

1: C	11: B
2: D	12: D
3: C	13: C
4: B	14: C
5: C	15: B
6: C	
7: A	
8: B	
9: C	
10: C	

1. C is correct.

If the hormone accumulates inside the cell without endocytosis (i.e., intake via invagination of the cell's plasma membrane), it must diffuse through the plasma membrane. Steroid hormones are hydrophobic and freely diffuse through the plasma membrane.

A: neurotransmitters are charged molecules that bind to a receptor at the cell surface.

B: second messengers transmit signals inside cells but are not hormones.

D: polypeptides cannot diffuse through membranes because they are large, hydrophilic molecules.

2. D is correct.

Excessive production of epinephrine results in clinical manifestations affecting the sympathetic nervous system (*fight or flight* response) with 1) elevated blood pressure, 2) increased heart rate, 3) dilation of the pupils and 4) inhibition of gastrointestinal tract function and motility.

3. C is correct.

Calcitonin is a peptide hormone secreted by the thyroid gland.

One of its significant effects is the inhibition of osteoclast (i.e., bone degradation) activity in bones.

Osteoblasts do not have calcitonin receptors, and therefore calcitonin does not affect them directly.

The processes of bone resorption and formation are interdependent.

Eventually, inhibition of osteoclastic activity by calcitonin leads to increased osteoblastic activity indirectly.

4. B is correct.

The epidermis consists of five layers of cells.

Each layer has a distinct role in the health, well-being, and functioning of the skin.

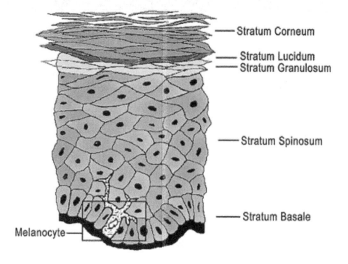

Stratum basale is the deepest layer of the five layers of the epidermis and is a continuous layer of cells. It is often described as one cell thick (though it may be two to three cells thick in hairless skin and hyperproliferative epidermis).

Stratum basale is primarily made up of basal keratinocyte cells that divide to form the keratinocytes of the stratum spinosum, which migrate superficially.

Other types of cells within the stratum basale are melanocytes (pigment-producing cells), Langerhans cells (immune cells), and Merkel cells (touch receptors).

B: *stratum spinosum* is where keratinization begins. This layer comprises polyhedral keratinocytes active in synthesizing fibrillar proteins (i.e., cytokeratin) built up within the cells by aggregating to form tonofibrils.

The tonofibrils form the desmosomes allowing strong connections to form between adjacent keratinocytes.

C: *stratum corneum* is the outermost layer of the epidermis, consisting of dead cells (corneocytes).

It forms a barrier to protect underlying tissue from infection, dehydration, chemicals, and mechanical stress.

D: *stratum lucidum* is a thin, transparent layer of dead skin cells in the epidermis named for its translucent appearance.

The stratum lucidum comprises three to five layers of dead, flattened keratinocytes, which do not feature distinct boundaries and are filled with an intermediate form of keratin (eleidin).

Stratum granulosum is a thin layer of cells where keratinocytes that migrated from the underlying stratum spinosum become granular cells containing keratohyalin granules.

These granules are filled with proteins and promote hydration and crosslinking of keratin.

At the transition between this layer and the stratum corneum, cells secrete lamellar bodies (containing lipids and proteins) into the extracellular space.

This results in the formation of the hydrophobic lipid envelope responsible for the skin's barrier properties.

Cells lose their nuclei and organelles, causing granular cells to become non-viable corneocytes in the stratum corneum.

5. C is correct.

The seminal vesicles secrete a significant proportion of the fluid that ultimately becomes semen.

About 50-70% of the seminal fluid originates from the seminal vesicles but is not expelled in the first ejaculate fractions dominated by spermatozoa and zinc-rich prostatic fluid.

6. C is correct.

A patient develops a peptic ulcer either when her gastric mucosa overproduces HCl or when mucosal defenses are inadequate to protect the stomach mucosa lining from the average concentration of HCl.

The pH in the stomach is about 2 because of the secretion of HCl, and this acidic environment is needed by the gastric (stomach) enzyme pepsin that functions optimally at pH 2.

Peptic ulcers can be treated with antacids, which neutralize the HCl and raise the pH.

By increasing pH, pepsin becomes nonfunctional, and therefore, pepsin activity is the most affected by an overdose of antacid.

The small intestine has a pH of between 6 and 7 and is relatively alkaline due to bicarbonate secretion.

Trypsin, procarboxypeptidase, and lipase are enzyme products of the exocrine pancreas secreted into the small intestine and function optimally in an alkaline environment.

A: procarboxypeptidase is an enzyme that hydrolyzes proteins.

B: trypsin is an enzyme that hydrolyzes protein.

D: lipase is an enzyme that hydrolyzes lipids.

7. A is correct.

The phenotype of the first child does not influence the probability for the second child.

Similarly, getting a tail on the first toss of a coin does not influence the second toss (i.e., independent events).

A Punnett square determines all possible gametes and their combinations.

If ½ of the woman's gametes carry the trait and ½ of the father's gametes carry the trait, the probability of a child receiving the allele from both parents is ½ × ½ = ¼.

8. B is correct.

Severe combined immunodeficiency (SCID) causes abnormalities in T and B-cells.

B-cells are produced in the bone marrow.

T-cells are produced in the bone marrow and mature in the thymus.

SCID is a genetic disorder characterized by the absence of functional T-lymphocytes.

The result is an inadequate antibody response due to either direct involvement with B lymphocytes or improper B lymphocyte activation due to nonfunctional T-helper cells.

Consequently, both B cells and T cells are impaired due to a genetic defect.

9. C is correct.

Blood returns to the heart via the inferior and superior vena cava (i.e., hollow veins) and enters the right atrium of the heart according to the following flow:

Superior/inferior vena cava → right atrium → right ventricle → pulmonary artery → lungs → pulmonary vein

10. C is correct.

The right atrium is the upper chamber of the right side of the heart.

The blood that is returned to the right atrium by the superior and inferior vena cava is deoxygenated (low in O_2) and passed into the right ventricle to be pumped through the pulmonary artery to the lungs for O_2 and removal of CO_2.

The left atrium receives newly oxygenated blood from the lungs by the pulmonary vein.

The blood is passed into the muscular left ventricle to be pumped through the aorta to the various organs of the body.

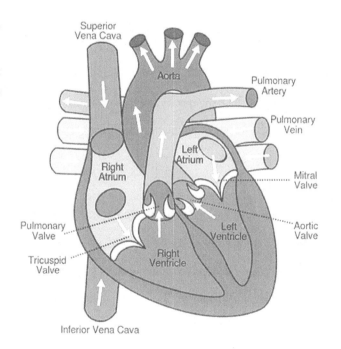

In the normal heart, the right ventricle pumps blood through the pulmonary arteries to the lungs during pulmonary circulation.

The left ventricle pumps blood through the aorta to the body for systemic circulation.

If blood mixes between the ventricles, some blood in the right ventricle (deoxygenated) is mixed with the blood in the left ventricle (oxygenated) for systemic circulation. This mixing lowers the O_2 supplied to the tissues.

11. B is correct.

Hypovolemic shock is a state of decreased volume of blood plasma from such conditions as hemorrhaging and dehydration.

The loss of blood plasma would be more rapid from arterial bleeding (i.e., high hydrostatic pressure) than from venous bleeding (i.e., low hydrostatic pressure).

12. D is correct.

Type 1 diabetes can occur from a deficiency of insulin produced by beta cells of the pancreas.

With a deficiency/absence of insulin, plasma glucose rises to dangerously high levels, and patients excrete excess glucose in the urine.

A: decreased blood glucose levels do not stimulate insulin.

B: the thyroid gland does not produce insulin.

C: decreased levels of circulating erythrocytes (i.e., anemia) are not related to diabetes.

13. C is correct.

The pancreatic duct leads from the pancreas to the common bile duct into the second portion of the duodenum.

The pancreatic duct carries pancreatic enzymes (e.g., pancreatic amylase, lipase) and some proteases (e.g., trypsin, elastin, amylase, chymotrypsin) from the pancreas to the duodenum.

The pancreatic secretions contain bicarbonate in response to the hormones cholecystokinin and secretin (i.e., released by the walls of the duodenum in response to food).

Bicarbonate neutralizes the acidic stomach contents (i.e., chyme) as they enter the duodenum.

The pancreas is an endocrine gland that produces hormones (e.g., insulin, glucagon, somatostatin) and an exocrine gland synthesizing enzymes for the digestion of proteins, lipids, and fats in the duodenum.

The pancreatic hormones do not pass through the pancreatic ducts but are secreted directly into the bloodstream.

I: diabetic crisis does not result from the obstruction of the pancreatic duct because the release of the pancreatic hormones (insulin or glucagon) is not affected.

II: acromegaly results from excessive secretion of growth hormone in an adult and causes excessive bone growth of some facial bones, resulting in a distorted facial appearance.

There is no connection between growth hormone from the anterior pituitary and blockage of the pancreatic duct.

14. C is correct.

Insulin is a hormone secreted by the beta cells of the pancreas in response to high blood glucose levels.

Insulin decreases blood glucose levels by stimulating cells to uptake glucose and stimulating glucose conversion into its storage form (glycogen) in liver cells and muscle cells.

An overdose of insulin can (and often does) lead to convulsions because of the resulting sharp decrease in blood glucose concentration.

A: people with diabetes would become dehydrated if untreated (with proper insulin dosage) because the excess glucose in the nephrons causes water (as filtrate) to diffuse into the nephrons. With high glucose levels, the net result is an increase in urine excretion.

Insulin decreases urine excretion by decreasing blood glucose levels, and glucose does not join the filtrate.

B: insulin increases the conversion of glucose into glycogen. Therefore, an overdose of insulin would not cause an increase in the conversion of glycogen back into glucose.

Glucagon, also secreted by the pancreas, stimulates the conversion of glycogen into glucose.

D: the presence of glucose is a clinical manifestation of diabetes because of high blood glucose concentration that arises from an insufficiency (or complete lack of) insulin production or because insulin-specific receptors are insensitive to insulin.

In untreated diabetes, there is a high blood glucose concentration and a high urine glucose concentration since the kidneys cannot reabsorb glucose because of its excess in the blood.

Controlled doses of insulin are used to stimulate glucose uptake by muscle and adipose cells and convert excess glucose into glycogen.

Insulin alleviates the symptoms of diabetes and would not cause an increased glucose concentration in the urine.

15. B is correct.

Increasing the concentration of reactants (or increasing pressure) increases the reaction rate because there is an increased probability that two reactant molecules collide with sufficient energy to overcome the energy of activation and form products.

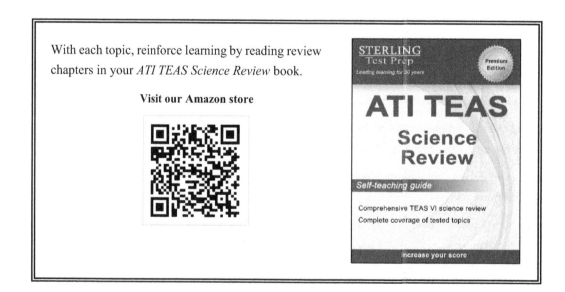

Notes for active learning

Notes for active learning

Analysis and Design of a Scientific Investigation – Explanations

Answer Key

1: C	11: C
2: D	12: B
3: B	13: C
4: A	14: D
5: D	
6: C	
7: D	
8: D	
9: B	
10: B	

1. C is correct.

To show that DNA, rather than RNA, protein, or some other cell component, was responsible for transformation, Avery, McLeod, and McCarty used several biochemical tests.

Proteases and ribonucleases (i.e., degradation enzymes for protein and RNA) did not affect the transforming agent that caused disease.

However, a DNase treatment did degrade the DNA (genetic material) and destroyed the extract's ability to cause disease.

Streptococcus pneumoniae (i.e., pneumococcus) is a Gram-positive pathogenic bacterium.

S. pneumoniae was recognized as a significant cause of pneumonia in the late 19th-century had been the subject of humoral immunity (i.e., antibody-mediated) studies.

2. D is correct.

Hershey and Chase showed that when bacteriophages (i.e., viruses), composed of DNA and protein, infect bacteria, their DNA enters the host bacterial cell while their protein does not.

They grew separate populations of viruses and incorporated either radioactive sulfur (^{35}S to label protein) or phosphorus (^{32}P to label DNA) into the bacteriophages.

The viral ^{35}S protein coats remained outside the bacteria while the ^{32}P DNA entered the bacteria.

The experiment demonstrated that the DNA, not protein, was the *transforming* molecule that entered the bacteria from viral infection.

3. B is correct.

For the same molecular weight, more of the positively charged compounds and less of the negatively charged compounds are filtered than neutral compounds.

This occurs because the *negative charge* on the cellulose filtration membrane attracts positively charged and repels negatively charged compounds.

4. A is correct.

A model organism for genetic studies (e.g., pea plants, Drosophila, zebrafish) has common features. Genetic studies rely upon statistics that favor large sample numbers. Therefore, a short generation time (i.e., the span between birth and fecundity) is preferred. The organism must be bred in large numbers, and ease of cultivation favors viable offspring that transmit genetic information between generations.

There should be discreet phenotypic differences among alleles (alternative forms of the gene). For example, among the seven traits that Mendel observed, he inventoried tall *vs.* short plants, round *vs.* smooth seeds, and green *vs.* yellow seeds. Mendel was able to control the crosses by manually transferring pollen from the anther of a mature pea plant of one variety to the stigma of a separate mature pea plant of the second variety.

The organism should have a genome well characterized (gene identity and function have been studied). Increasing the number of chromosomes increases the genes that can influence the observable phenotypic outcomes. An organism with fewer chromosomes makes statistical analysis direct and supports causation when the genome is manipulated.

5. D is correct.

Isotopes are variants of an element that differ in the number of neutrons.

Isotopes of the element have the same number of protons and occupy the same position on the periodic table.

The experimental results should depend on the mass of the gas molecules.

Deuterium (D or ^{2}H) is known as heavy hydrogen. It is one of two stable isotopes of hydrogen.

The nucleus of deuterium contains one proton and one neutron, compared to H, which has 1 proton and 0 neutrons.

The mass of deuterium is 2.0141 daltons, compared to 1.0078 daltons for hydrogen.

Based on the difference of mass between the isotopes, the density, rate of gas effusion, and atomic vibrations would be different.

6. C is correct.

For the ideal gas law, there is no difference between He and Ne since pressure, volume, temperature, and the number of moles are known quantities.

The identity of the gas would only be relevant to convert from moles to mass or vice-versa.

7. D is correct.

In thermodynamics, an isolated system is enclosed by rigid, immovable walls that neither matter nor energy passes.

Temperature is a measure of energy and is not a form of energy; it cannot be exchanged between the system and surroundings.

A closed system can exchange energy (as heat or work) with its surroundings, but not matter.

An isolated system cannot exchange energy (as heat or work) or matter with the surroundings.

An open system can exchange energy and matter with the surroundings.

8. D is correct.

A reaction proceeds when the reactant(s) have sufficient energy to overcome the energy of activation and proceed to products.

Increasing the temperature increases the kinetic energy of the molecule, increases the collision frequency, and increases the probability that the reactants will overcome the barrier (i.e., the energy of activation).

9. B is correct.

As the temperature (i.e., average kinetic energy) ινχρεασεσ, the particles move faster and collide more frequently per unit time and possess greater energy when they collide. This increases the reaction rate.

Hence the reaction rate of most reactions increases with increasing temperature.

10. B is correct.

The activation energy is the energy barrier that must be overcome to transform reactant(s) into product(s).

The molecules must collide with the proper orientation and energy (i.e., kinetic energy is the average temperature) to overcome the energy of activation barrier.

Solids describe molecules with limited relative motion.

Liquids are molecules with more relative motion than solids, while gases exhibit the most relative motion.

11. C is correct.

Convection is the movement of heat through liquids and gases.

The lid prevents the fluid (e.g., air) from escaping the vessel.

12. B is correct.

A closed system can exchange energy (as heat or work) but not matter or temperature with its surroundings.

An isolated system cannot exchange heat, work, matter, or temperature with the surroundings.

An open system can exchange energy, matter, and temperature with the surroundings.

It is not an isolated system because work is being done on the system; it is a closed system because no matter moves in or out.

13. C is correct.

An insulator reduces conduction (i.e., transfer of thermal energy through matter).

Air (or a vacuum) between the two partition walls is a highly effective insulator.

14. D is correct.

A closed system can exchange energy (as heat or work) but not matter with its surroundings.

An isolated system cannot exchange energy (as heat or work) or matter with the surroundings.

An open system can exchange energy and matter with the surroundings.

Notes for active learning

Notes for active learning

For best results, use ATI TEAS Science Review

A thorough review of science topics tested on TEAS VI. Learn the important foundations and essential details for targeted test preparation to *increase your score*.

Visit our Amazon store

HESI A2 prep books

- Biology, Anatomy & Physiology Review
- Biology, Anatomy & Physiology Practice Questions
- Chemistry and Physics Review
- Chemistry and Physics Practice Questions

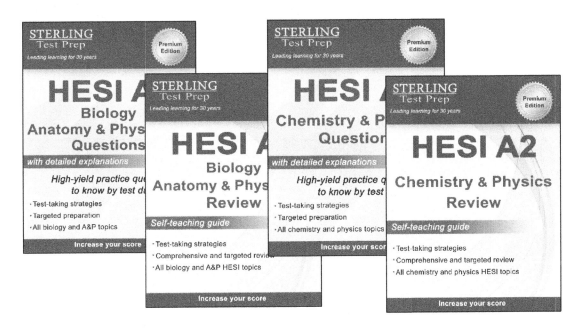

Frank J. Addivinola, Ph.D.

The lead author and chief editor of this preparation guide is Dr. Frank Addivinola. With his outstanding education, laboratory research and decades of university science teaching, Dr. Addivinola lent his expertise to develop this book.

Dr. Frank Addivinola conducted original research in developmental biology as a doctoral candidate and pre-IRTA fellow in Molecular and Cell Biology at the National Institutes of Health. His dissertation advisor was Nobel laureate Marshall W. Nirenberg, Chief of Biochemical Genetics Laboratory at the National Heart, Lung, and Blood Institute (NHLBI). Prior to NIH, Dr. Addivinola conducted research on prostate cancer in the Cell Growth and Regulation Laboratory of Dr. Arthur Pardee at the Dana Farber Cancer Institute of Harvard Medical School.

Dr. Addivinola holds an undergraduate degree in biology from Williams College. He completed his Masters at Harvard University, Masters in Biotechnology at Johns Hopkins University, and five other graduate degrees at the University of Maryland University College, Suffolk University, and Northeastern University.

During his extensive teaching career, Dr. Addivinola taught numerous undergraduate and graduate-level courses, including biology, biochemistry, organic chemistry, inorganic chemistry, anatomy and physiology, medical terminology, nutrition and medical ethics. He received several awards for his research and presentations.